FLY FISHING THROUGH THE MIDLIFE CRISIS

FLY FISHING THROUGH THE MIDLIFE CRISIS

HOWELL RAINES

William Morrow and Company, Inc.
New York

Publisher and author are grateful to acknowledge the use of the
following copyrighted material:

"In My Hour of Darkness"; Words and Music by Gram Parsons and
Emmylou Harris; © 1974 Wait and See Music (BMI).

The northern pike filleting instructions appearing on pages 136–137
from *A Boundary Waters Fishing Guide* © by Michael Furtman.
NorthWord Press, Inc., Box 1360, Minocqua, WI 54548.

"Five Songs"; Copyright © 1981 by Gian Carlo Menotti; G. Schirmer
Inc., publisher.

"The Song of Wandering Aengus" from *The Poems of W. B. Yeats: A New
Edition*, edited by Richard J. Finneran. New York: Macmillan, 1983.

The "Pensacola Fish Chowder" recipe appearing on pages 183–185
from *The Compleat McClane* by A. J. McClane, Copyright © 1988 by
A. J. McClane. Used by permission of Dutton Signet, a division of
Penguin Books USA Inc.

The first chapter of *Fly Fishing Through the Midlife Crisis* was previously
published in a slightly different form by *Southpoint* magazine and
reprinted by *Fly Rod and Reel* magazine.

It is the policy of William Morrow and Company, Inc., and its
imprints and affiliates, recognizing the importance of preserving what
has been written, to print the books we publish on acid-free paper, and
we exert our best efforts to that end.

Library of Congress Cataloging-in-Publication Data

Raines, Howell.
    Fly fishing through the midlife crisis / Howell Raines.
        p.   cm.
    ISBN 0-688-10346-4
    1. Fly fishing—Southern States—Anecdotes.   2. Fishing—
Southern States—Anecdotes.   3. Raines, Howell—Anecdotes.
I. Title.
SH464.S68R35   1993
799.1'2—dc20   93-15162
                                                              CIP

Printed in the United States of America

First Edition

1 2 3 4 5 6 7 8 9 10

This book is dedicated to my
brother, Jerry W. Raines,
who was born knowing
where fish live and what they want.

Acknowledgments

Many of the people who helped with this book are named in the pages that follow and my debts to them are obvious. I also want to thank the following for reading the manuscript and offering advice: Robert H. Berls, Sigrid Blalock, Maureen Dowd, Rick Duffield, Jane Stanton Hitchcock and Tennant S. McWilliams.

For their hospitality or advice, I am also indebted to Orval L. and Louise Baker, Linda Burgess and Bill Dunlap, Jane and Redge Hanes, John Huey, Ann Lewis, George F. Randolph and Harry Whyel. For help with research and correspondence, I am grateful to Monica Borkowski, Judith Greenfeld, Roger Pang, Earl Smith, Barclay Walsh and, above all, to Ferne Horner and Rosemary Shields.

I am grateful, as well, to the Rockefeller Foundation for a one-month residency at the Bellagio Study and Conference Center.

Contents

CONTENTS

How can one age the heart?
What wound, what memory will ever teach it
   wisdom?

—Gian Carlo Menotti

Then there was an old man,
Kind and wise with age,
And he read me just like a book
And he never missed a page.
And I loved him like my father
And I loved him like my friend
And I knew his time would shortly come
But I did not know just when.

In my hour of darkness,
In my time of need,
Oh, Lord, give me wisdom,
Oh, Lord, give me speed.

—Gram Parsons and Emmylou Harris

FLY FISHING THROUGH THE MIDLIFE CRISIS

1
How It Starts: The Song of Rapid Anne

Like many Southerners, I was ruined for church by early exposure to preachers. So when I need to hear the sigh of the Eternal, I find myself drawn to a deep hollow between Fork Mountain and Double Top Mountain on the eastern flank of the Blue Ridge. This is where the Rapidan River plunges through a hemlock forest and through gray boulders that jut from the ferny earth like the aboriginal bones of old Virginia. This is a place of enlightenment for me, the spot where I received the blessing of my middle years. Here, after three decades of catching fish, I began learning *to fish*.

At this point it is necessary to introduce Mr. Richard C. Blalock, a man given to pronouncements. There are two reasons for this trait. As a former officer of the Foreign Service of the United States, he is a natural-born pontificator. Also, Dick Blalock serves as the fly-fishing guru for a handful of people around Washington, and some of us provoke his speechifying for our own enjoyment.

I'll try to give you a sample of the conversation in Dick's loose-jointed old Chevy as it grinds along the road that the Marines scraped across the mountains in 1929 so that Herbert Hoover could reach the Rapidan. In those days, the stream was reserved for his exclusive use. President Hoover liked to fish. He also needed a place where he would not be bothered by the little people while he planned the Great Depression. I find it impossible to visit the Rapidan without a haunted feeling in regard to Herbert Hoover, but more on that later. First, the fish and the river, according to the teachings of Dick Blalock.

"This species of brook trout has never been stocked in this stream. They go back to the Ice Age. That means they have been here in this form, just as we see them today, for ten thousand years. They are survivors." That is what Dick always says to newcomers by way of inspiring respect for the Rapidan and its tenacious little genetic warriors.

"They are the most beautiful fish that God ever put on this earth. When they are in their spawning colors, they are just breathtaking," he adds for those who need prompting to adore the lush greens and pinks, the unmitigated reds of *Salvelinus fontinalis*—"the little salmon of the waterfall."

Then he enunciates Blalock's Rapidan Paradox. "These brook trout will strike any fly you present, provided you don't get close enough to present it." This means the fish are predatory, but skittish. More to the point, pursuing them prepares us to receive the central teaching of Blalock's

Way. To achieve mastery is to rise above the need to catch fish.

This part did not come easily for me. I was born in the heart of Dixie and raised in the Redneck Way of Fishing, which holds that the only good trip is one ending in many dead fish. These fish might then be eaten, frozen, given to neighbors or used for fertilizer. But fishing that failed to produce an abundance of corpses could no more be successful than a football season in which the University of Alabama failed to win a national championship.

Of course, not even Bear Bryant won every year. Similarly, the greatest fishermen get skunked. So it is inevitable that the Redneck Way, which is built around the ideas of lust and conquest, will lead to failure. In that way, it resembles our physical lives. In the days of youth, when the blood is hot and the sap is high and the road goes on forever, it is easy enough to slip the doomy embrace of frustration. But time, as a British poet once said, is a rider that breaks us all, especially if our only pleasure—in football, fishing or love—comes from keeping score.

By the time I reached my late thirties, my passion for fishing brought with it an inexpressible burden of anxiety. As Saturday approached or, worse, a vacation, the questions would whirl through my brain. *How many* would I catch? *How big* would they be? Would my trip be *wonderful?* Would I be a *success?* I had reached the destination of all who follow the Redneck Way. I had made my hobby into work.

Then one day in the summer of 1981 I found myself at the L. L. Bean store in Freeport, Maine. I was a correspondent at the White House in those days, and my work—which consisted of reporting on President Reagan's success in making life harder for citizens who were not born rich, white and healthy—saddened me. In fact, hanging around the Reagan crowd made me yearn for connection with something noble and uplifting. I bought a fly rod.

I do not know if you are familiar with the modern fly rod, but it is one of the glories of industry. The maker starts with a toothpick of steel called a mandrel. Around this mandrel are laid miles of thread spun from graphite. The mandrel is slipped out, and this long taper is then painted with epoxy, producing a deep, mirrored finish of the sort one saw on the German automobiles of thirty years ago.

The result is a piece of magic, an elegant thing, willowy and alive—a wand that when held in the hand communicates with the heart. And the more I waved such a wand over the next few years, the more the scales of my old fish-killing heart fell away. At last I stood on the threshold of being what I had tried so hard, yet so blindly, to be since that sublime spring day in 1950 when my father and mother helped me catch twenty crappies from the Tennessee River. In the ensuing decades, I had killed hundreds of fish—bass, crappies, bluegills, shellcrackers, pike, king mackerels, red snappers, black snappers, redfish, bluefish, pompanos, amberjacks, jack crevalles, barracudas. I had been blooded in the Redneck Way by those who understood fishing as a sport and a competition. Now I was about to meet a man who understood it as an art, a pastime, a way of living easefully in the world of nature. One day my telephone rang and it was Dick Blalock.

I like to say I got my guru from the U.S. government. He was fifty-five years old when I first saw him and already a walking medical disaster. Dick played football for a season at the University of Oklahoma, but in the ensuing years he had open heart surgery and gained weight. The big event in his medical history—and his angling history, for that matter—was a liver parasite contracted in North Yemen, where he was working as a Foreign Service officer. The government pressed him to take medical retirement and a pension when he was thirty-seven.

"So I decided that if they were so determined to pay me not to work, I'd take advantage of the opportunity and go fishing for a while," Dick told me on the day we met. "That was over seventeen years ago."

"So, how's it been?" I said.

"Terrific," he said. "I'd recommend it to anyone."

As Dick Blalock spoke these words, we were rolling through northern Maryland on the enticing roads that Robert E. Lee followed to his mistake at Gettysburg. Dick had spotted an article I had written for the sports section of *The New York Times* on bass fishing in the Potomac, and he called out of the blue to say maybe it was time I tried my hand on trout. He suggested the limestone creeks of Cumberland County, Pennsylvania, holy territory for fly fishers since before the Civil War.

It was a day I will not forget. At the Letort Spring Run, we watched huge brown trout fighting for spawning sites. In deference to the wishes of Charlie Fox, a venerable fly fisherman who lives near the Letort and dislikes having his trout disturbed during procreation, we did not fish. Later, on nearby Yellow Breeches Creek, I caught my first brown trout on a fly. Actually, at the time, I wasn't entirely sure whether it was a brown or a rainbow. But I guessed correctly, sparing myself embarrassment under the eyes of my new friend. Then, in accordance with the catch-and-release rules of the limestone creeks, I set the fish free. This occasioned the first Blalockian pronouncement I was to hear.

"I will never kill another trout," he said. "I release every one I catch, no matter what the regulations call for. There are too few of them in the world, and each one is too precious to do something as wasteful as eating it."

Driving back to Washington that night, I was seized by a sneaky kind of joy, a feeling not altogether in keeping (I thought then) with the fact that I had caught only one fish—quite by accident, really—and killed none. This feeling was a clue. Soon I would be ready for the Rapidan.

Like many things in Virginia, the river was named for a member of the British royal family: Queen Anne. Being swift, it was called the Rapid Anne and, in time, the Rapidan. When we first got there in 1985, spring had come with an abrupt glory. Daffodils and forsythia bloomed on the banks, marking the homesites of the mountaineers who had been evicted by creation of the Shenandoah National Park. My sons Ben and Jeff were fifteen and thirteen. I was forty-two.

We began our apprenticeships at stream fishing together. It was a painful business, learning to cast without hanging the flies in the trees, conquering the clumsiness of foot that is as much an enemy in wading as in dancing. One of the saddest sights I have ever seen was Ben returning to camp with his new Orvis rod—a Christmas trophy—shattered in a fall on slick boulders.

But in time we were skilled enough to defy Blalock's Rapidan Paradox. We learned to creep to the rim of crystal-clear pools without spooking their fish. We learned to whip our flies under limbs and drop them like live things into a living current. These matters take concentration, and the stream graded us unforgivingly. The only passing mark was a fish flashing into the visible world to strike more quickly than a finger-snap.

It is fishing I would have disdained in years past for the fragility of the tackle and the tininess of the fish. Eight inches is an average brook trout, ten a large one, anything over eleven inches a whopper. A few people, including Dick Blalock, have caught accurately measured twelve-inchers, or so they said.

Dick told us of his catch at a time when I was boasting about my liberation from the competitiveness that is part of the Redneck Way. I no longer had to catch the most fish or the biggest fish. That is what I said. In fact, Dick's twelve-inch brook trout filled me with a sudden bolt of envy.

So there came the day when Dick and I took Bill Dunlap, my friend from Mississippi, to the river. Bill is a painter with a special eye for the Virginia landscape, and I wanted him to see the shapes and colors of the Rapidan. At the time, he was in that stage of his fly-fishing novitiate in which every cast develops into an accident, so he contented himself with watching me fish one particularly sweet pool.

Straightaway, I caught my largest Rapidan trout, a deep-bellied fish that I guessed to be at least thirteen inches long. Before releasing it, I carefully marked its length on my rod, and we hurried downstream to borrow Dick's tape measure. My trophy measured eleven and one-half inches.

Later, I admired the symmetry of the experience. I had created a competition for myself and then lost it. It was yet another lesson in listening to the song of Rapid Anne. It is a song, among other things, about conquering greed and learning one's place.

The fact is, this is a river that can make people greedy. To see it is to want to possess it. So it was with Herbert Hoover when he first came in 1929. In no time, a crew of five hundred Marines was splitting the silence with bulldozers and hammers. Camp Hoover became a layout of a dozen cabins, barracks for 250 men, and riding stables. Hoover liked to think big. The Marines carted in fifty-one tons of boulders for a single fireplace in the President's lodge. By 1930, plans were underway for a 100,000-trout hatchery on the riverbank.

A few Democrats grumbled about this use of tax money to create a private 164-acre playground, but Hoover assured them that he had done his part. He had paid $5 an acre for the land and chipped in $15,000 worth of lumber for the Marine carpenters. As for the road building, the White House explained that this was a training exercise that the President had generously allowed to take place on his land. As they settled into their new retreat, the Hoovers did not let the political carping or the nation's rising unemployment spoil their taste for trickle-down humor. Mrs. Hoover, known to the locals as The Lady, issued written instructions for guests, advising that the proper course on chilly nights was to "throw your fur coat" over the foot of the bed.

Hoover delighted in making members of his cabinet and distinguished visitors such as Charles Lindbergh join him in building rock dams in the stream. Their labor did result in better holding water for trout in a few pools. So far as I know, this was the only undertaking of the Hoover administration that actually improved conditions in a Southern state. Except for his fishing camp, Hoover opposed, as a matter of principle, the spending of tax money on public-works projects in the South. His firmness in this regard allowed the region to enjoy an especially intimate experience with the Depression, and no doubt many older Southerners can identify with the sentiments expressed by my then eighty-two-year-old father when I described Hoover's idylls along the Rapidan. "Yeah, we heard back then that Hoover liked to fish," he said. "We were hoping he would fall in and drown."

The more time Hoover spent on the Rapidan, the more his greed increased. First, he got permission to fish year-round, ignoring the three-month trout season that applied to everyone else in Virginia. Then, being a Westerner, he became unhappy with the size of the native brook trout. Through a mix-up, both the Virginia game department and the National Park Service loaded the stream with rainbows and browns, stunting the lot with this double stocking and causing the President to yearn belatedly for the stream he had spoiled. According to Darwin Lambert, author of the National Park Service history of the area, "Hoover jumped on them, saying, 'Where are you getting all these fish? Why don't you just leave it alone?' "

Of course, the fishery people were just trying to please The Chief, as Hoover liked to be called. It was not an easy task. Lambert provides this glimpse of a frantic Hoover arriving by limousine from Washington. "He'd disappear within three or four minutes, in the very clothes he was wearing. You'd look for him and he'd be gone. He's gone out there in his dark suit and white shirt. Maybe he's loosened the tie, but he's out there on the stream. He couldn't stand people any longer. He had to be out there with his fish."

There's something touching in the image to me—Hoover fly fishing while the country goes to hell, casting frantically, not understanding the frustration that churned in him and produced his lust for deeper pools, more fish, bigger fish. The President of the United States had transformed himself into a follower of the Redneck Way. I often wonder if he ever learned how deeply he erred with his stocking of those big, innocent hatchery trout. For he was already in the presence of a perfect thing, the Eastern brook trout living as it lived while the centuries rolled over the earth, living as it lived in those very waters before Christ, before Caesar, before the Pharaohs.

Like them, Herbert Hoover has come and gone. Luckily, the Rapidan, like America, survived him. The brown trout and rainbows did not take over and drive the brook trout to extinction, a common occurrence in other Eastern streams. Now, in our eyeblink of eternity, Dick Blalock and Bill Dunlap and my boys and I will have our moment to contemplate these perfect beings and to understand that they do not exist for our pleasure.

This is a lesson that Henry Beston set down more than sixty years ago in a book called *The Outermost House.* "For the animals shall not be measured by man," he wrote. "They are not brethren, they are not underlings; they are other nations, caught with ourselves in the net of life and time, fellow prisoners of the splendor and travail of the earth."

To embrace this knowledge in one's inmost heart is to depart from the Redneck Way and to know, as Dick Blalock says, that "fishing is not about food." It is a way of interrupting the invisibility of these shining creatures and existing for a moment with them in their wildness and transience, their indifference to our approval and their dependence on our restraint if they are to add another hour to their ten thousandth year.

Henry Beston wrote of splendor. On the Rapidan one day I saw snow fall through blooming dogwoods. I do not expect to see such a multiplication of whiteness again in my lifetime, but it is a part of me to be lived again whenever I pull a Rapidan trout into our half of the world or, for that matter, when I contemplate these words which somehow seem to tumble together toward poetry, or song:

> Rapidan.
> Rapid Anne.
> Rap-i-dan.
> Rapidan.

2
The Arc of My Story

Perhaps I should say something here about the story I want to tell in these pages.

First, it is important to understand that I am a son of the hillbilly tribes of Alabama, rough men and women named Raines and Walker and Barton and Best and Abbott and Flannagan and Fell and Rooks and Jackson and Key who came down the spine of the Appalachians in the early nineteenth century to undertake the "settling of a wilderness continent . . . [by] force and violence," as A. N. Boney, a Georgia historian, puts it in his succinctly titled essay "The Redneck."

This is my declaration. The blood that beats in me is hillbilly blood, and when I use the words "hillbilly" or "redneck" in this book, or speak of the Redneck Way of Fishing, it is with binding affection and due reverence for those who have gone before.

If I have any skill as a writer, it is their genes

speaking through me. If I have any energy for this task, it is the raw energy of that immemorial Celtic ancestral urge to tell, to bear witness, but also to entertain, to sing, to fiddle, to push into the dark and narrow places where whiskey is made, to be drunk and dance in the roads by moonlight.

I do not want to make too much of this, or too little. Although I know the hills very well, I am a city boy. I am a passably educated man. The life I have lived as a journalist on a newspaper of distinction is not a life that could have been imagined by my kinsmen who sleep in the graveyards of forgotten Alabama hamlets with names like Curry, Meek, Mary Lee, South Lowell, Sunlight, Gallant, Day's Gap, Rock Creek and Old Nathan.

Chief Seattle said, "The dead are not powerless," and sometimes I almost believe him. At least, it is worth thinking about if you were raised by distinctive people, people who had a certain kind of relationship to the world of nature. If the old ways of these people were a palpable presence in the world of your childhood, if at a young age you went into the hills on dirt roads to places beyond the reach of the last telephone line, if you stood in a pioneer cabin that was still being lived in and the people who lived there were your kin, these experiences are something you have to reckon with when you come up against the problem of what kind of man you want to be. If you were a boy who glimpsed the end of something out in wild America and if, years later, you are among those thousands of urban men who find themselves at midlife with the taste of ashes on the tongue, it may be that your hereditary psychic map is all you have to lead you out of the gloom.

I have said already that this is an account of the journey I made from the Redneck Way of Fishing to the higher path traveled by my remarkable friend Dick Blalock. To state the obvious, my exploration of the sport of fly fishing is a metaphor for another, more painful journey experienced by me and people I care about.

Of course, I am not the first person to discover in fly fishing a framework for thinking about life. On its surface the analogy is obvious. If we can discipline ourselves to cast a line with perfection, perhaps we can impose order on—or perceive some inherent order within—the chaos of daily existence. Nor am I the first writer to seize upon fly fishing as a literary vehicle by which we drive close to the heart of life's abiding mysteries. It is informative in this regard to note the publication dates of the two works in American literature that best succeed in the use of fly fishing as the controlling metaphor for a spiritual quest. These are "Big Two-Hearted River" by Ernest Hemingway, and *A River Runs Through It* by Norman Maclean.

Published in 1927 and 1976 respectively, these two stories bracket the years in which the United States of America came to be the most accomplished and most ardent fly-fishing nation in the world. Between them, these stories also cover the arc of our progress in refinements of taste and technique. Hemingway's hero, Nick Adams, cast a fly rod, but his methods were raw and unsophisticated. He used live grasshoppers as bait, rather than artificial flies. For Norman Maclean and his father and brother, it was dry flies or nothing at all. People who used live bait or sinking flies might own and use fly rods, but they were not fly fishers.

Despite their differences on the aesthetics of fly fishing, both works struggle with the same central question. What do we seek when we fish with the most fragile of rods in the most difficult waters we can find? Norman Maclean, the son of a Presbyterian minister, suggested one answer when he wrote of his father's conviction that "all good things—trout as well as eternal life—come by grace and grace comes by art and art does not come easy." But peace of mind does not come easy either, especially for those of us who lack the elder Maclean's faith.

Hemingway used fly-fishing scenes to illustrate the impotence of faith and the power of fear, addressing those of us who have known the dread that Nick Adams felt when he came to the place where the Big Two-Hearted River flowed into a cedar swamp and he realized that beyond there "in the fast deep water, in the half light, the fishing would be tragic."

Who had it right, the Reverend Mr. Maclean or Nick Adams? Is fishing about faith or fear, death or salvation? The answer is as mutable, as variable, as the symbol of the fish itself.

Since the birth of Christianity, the fish has symbolized immortality. Jesus consorted with fishermen. The five fishes became the miracle food with which he nourished the faith of unbelievers stranded in a "deserted place" on the Sea of Galilee. In the end, the fish became the signature of Christ himself, the very hieroglyph by which believers try to convince themselves of their invulnerability to death.

But in many folk and fairy tales, we see the fish and the water in which it swims as the abiding symbols of the finite Self and the inescapability of death. In "The Fisherman and His Wife," the Brothers Grimm told how the luckiest catch in history—a talking flounder that could grant any wish—led an impoverished couple to destroy themselves with greed. In *Women Who Run with the Wolves,* Clarissa Pinkola Estés writes of tales from several cultures in which a fisherman gets a bite on a deep-drifting line and eagerly pulls in his catch. But his excitement turns to terror when he fetches up Skeleton Woman, an archetypal figure symbolizing death's presence in the very midst of life, or what Estés calls the Life/Death/Life cycle. Skeleton Woman follows him home, eats all his fish, drinks his tears, takes his heart out of his chest and beats it like a drum, and when he falls asleep, she crawls into his bed and has her way with him. The next morning she has gotten some flesh on her bones and they get married.

"The fisherman is slow to realize the nature of what he has caught," concludes Estés, a Jungian analyst. "This is true of everyone at first. It is hard to realize what you are doing when you are fishing in the unconscious."

You can say that again. For my part, I do not believe entirely in the venerable religion preached by the Reverend Mr. Maclean or in that more recent but equally lucrative faith evangelized by the psychoanalysts. Therefore allow me to say they are all selling the same story. It is a story about the search for wholeness, if not holiness. Allow me also to promulgate in five rules what I perceive as their collective wisdom for one about to embark on the adventure of fly fishing through the midlife crisis.

Rule One: Always be careful about where you fish and what you fish for and whom you fish with.

Rule Two: Be even more careful about what you take home and what you throw back.

Rule Three: The point of all fishing is to become ready to fly fish.

Rule Four: The point of fly fishing is to become reverent in the presence of art and nature.

Rule Five: The Redneck Way and Blalock's Way run along the same rivers, but they do not come out at the same place.

These are heavy matters, but I ask you not to forget the joy and vitality and primitive, soul-making power that I wish to invoke when I speak of the Redneck Way. As I write these words, I think of a ride my father and I took one autumn day along the back roads of Winston County, Alabama. The road twisted through hills and hollows where in bygone times some of my forebears had been involved in the production and consumption of corn whiskey.

Yonder, my father said as we passed an aged dwelling, is the house of Amos LaMunion. Then he leaned close to me as I drove and said, "He and your grandfather used to screw the lids off of fruit jars together."

So what I propose, gentle reader, is to screw the lids from the jars of memory and experience and pour this distillation of sport and love, frailty and fraternity, mortality, travail and the kinds of joy that can happen when you try to learn to fish. For me, that learning will never be done, but I tell you this. I cast a cleaner line today than when I started.

Now, I want to show you the arc of my cast and in it perhaps you can see the arc of my story, and over and beyond that, across the long glassy tongues of every fish-harboring stream I have waded, perhaps you will see the arc of a life.

3
The Gene Pool of the Redneck Way

Psychologists call it "the primal scene," that moment when a youngster first sees his parents in the grip of love. The fishing equivalent of such a moment came to me on the causeway across South Sauty Creek on a Monday when I was allowed to play hooky from school in the spring of 1950. On that day and in that place, I witnessed my first great fish carnage, and the experience marked me forever. Even now, it glows in my memory as a transforming experience, a day of pleasure pure and powerful. I will not be surprised if, as I die, my last thoughts are of this day.

I cannot explain the grandeur and tragedy of which I speak when I speak of the Redneck Way of Fishing without telling about this day and about my uncle, Erskine David Raines. He is old now, his lungs so ravaged by sixty years of cigarettes and the industrial air of Birmingham that he can hardly walk a hundred feet. But in his day, he was a true Master of the Redneck Way, and in later years, he was the first to bring into our family the news of a higher magic called fly fishing.

But this was before all that. Uncle Erskine was my father's baby brother. He was a man of great rages and awesome profanity. It was thought that his fierce temper stemmed from bad fortune. He was drafted out of the Alabama hills and assigned the job of walking in front of Patton's tanks in case there were land mines about. He went all the way across Europe in this fashion and wound up at the Elbe, getting drunk with the Russians and watching them shoot up a bar with a machine gun. But so many of his friends in the infantry perished in the process of finding safe pathways for Patton's tanks that it left him with a moody turn of mind and a dicey temperament. Once he and my father, both big men, went after each other with two-by-fours in my father's lumberyard. My older brother witnessed this, and for all of his life, he has carried himself like a man who has seen the fighting of giants. That is to say that even at sixty my brother is not a man you would want to trifle with, much less so my Uncle Erskine in his prime, which is the time of which I wish to tell.

Uncle Erskine liked Camel cigarettes, strong coffee, homemade ice cream, Nash automobiles, Dalmatian dogs and his only child, my wild-as-a-buck cousin who was named David Ralph and called Daveydraf. Daveydraf was the only person I ever knew to be permanently expelled from our alma mater, Ensley High School in Birmingham, for bad behavior. This was no mean accomplishment since people sometimes went directly from Ensley High to prison.

But I digress. Uncle Erskine's overriding passions in 1950, when I was seven years old, were barbecued ribs and crappie fishing. He built a barbecue stand for family use on the shady spare lot beside his house. It was a miniature version of his favorite commercial barbecue joints, which included Jack's, Ollie's, Riddlehoover's, Carlisle's, the Old Plantation, the Golden Rule and the redundantly named emporium of the two Lovoy brothers, The Double LL. Like most of those places, Uncle Erskine's barbecue house was a tidy brick building with pine paneling and a plate-glass window across the front wall and a big open-hearth pit with a galvanized metal hood to catch the smoke. It had a Marlite counter and several stools, and when Uncle Erskine invited our family over for Sunday dinner, we sat on the stools like customers in a diner, and he stood behind the counter and served us. The recipe for his sauce was secret. Judging from the red splatters on his white butcher's apron, it depended on ketchup.

As for the crappie fishing, sometimes in the spring, Uncle Erskine would go off to Guntersville Lake and not come back for a week or so. This was an inconvenience for customers of his carpentry shop, but most of the regulars had learned not to cross him. In April of 1950, Uncle Erskine and Aunt Grace and Daveydraf returned from such a trip with so many fish that normal fish-cleaning procedures failed and Uncle Erskine took to chopping their heads off with a hatchet and then throwing the carcasses to Grace and Daveydraf for scaling. Several days later, their new Nash Ambassador began to stink, and Uncle Erskine found a crappie under the spare tire. It was a nice one, too.

It was then that Uncle Erskine told my father that he had found The Place, and it was called South Sauty. The body of water he described was an embayment of the Tennessee River. South Sauty Creek had originally been a modest stream draining a mountain cove called Buck's Pocket. But now the creek bed and most of Buck's Pocket were under deep water as part of the vast lake created by Guntersville Dam.

This place was over one hundred miles north of Birmingham, the last thirty miles on an unpaved road of choking dust. Erskine decreed that we leave at 1:00 A.M., so as to arrive in time to claim the prime spots on the long causeway and bridge that spanned the waters of South Sauty.

A washtub was set in the trunk of each car, and in the middle of this tub went a fifty-pound block of ice and many six-ounce Coca-Colas. We rolled through the night, through Oneonta and Fort Payne and Arab, grinding up the long, fertile slope of Sand Mountain, descending at length to the waterfront town of Guntersville and turning at last up the stony rim of the lake toward our destination.

I slept most of the way. I arrived in my pajama shirt and never bothered to change it. My mother or someone had seen to it that I put on my jeans and shoes or else I might have fished stark naked, so arresting was the scene that lay before me at daybreak.

There, on that causeway, was a gathering of hillbillies the like of which I have never seen. There were lank-jawed countrymen and their bony wives, knotty little children and teenage boys who looked strong enough to jerk stumps out of

38

the ground, roots and all. There were twisted old men with tobacco-stained chins and snuff-dipping granny women in sunbonnets. They carried cheap rods and reels or long poles still scarred by the rough ax work it took to hack them from the canebreak.

At this point, my father put my first pole in my hands. It was a piece of varnished bamboo in three pieces. These pieces were joined by aluminum fittings that screwed together. My mother and Aunt Grace also used poles like mine. The men used bait-casting rods and level-wind reels with linen lines. We took our places on the bridge, part of a long line of people on both sides of the bridge and causeway for as far as one could see.

I did not know it then, being only a slip of a lad, but I swam that day in the very gene pool of the Redneck Way. These were my people, the English, Scotch, Irish and Scotch-Irish yeomanry of the Alabama hills, a lean and freckled people, a tribe of singers, preachers, fighters, whiskey makers like my great-grandfather, Andrew McKinley "Doc" Fell, and whiskey drinkers like certain of my uncles.

Many of these hill people were hereditary Republicans whose ancestors had either refused service in the Confederate Army or had, like some of my own kin, actually enlisted in the Union Army. But this scene on the causeway pointed up the reasons for the Democratic shift that swept the hills with the New Deal and establishment of the Tennessee Valley Authority, which built a great string of hydroelectric dams along the river and strung power lines into every hollow and branch head. Herbert Hoover had brought the hillbillies hunger and a firm economic policy. Franklin D. Roosevelt had brought electric lights and the best crappie fishing in the world.

And oh, brothers and sisters, what a slaughtering of crappies took place there that day.

To my left was a humpbacked old woman sitting on an overturned bucket, her rod protruding between the bridge rails. From time to time, she would crank her reel like a coffee grinder and a crappie would come twisting out of the water. These were big fish of one to two pounds, speckled as dominicker hens and redolent with the spermy smell of the spawning season. All around us, these big fish flopped on the boards of the bridge, coating themselves with dust. Only when someone had a pile of five or more would that person pause from the furious catching to string up these bedusted fish.

At midmorning, this old woman cranked up a fish and announced, "That's twenty. I've got my limit."

I took that number as my goal, too. Barely able to reach over the top rail, I dangled my pole toward the brown water ten feet below and slowly built my count to nineteen. My red-and-white bobber went under and I heaved back on fish number twenty. I felt a weight I had not felt before and at length the stout line and my mighty heaving drew to the surface a thrashing behemoth of a crappie. I could not lift it.

My father, who was standing beside me, was playing a fish of his own. But he reached over with his left hand and gave my pole a sharp tug. My fish flew into the air like a missile, arched over our heads, and plummeted to the roadway behind me, my broken line hanging from its mouth. It was the largest crappie I saw that day and to this day the largest of its species I have caught.

I strode up and down the bridge then, announcing to one and all that I had my limit. It seems clear, therefore, that boasting and fish killing came as naturally to me as breathing. But I see now how puzzled my fellow Alabamians must have been on another score. Of the hundreds of people on that bridge, only the old woman and I gave a damn about the limit.

Late in the afternoon, Uncle Erskine, my father, my honorary uncle Lonnie Best, and Daddy's friend Marvin Young invented a contest. They were using bait-casting rods, which are shorter and less delicate than fly rods and are used to cast heavy lures and live baits like minnows. They wanted to see who could make the longest cast that actually took a fish. They stood on the gray rocks of the causeway and hurled their floats and minnows far into the lake and cranked back still more crappies. I carried their fish to the car and threw them into the washtub.

I learned one of the unfailing truths of fishing that afternoon. If you put a drink bottle in a cooler with fish, the drink will always taste of fish slime, no matter how much you wipe the neck of the bottle.

I also learned the emotion of rank greed. On the drive home, we happened upon Daddy's uncle, an old man who had been to another part of the lake and caught nothing. My father gave him twenty or more crappies from our washtub. I was stunned at the misguided generosity of this act. These were *our* fish.

There on the side of the highway as my father gave part of our fish to Uncle Walter Hester, I faced a harsh truth. I had blown my chance to catch every damn crappie in South Sauty and take the lot, a great slathering pile of fish, back to Birmingham. I realized what a fool I had been to listen to the granny woman with her talk about the limit. What had there been to keep me from catching twenty more, or a hundred?

I was a child, but I knew that my uncle Erskine would have come to my house to help me, and we could have cut their heads off with a hatchet. All this is to say that on the bridge at South Sauty my feet were planted upon the Redneck Way, and I was initiated into what Professor Boney, the aforementioned historian of the Southern psyche, has called our "unique regional bloodlust."

The next day, my mother came to my school and took me home for lunch so she could snap a picture of me and my twenty dead fish. It is the picture of a boy who understood the work that lay before him.

4
My Brother's Keeper

It was along about this time that I saw my first fly rod.

It belonged to my brother, and I broke it.

That's right. I broke it.

It was his favorite possession. It was a split bamboo rod that he bought with money he saved from his summer job at the lumberyard. It was his favorite possession in the world, and I broke it.

If you ask me, it was his fault.

Here's how it happened.

My father and his two brothers owned some beach cottages at Panama City, Florida, a place of beautiful snow-white beaches and clear Gulf water that has been known as the Redneck Riviera ever since I called it that in *The New York Times* in 1979. In some parts of the South, I am mildly famous as the man who popularized the term Redneck Riviera. People print these words on T-shirts or on their boats or on their houses. But that came

43

many years after the breaking of my brother's rod, which, as I say, was really his fault.

At any rate, my uncle Carl and my uncle Joe and my father owned these cottages. (Uncle Erskine was not part of their lumber-and-building business, partly because he was in the Army when they started it and partly because of his habit of impromptu fishing trips.) Every summer, each brother took his family to the beach for one month to oversee the renting of the cottages and also as a vacation. Usually we went in June, when the bass and bluegills and shellcrackers were spawning in the coastal rivers, or in August, when the speckled sea trout were schooled up in the bays and the whiting and pompano were running in the surf.

It was during one of these summers when I was about eight that I got my first bait-casting rod, and my brother, who was ten years older, purchased his fly rod. He often took me surf fishing and helped me with my casting, but in general I was not happy with the way my father and brother treated me that summer. Even though I had already slain the twenty crappies at South Sauty, I was pronounced "too little" for the serious fishing they were doing with J. Manning Vickers.

Mr. Vickers was a leathery old cracker who had a big family in town. He could also sometimes be found in the black neighborhoods on Massalina Bayou, which suggested that maybe he had an unofficial residence, as well. But mostly we saw him out on the beach, where he had done a miraculous thing. He had built a dam across the mouth of a brackish tidal lake and pumped all the salt water out of it and allowed it to fill up again with fresh water. Thereby he had created, in the midst of the sand dunes only two hundred yards from the ocean, a freshwater lake that was crawling with largemouth bass and big bluegills.

Every afternoon, my father and brother went to the lake and threw Dalton Special plugs and caught bass of three to five pounds. After my brother got the fly rod, they caught these powerful, chunky fish on popping bugs. But they never took me. Sometimes my mother would walk me over to the lake, and I would throw my Dalton Special haplessly from the dock with my little rod while I watched my father and brother, far across the lake, in their boat, where the bass were.

Naturally, when Mr. Vickers announced that it was time to go back in the pine hills to Lake Wimico for the bedding of the shellcrackers, they ruled that I was too little to go. Mr. Vickers said he would pick them up at daylight and they were not to worry about bringing drinks or lunch or bait. He would take care of everything.

They returned shaken from this trip, for it seems that at midmorning, Mr. Vickers had relieved himself in a mason jar and poured it over the side. Later, when the Panhandle sun was blasting down, my brother said he was ready for something to drink. Mr. Vickers took the same mason jar, swished it in the water, filled it again and passed it to my brother.

It pleased me no end that they had to drink from Mr. Vickers's pee-pee jar, and I hoped that they had learned their lesson about the bad luck they got from leaving me behind.

Then Mr. Vickers volunteered to lead an expedition into the heart of the Apalachicola Delta to a place called Tate's Hell Swamp. This was big medicine. Tate's Hell Swamp was the place where the last ivory-billed woodpecker in North America was sighted. There were cottonmouths as big as your arm and mosquitoes that mated with turkeys. And, great God, man, there were fish.

Being the baby of the family teaches you certain skills. For days before the morning of the departure, I mounted a campaign that was the whining-and-begging equivalent of Sherman's March to the Sea. I thought I had broken them down until I awoke to the bright sunlight of a beach morning to discover that the bastards had left before dawn. And this time, they took their own drinks.

I was a small boy. The passion to fish burned within me. I hated their guts.

Then one day my luck seemed to change.

My brother came bursting into the cottage and said he had just come from Mr. Vickers's lake and there was a school of yearling bass feeding in a slough there.

Over forty years later, I remember his exact words. "Let's take the fly rod over there. We'll have more fun than a barrel of monkeys."

How to describe the joy that I felt? It seemed that I had, at long last, broken the baby barrier. We raced to the lake, my heart full to bursting. The bass had quit striking. I never got to touch the fly rod.

We trudged home. Jerry asked me to hold the screen door open while he carried the fly rod through. So I'm standing there holding the door, which has one of those strong springs on it, and it kind of slips out of my hand. Wham! It shears six irreplaceable inches off the tip of my brother's bamboo rod.

He couldn't speak. He stood for several hours staring out the window at the sea as if in a trance.

He would accept no apology from me or consolation from my parents. No one ever spoke of that rod again for the rest of my childhood or, indeed, for the next four decades.

During those years, my brother and I fished many places together and had many wonderful adventures. We were very close for a long time, then we had a silly feud over a piece of property and did not speak for seven years. Then we patched that up because we really love each other, and we will be fishing together for the rest of our lives.

There is gray in our hair now, and as I think back on those long-ago Florida afternoons, when I was left to play on the beach while my father and brother went out on Mr. Vickers's pond or to Lake Wimico or on the great safari to Tate's Hell Swamp, I want to say this to my brother.

I'm glad I broke your fucking rod.

5
My Boys Appear in the Watery Part of the World

That is how I became a man who did not believe in leaving his boys behind. Perhaps we should speak here of the world of boys and men. In the men's movement, they say we must acknowledge our anger toward the "missing father." I still hold a grudge, as I admitted, about the trip to Tate's Hell Swamp in 1950. But otherwise, I have few complaints about being barred from the company and instruction of my father, brother, uncles, cousins and that vast masculine tribe referred to by the late Robert Ruark as the "honorary uncles, black and white, who took me to raise."

In my family, as I have said, it was my blood uncle, Erskine, who was our guide to higher magic, such as that of fly casting. I realize now that his teaching was crude, but powerful. He was, for example, the first person to mention Ephemeroptera in my hearing. Wherever and whenever specimens from this vast order of insects appear on the waters of North America, fish try to eat them. The many species of Ephemeroptera are commonly known as mayflies. In Alabama, we called them willow flies.

Uncle Erskine became a devotee of the willow flies. These insects, which possess triangular wings that look like gossamer sails, hatched each May and June along the shore at South Sauty and other places on the Tennessee River. We thought they were born from microscopic eggs on the willow trees and then fluttered down to the water to offer themselves as fodder for the bass, bluegills and catfish that fed with wild abandon, taking any fly in sight. In fact, mayflies are born from tiny, gilled nymphs that live in the water. When the nymphal husk breaks open, the newly hatched fly floats upon the surface for a few minutes, waiting for its wings to dry so that it can flutter upward to the safety of the willow trees. In short, we had our facts back-asswards. This was not uncommon in Alabama at that time. Suffice it to say that during willow-fly time, Uncle Erskine cast his flies upon the water and did his worst.

He was a happy man until his fly lines began to sink. In those days, the Cortland Line Company sold lines that were "guaranteed to float." But Uncle Erskine's did not float to suit him, and his raging letters to the company headquarters in Cortland, New York, brought him many apologies and free lines by return mail. This correspondence continued until Uncle Erskine bought a Corning Ware coffeepot that did not suit him. Then he started getting free coffeepots in the mail from Corning, New York.

There was something about his letters that made Yankee businessmen roll over in an instant.

I think it was the fear that a man capable of such rage might show up in their office one day. Indeed, they were on to something. It is sound policy to take seriously the rages of certain Alabamians.

In any event, by the time Uncle Erskine got caught up in the coffee wars, my father, my brother Jerry and I were moving down the fly-fishing path on our own. When I was twelve, my father took me out on Mr. Vickers's lake, and I caught a couple of solid bass on a yellow popping bug with black polka dots.

Shortly thereafter, I broke my second fly rod, a nice bamboo belonging to my father. I did this by tying the end of the line to our Pomeranian and then reeling her in while she struggled to chase down the ball I had thrown for her. I was interested in the problem of how heavy a weight one could handle on a fly rod. The answer, for the rod my father owned in 1955, was less than one Pomeranian.

My brother gave me a Garcia fly rod when I graduated from high school. It was nine feet long and had a butt as thick as your thumb. It was the kind of rod that would, in later years, be called a thunderstick. It had a spring-loaded reel that would snatch in fifty feet of line in the blink of an eye. This rig could overpower any bass or bluegill ever hatched, and it was the agent of many deaths.

Then I fell in love for the first time. It happened at Stewart's Sport Shop on Twentieth Street in downtown Birmingham. There I spied a willowy little Shakespeare rod, seven feet long, three ounces of white fiberglass with shiny maroon wrappings. I did not know fly rods came in such tiny sizes. I put upon it a cheap single-action reel. My brother ridiculed me for the effeteness of this rig. In particular, he said, only a dolt would buy a hand-cranked reel when there were plenty of good spring-loaded ones on the market. Such was the state of our mutual ignorance that he said this with great authority and I half believed him. In fact, there is a good chance that by purchasing this delicate rod and light, functional reel, I became the owner of the most sophisticated piece of fly-fishing gear then in existence within the borders of what George Wallace liked to call "the sovereign State of Alabama." I used this wonderful rod mainly in secret.

This led to my aesthetic period. By 1968, I was city hall reporter for the *Tuscaloosa News* and a graduate student in English at the University of Alabama. I thought of myself as a man of poetry and politics. I became a student of William Butler Yeats. This is one of the poems I liked in those days:

> I went out to the hazel wood,
> Because a fire was in my head,
> And cut and peeled a hazel wand,
> And hooked a berry to a thread;
> And when white moths were on the wing,
> And moth-like stars were flickering out,
> I dropped the berry in a stream
> And caught a little silver trout.

> When I had laid it on the floor
> I went to blow the fire aflame,
> But something rustled on the floor,
> And some one called me by my name:
> It had become a glimmering girl
> With apple blossoms in her hair
> Who called me by my name and ran
> And faded through the brightening air.

In my case, the glimmering girl was named Susan, and even by the standards of Alabama, where beautiful women are not a rarity, she was considered an extraordinary beauty. She was not interested in going out with me. But I came up with something that was hard to find—two press passes that meant we did not have to stand in line for hours to get into Bobby Kennedy's campaign rally in the University of Alabama field house. That was our first real date and it was quite a show. There was so much energy in the place you felt like you were hooked to jumper cables. It was a funeral service for Old Alabama. Fifteen thousand white kids raised on the rantings of George Wallace cheered for racial justice and endorsed Kennedy's criticism of the Vietnam War with chants of "Hell, no, we won't go." I wrote it up for the newspaper.

Before long, we were inseparable. Her grandfather owned two ponds outside of town that no one was allowed to fish. I went there in the afternoons of that tender spring, alone or with Susan in a skiff of rough planks, and caught big fish with my white rod and the cheap reel.

Call it fly fishing through the apocalypse. In a few weeks, King and Kennedy were dead. I remember getting up on the morning of June 6 and hearing the radio report that Bobby Kennedy had been shot. I paced back and forth in my apartment, as if I could get away from the news. And yet, and yet . . . I will not lie. When I think of the spring of '68, I do not think first of those deaths or the war or the riots in Detroit and Watts. I visualize the tender, limey green that coats the hardwood forests of Alabama when the first leaves break from the buds. This was the color of the forests that wrapped around those ponds near Tuscaloosa. It is a color I first remember seeing years before on the morning of the run to South Sauty. We were rolling through a poplar flat north of Oneonta when I awakened and peeked over the windowsill of the Oldsmobile. There I saw the gray branches of the trees motionless in the gray light of dawn and, over it all, the brushings of that green budding which is the most ephemeral color in the natural world.

It is the color of beginnings, of fleeting moments. I think of it as the color of a time when I believed my two great passions—*amare e pescare*—could be contained in one sweet bundle with knots that held forever.

Let us shift our attention now to another spring morning. It is 1976. A man and two boys are out in Tampa Bay off the mangrove tangle along the shore of Coquina Key. They are in a green fiberglass skiff originally purchased on the installment plan for $328 from Mack's Bait Shop in Tuscaloosa, Alabama. The boys are small enough that a casual observer might wonder at the judgment of any man who would have two tykes out on the bleak ocean in a fourteen-foot boat.

But I make no apology. For these are boys born of a waterborne courtship, and they have fishing in them, and it's got to come out. They are my favorite beings in all of creation, Ben Hayes Raines, born in 1970, and Jeffrey Howell Raines, born in 1972.

We are drifting on calm, clear, green water above a bottom of sand and turtle grass. The boys are too young to cast, so I have baited their lines with cut pinfish. We are after spotted weakfish, known locally as speckled trout or, simply, specks.

Suddenly, Jeffrey's rod arcs over and his Zebco reel begins singing a high, going-away song. A fish that is much too fast and heavy for his discount-store rig is taking line against the drag.

Here is the snapshot I will always have in my memory of that moment. Jeff's hands have a death grip on the shaft of his rod. The butt is digging into his stomach. He is tiny, and his narrow, tanned legs dangle from the boat seat without touching the floor. His eyes are round with fear, wonder and determination. He does not flinch, let go, appeal for help. My chest thickens with pride.

Before I can crank the motor to chase the fish, it runs out all the line and breaks off. "Was that a fish?" he says, stunned.

I know what he is feeling on this his first brush with the immemorial One That Got Away. Everyone has a first one, and Jeffrey, at four, had started with a gorilla. Now he was feeling that mixture of awe and regret and indelible relief that touches every fisher or sailor when he feels the deep surge of what Mr. Yeats called "the murderous innocence of the sea."

"A very big fish," I say. "You did a good job holding on. There was no way to stop it. It was probably a redfish or a big snook or maybe a tarpon or a jack crevalle. I'm sorry I couldn't get the motor started in time to chase it."

"Maybe it was a shark," Ben says.

"I don't think so," I say. "It was too fast. Sharks are usually slower."

It seems odd to me now to have had this kind of experience with such tiny beings. But they were boys who grew up around water. In St. Petersburg, our lawn went down into a pond that held bluegills and tilapias and a few big snook that you could hear crashing bait in the night, but never catch. On foggy mornings, hordes of pelicans flew into our pond from the bay, and when they came ghosting out of the watery mist on their pterodactyl wings and settled around the papyrus grove at the rim of the lake, it looked like opening day at the Garden of Eden.

In the evenings, Susan and I sat in the grass with our drinks while the boys fished, and it was then that I gave up the last of my fly-fishing equipment. Somewhere along the way, I had broken the tip of the white rod I used in Tuscaloosa, and now I took the Garcia thunderstick that Jerry gave me for graduation and tied a line to the end and let the boys use it like a cane pole.

It lay out in the rain and the baking Florida sun, and its gold finish faded, and the wrappings came unwound, and that was that.

6
The Kiss of Time

In 1981, shortly before the inauguration of Ronald Reagan, my family and I arrived in Washington. I was thirty-eight. I attributed any twinges of unhappiness I felt in those days to bad timing and the cycles of politics. My parents raised me to admire generosity and to feel pity. I had arrived in our nation's capital during a historic ascendancy of greed and hard-heartedness.

In our first months in Washington, the boys and I towed our boat—a fast, seaworthy runabout that had long since replaced the skiff from Mack's Bait Shop—to a place in Virginia called Lake Anna. We caught great numbers of small crappies on minnows and a few bass, and once Jeffrey caught a large chain pickerel on four-pound line.

Another time, we took the boat over to the Chesapeake and caught a pile of bluefish. Later that summer, Tennant McWilliams, my closest friend, came up from Alabama, and we went back to the same place and caught huge sea trout of nine to eleven pounds.

One afternoon, with a cooler full of fish, Tennant and I cruised across calm Chesapeake waters and got blistering drunk on Beefeater martinis. We said it was just like old times, like the summer of 1963 when we left college and went on a long ramble through Florida that we called the Great Fish. We rented a skiff in Carabelle, Florida, and made the seven-mile run to the channel off Dog Island for Spanish mackerel and cruised slowly home in the evenings, drinking rum.

But it wasn't like old times. Not really. Not quite.

What I know now is that the midlife crisis typically begins with mild twinges of dread, disappointment and restlessness that tiptoe in on little cat feet. Then in some cases, the cat feet turn to elephant feet. The process takes about five years. That part is science.

Many men respond to these twinges by purchasing something. That part is personal opinion, based on my experience with the fly rod at the L. L. Bean store in the summer of 1981. I have heard of men purchasing Porsches, land in Montana and gifts for women they hardly knew.

For a couple of years, while I was feeling those twinges, the fly rod lived in the basement, still in its box. Then one day, an old newspaper friend invited me to ride with him up to Frederick, Maryland, where a guy named Mark Kovach was giving a one-day course in fly fishing for $65. I figured after a twenty-year layoff, a day of casting instruction would not hurt. The casting was the least of it.

When it came to the complicated system of

insect identification upon which fly tying and fly selection are based, Mark Kovach was a devotee of the instructional method known by the acronym KISS. It stands for Keep It Simple, Stupid.

The premise of the KISS system is that a lot of the techno-scientific jargon with which fly-fishing writers punish their readers is unnecessary. You do not have to know the Latin names of all the insects that trout eat in order to select a fly and catch a fish on it, even though an expert may on a given day in June observe an insect, realize instantly that it is an *Ephemerella attenuata* and choose a dry fly called a Blue-Winged Olive tied on a number 18 hook, which is a very small hook indeed. This is called "matching the hatch," after a landmark book on this subject by Ernest Schwiebert, an architect in Princeton, New Jersey.

KISS is a training-wheels version of the Schwiebert method. A truly expert fly fisherman can match the hatch with the precision of an entomologist, because he knows the Latin name of every streamside insect and its exact artificial counterpart, and there are people who would rather cut off their toe with a hatchet than tie on the wrong fly.

But if you follow the KISS system, you settle for an imitation that is about the right size and about the same color, and unless the fish in your stream are extremely picky, you're likely to catch one. Imagine my surprise when I figured out that the vaunted Schwiebert method was based mainly on the life cycle of the mayflies, and that whatever their individual category—say, *Ephemerella attenuata* or *Epeorus pleuralis* or *Stenonema vicarium*—

they were all members of one widely distributed order. That order, of course, was Ephemeroptera, or Uncle Erskine's willow flies. Everything runs together, if you manage to live long enough.

When trout are feeding under the surface, it seems, they are often eating aquatic insects called nymphs, which range from a quarter inch to one inch in length. They are shaped like miniature scorpions, with segmented abdomens and pincer-like front legs.

Here is my drawing of what they look like, more or less:

By wrapping bits of fur, feathers, and sparkly thread around a hook, you can make a fly that imitates these creatures. This fly is called a nymph, and fishing with it is called nymphing.

The nymph fly looks like this:

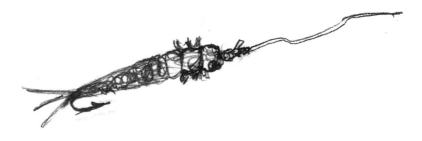

Now, the nymph belongs to a group of insects with a life cycle not unlike that of the caterpillar, which through a process that has always been difficult for us agnostics to explain hatches into a butterfly.

Nymphs, at a certain point in their development, swim to the surface. Their skins pop open and out comes either a mayfly or some other kind of insect.

Mayflies look like this:

The flies that imitate them look like this:

So much for mayflies. Not all nymphs become mayflies. Some become a less elegant, but from the trout's point of view equally toothsome, creature called the caddis. Live caddis flies look like this:

The flies that imitate them look like this:

The flies imitating the mayfly and the caddis fly come in a wide variety of sizes and colors, because the living insects come in a similar variety. Sometimes these flies are named for the places where they were invented and sometimes for the people who invented them. The most popular and reliable in the latter group is the Adams, named after the fisherman who first used it on the Boardman River in 1922.

There is also another category of artificial flies that are shaped like the mayfly imitations, but are arrayed in colors that are not found in nature. These flies are called attractors, and fish seem to strike them not because they are deceived, but because they bloody well feel like it.

Perhaps the most famous in this family is the Royal Wulff, named after Lee Wulff, who crashed and died in 1991 at the age of eighty-seven while renewing his pilot's license. (In fly fishing, we believe it is better to flame out than rust out.)

There is yet another family of fishermen's flies called terrestrials. These flies imitate grasshoppers, crickets, beetles and ants—insects that hatch on the land *(terra)* rather than emerging from aquatic nymphs.

I can attest that it is possible to read outdoor magazines for several decades without getting this kind of primer, which was why Mark Kovach's course was a bargain at $65.

Mark had another bargain in mind. He sold me a fly box with a basic selection of a dozen flies so that I could try the KISS system on my own.

He also informed me that the rod I had bought at L. L. Bean was a pretty primitive one and that he'd be glad to sell me one of his nice Walton Powell graphite rods custom-made in California for $250 or so.

In this way, I learned the most important rule of modern fly fishing: You always need to spend more money.

I think it was Mark, too, who pointed me toward waters that move.

One Sunday afternoon, Ben and I drove out to the edge of the Shenandoah National Park and found a little stream that came tumbling out of the mountains.

I had the Bean rod, and I sent him off with my old white Shakespeare with the broken tip. It cast like a broom. With the better rod, I took a couple of eight- or nine-inch brook trout, but in little while Ben came back with an eleven-incher.

He caught the bigger fish because he is one of those people born with the gift of knowing where to cast. It was the most handsome fish he had ever caught. He killed it and took it home to eat for the obvious genetic reason. It was the way of our people.

7
Mark Shows Me the Gap

Mark Kovach was the first really good fly caster I ever met. He had a big handlebar mustache and a theatrical, hucksterish manner that I found by turns appealing and off-putting. He could lay out long snakes of line with a deft casting motion that seemed the soul of delicacy. I sensed that there must be grim pulses of muscle power shooting from his shoulder, biceps and wrist. But somewhere between his fingers and the tip of his rod, there was a balletic, soundless transference of force that sent line and leader shooting out fifty or seventy feet on the shoulders of some mysterious negotiation with gravity. Watching Mark, I knew that the physics of fly casting was a science I but dimly grasped, a science such as might reside in the feathers of birds.

Mark was vain about his casting. You sensed that even when he was ABCing for the beginners. But I figured if I had his motion, I would be vain, too. As Dizzy Dean said, "It ain't bragging if you really done it."

Mark also owned the most outlandish boat on the Potomac River. It was a rubber raft of the sort used for hauling tourists down the brawling rivers of the Western mountains and canyons. For $190, Mark met me and another fisherman at a boat landing above Harpers Ferry. Mark sat in the middle of his bulbous craft and guided us with two long oars as we moved off downstream with the quickening current.

This was not the brown tidal pond of a river that one sees at Washington, the turgid soup in which Congressman Wilbur Mills made his Midnight Mystery Swim and upon which Richard Nixon and his crimped buddies took their joyless martini cruises aboard the *Sequoia*.

No, this was a giant, wet road of a river that swept us in a white spray past its boiling confluence with the Shenandoah. We pulled smallmouth bass from chutes of green water in front of the stony palisades surmounted by the town of Harpers Ferry.

One hundred and fifty years ago, this was the most industrialized spot in the United States, the site of huge mills and foundries driven by the sea-seeking waters of the Shenandoah and the Potomac. During the Civil War, so many soldiers bivouacked here that their campfires consumed the forests for forty miles around, and their ablutions turned the river itself into an undrinkable stew.

But now the trees and the fish were back, avatars of the healing powers that sleep in our damaged land. Even so, I was not prepared for what happened a few miles below Harpers Ferry. Mark spun the boat around so that we faced back upstream, and he bade us lift our eyes. "Behold," he said, "the Potomac Water Gap."

Such a vista might have lain before Bierstadt or Eakins. From the west, the last folds of the Blue Ridge came down to the water. On the east side, the Catoctins truncated abruptly, as if cut by the knife of God. The haze of the high-summer afternoon lay over the hills and over the V-shaped cleft through which the river passed, rolling down toward us over terraces of stone and marsh grass.

This was the very scene described over two hundred years ago by Thomas Jefferson in his *Notes on Virginia:* "The passage of the Potomac through the Blue Ridge is perhaps one of the most stupendous scenes in nature. . . . The first glance of this scene hurries our senses into the opinion, that this earth has been created in time, that the mountains were formed first, that the rivers began to flow afterwards, that in this place particularly they have been dammed up by the Blue Ridge of mountains, and have formed an ocean which filled the whole valley; that continuing to rise they have at length broken over at this spot, and have torn the mountain down from its summit to its base. . . . [T]he mountain being cloven asunder, she presents to your eye, through the cleft, a small catch of smooth blue horizon, at an infinite distance in the plain country, inviting you, as it were, from the riot and tumult roaring around, to pass through the breach and participate of the calm below. . . . The scene is worth a voyage across the Atlantic."

I cannot make it any nicer than that. It was through this gap that George Washington and the other founders pushed the Chesapeake and Ohio Canal, the water road that opened up the Middle

West and later the true West itself to the commerce of the Atlantic shore. Here were the birthing waters of a nation, arrayed at twilight in a scene of abiding grandeur. I looked at the Potomac Water Gap, with Reagan's Washington at my back, and thought of the line from Russell Hoban's doomsday novel *Riddley Walker:* "Oh, what we ben! And what we come to."

We fished until dark, mainly with spinning tackle, and we caught 156 fish, the most ever taken from Mark's boat in one day. He kept count on a hand calculator of the sort used by doormen.

Late in the day, I began fly fishing, dropping a slender, colorful streamer called a Wooly Bugger into the purls and eddies around the boulders and sandbars. The Wooly Bugger is an elongated fly intended to remind smallmouth bass of a leech or crayfish, and the fish tend to take it with a murderous shaking of their heads and then jump clear of the water in a panic of dismay at the power of this thing they have consumed.

It is hard to experience such an elemental contact and feel altogether doomy. I had always thought myself a coastal man, drawn to low stretches of salty water. Now, suddenly, I preferred rivers with conjuring names—Potomac, Rappahannock, Rapidan—to the blue expanse and, perhaps, to the tides of labor and loss that were purling around our little brick Colonial in Chevy Chase.

All living waters whisper individually to us. I believe that now if I did not then. Call it the Ancestral Whisper, and it is as real as anything else that we adorn with capital letters and choose to believe. So here was a call to follow, blindly, instinctively, the ancient way of my people, which is to head for our primeval Appalach, which is to follow the smooth waters up toward the hills into places where streams reduce themselves to lanes of fast water running through boulders, to push upward into mountain hollows, to go along the ribbony streams in the branchheads until you find the hole under a mossy bank where water from the center of the earth leaps up to meet the light.

If you'd like things to feel new again, that's a place to go.

8
Cornering the Streaker

I realize now, only as I write these words, that we first saw the Streaker in the Rapidan River. Literally *in* the Rapidan. The reason this seems odd to me is that I always associate the Rapidan with the period when my sons and I became trout chasers and went up into the Blue Ridge Mountains, to the headwaters of the Rapidan at Camp Hoover.

But this was a step along the way and earlier by a year or so. Susan and the boys and I were canoeing the flatter country down near Fredericksburg, Virginia. The outfitter, Gene Clore, had launched us on a sleepy stretch of the Rapidan.

We were to follow it for a few miles, until its pace quickened as it merged with the larger Rappahannock River. We planned to camp overnight at the confluence of these streams, a roomy area of runs and pools that was strewn with huge boulders and the tumbledown remains of an old sys-

Howell Raines

tem of locks and dams. For at this point, as they passed through the last range of foothills before reaching the coastal flats of the great Chesapeake drainage, both rivers furnished decent canoeing and ideal water for smallmouth bass.

After the outing with Mark Kovach, I became much taken with smallmouth bass and my discovery that they lived in almost unbelievable abundance in the rivers around Washington. I was in some sort of transition period, fishing with lighter tackle, going by canoe rather than motorboat. But the frying pan still figured mightily in my plans, and Ben and Jeff and I began many conversations with the question "Is this one big enough to keep?"

Gene Clore had warned us that there had been some sightings of the Streaker, a locally renowned exhibitionist who sometimes disported himself around the junction of the Rapidan and Rappahannock. He had been known to dash naked through people's campsites, but had never harmed anyone.

Even so, I was doubtful when Ben reported that he and Jeff, in the lead canoe, had seen a nude man scramble from a deep pool near the junction of the rivers and melt into the forest, all the while watching them over his shoulder like one of those creatures in the home videos of Bigfoot sightings. I said I was sure it was a swimmer in a flesh-colored bathing suit.

"No, Dad," Ben said firmly. "This guy was naked."

"Well, a skinny-dipping camper, then," I said.

We put up our tents on a shaded spot overlooking the vast coming together of the rivers. They met in a stony Y a half mile across at the main intersection. From this point, the Rappa-

70

hannock, having swallowed the smaller river, falls away in a long degression of terraces and rock-bordered channels, all this punctuated with gardens of shoal rubble and river grass, and here and there the skeletons of trees carried down from the mountains in the last big flood or boulders as big as cars dropped by the glaciers that moved through a while before that.

From this place, you can look westward toward the uplands where the Battle of Chancellorsville took place in 1863 and the Battle of the Wilderness in 1864. Here the Union and Confederate armies fought for days in forest so thick that their soldiers were at rifle point before they could see one another. Here transpired an incident that the propagandist/historians of Confederate glory seldom include in their histories. But no son of the redneck South should ever pass through these parts without recalling the story of John Robert Jones, a brigadier general in Stonewall's command. On May 2 at Chancellorsville, after the first of three days of fighting that would take down thirteen thousand Rebel boys, General Jones complained that his leg was hurting and asked to go home to his plantation in the Shenandoah Valley. And they let him "retire the field," as the saying goes among Southern gentlemen.

Do you think General Lee or Stonewall let privates quit in the middle of a battle if they got scared? Those poor bastards got to choose between the front line or the firing squad. Hundreds of Alabamians died at Chancellorsville and in the Wilderness. So far as I know that number included none of my relatives.

Most of them, I think, were among the estimated ten thousand north Alabamians who hid out in the bluffs and hollows of their native region and declined to present themselves for conscription into the Confederate Army when that noted slave-owning draft-dodger, Governor John Gill Shorter, announced from Montgomery that it was time for all the hillbillies to sign up as Johnny Rebs and die for Massa Robert. Some, including a few of my cousins, made their way to Union lines and signed up to fight the Confederates. God bless such hillbillies, in whose veins ran blood of a truly rebellious nature.

In any case, I was fishing in the slanting sun of late afternoon when the Streaker appeared again. This time there was no mistaking. Several hundred yards away across the watery slope of the rivers' junction, he stood atop a huge boulder and struck poses. Not bad ones either. Some had a classical cast, as if he were showing us a *tableau vivant* of *David* or *The Discus Thrower*.

Sometimes he would dive into the water and swim about, reemerging on another rock and taking new poses. He never came closer or called to us, and his posing, after a while, did not seem threatening nor an effort to arouse in me some testosterone-driven rage to prevent him from showing himself in such a way to my wife and children.

Rather it had the quality of a dance to the unheard music of twilight. In time, Susan went back to our camp. I fly fished and Ben wandered off downstream with his spinning rod. Jeffrey, who always had something of the otter in him, found a long slick rock washed by a fast current, and he stopped fishing altogether and went sliding. And whenever I glanced up to find another spot to cast or to check on the location of my boys, I saw the Streaker in his dance, until night drove us all from the river.

I heard later that the sheriff's men tried to catch him. But they could not find where he parked his car or left his clothes or even by what path he made the long hike to the river.

Gene Clore told me there was an unsubstantiated story that the Streaker had rescued a novice canoer who found himself stranded on the river at dark with two small children. According to the story, this man had called out to the Streaker during the dance of the poses. The Streaker disappeared from the river, and in time a clothed man, a man of few words, appeared and led the worried father and his two children on a long hike to a parked car. He seemed a mild-mannered unexceptional fellow of middle years. He drove them into town. I think the car was supposed to be a Volkswagen.

My last sighting of the Streaker came the next summer. My friend Patrick Tyler, then with the *Washington Post* and now a foreign correspondent for *The New York Times,* joined the boys and me for a three-day canoe trip that took us down the length of the Rappahannock and, on the second evening, once again past that point where the Rapidan debouches into the larger stream.

The current brought us swiftly down into their wide conjoinment, and there picking his way among the rocks was the Streaker in his accustomed state of nudity. Ben and Jeff, now in their early adolescence and with half a dozen years of canoeing already behind them, began digging hard with their paddles, and this effort, along with the racing current, brought them atop the Streaker in no time.

I expected—I think we all expected—some bold display, perhaps a big cock-proud pose atop his home boulder. Instead, he plunged into the water and hunkered up against the roots of a big tree that had been knocked down and stranded. He sheltered there like a troll, only his head above the surface, and watched us pass, following us with his eyes. And he seemed powerless and a little bit pitiful, as if in pushing so close, we had broken the magnetic field of his magic and confounded his ability to show himself. He was a man about my age, a man with a sullen look. Neither a dancer nor swimmer now, he looked ordinary and a little frightened that we might try to catch him or speak.

We made camp a half mile downstream on a wide sandbar at a place called Blankenbaker's, after the people who had owned this land since the Civil War.

On that sandbar, I performed one of my legendary fish fries, serving bass fillets straight out of the skillet until we all four lay in the sand like dogs. After a while, both boys waded to the far shore for the last fishing of the day. Pat and I each smoked a cigarette, something we sometimes did when our wives were not around to catch us, since we had both officially quit.

Having seen him close up, I thought I had the Streaker's story now. I imagined him as a librarian or English teacher at some rural high school, a bachelor who lived with his mother. Or if married, he was the clerk at a Sears catalog store, wed to one of those Baptist girls with stout upper arms who spent all day Sunday at church and prayer meeting whether he accompanied her or not.

He was a dutiful, sober man, sharing his paycheck and taking whatever reprimands his wife or mother dealt him. Fishing was his cover. On certain days, he took his tackle and went down to the river. At first, he even fished in the waters of the river with his line, but at some point, he began fishing these waters by entering them.

I understood that he did this not to display some part of himself, but to shed it. Such a man in the city could skulk off to his therapist and say, "I feel as frightened and incomplete and confused as a child. Earn your money. Find the man within me."

But think of such a person stranded out in the Virginia countryside, caught between the paudeens and the preachers who still rule in the small towns there. What is he to do but pose naked on a rock and hope that the chrysalis of his afflicting boyhood will break open so that the man within can stand newborn and finished before nature?

Such a man as he yearned to become would be able to hear the voices of river and forest and dawn light and darkness and offer comfort to the ghosts of the Wilderness, those poor Rebel boys who had lacked the old hillbilly cunning to stay rooted on their home ground and found themselves led into blinding thickets and there betrayed unto death by the awful unpunished ignorance of their generals.

9
The Black Dog

In 1983, I turned forty and directed my attention to the question of why the sadness of the Streaker was upon me. It was not a big sadness, but it was there, even with two hundred people in the house. Everyone at the party admired the present that Susan had secretly prepared: a photograph album entitled "Forty Years of Fishing." The first page was a picture of me and the twenty crappies from South Sauty. Succeeding pages showed me holding large dead fish all over Alabama, Florida and Louisiana. As you flipped through the pages, the fish grew larger and I grew older. There were pictures of Jerry and me with fish and the boys and me with fish.

I was touched by the gesture. A great deal of work had gone into the album. But I was oppressed by the message it held for me alone.

I, who had set out to be a great fisherman, was a middling one, at best. I had never caught a marlin or a tarpon or a bonefish. I had spent countless hours at fishing of all kinds, but I was truly expert at no kind.

And I, a boy-wonder writer who had set out to create novels about the great struggles of our time, was a middle-aged man in a gray suit who trudged to the White House press room to write stories that began, "President Reagan said today . . . " They call it journalism, but some days it felt like stenography.

For years, sadness such as that which settled over me was a secret, silent force among men in America. Then it became an industry with its own speakers' bureau. I try hard not to ridicule the men's movement. I think it is theoretically possible to touch your inner force by getting a gang of guys together and passing a writhing, sweaty, half-naked Harvard-educated attorney from the Department of Housing and Urban Development over your heads while someone bangs on a drum. That's the way they do it in Washington, D.C.

But in my case, growing up in the Redneck Way had me hard-wired to all the raw masculine force I could handle, and in the course of bouncing around the fishing camps and hunting lodges of the South, I had hell's own abundance of male bonding. I did not then nor do I now want to paint myself blue and listen to Robert Bly. But I wanted something, and I feared something, and I did not know what.

Another thing happened in my fortieth year. My father told me that he was selling the beach property in Panama City to condominium builders. This was the place across from Mr. Vickers's lake, the place where I had broken Jerry's rod. I thought he was selling too cheaply and reneging on a plan to pass this property on to my sons and his three other grandchildren. I felt doubly aggrieved when I found out that my brother was to be a partner in the condominium project.

We argued bitterly, as Southern families will over land and all families will over money, and I washed my hands of them. For seven years, I saw my father infrequently and my brother not at all. Yet even when we were estranged, they had left me something.

It was a memory of a time when my father, not much past forty, had settled into a profound moodiness. I asked Jerry, who was then in the family business, what was wrong with Daddy. "He's decided he's about to die," my brother said with the invulnerable confidence of a man in his twenties.

My father—a classic self-made man, a tenth-grade dropout, even to this day strong as a bull—began to suffer illnesses. Finally, there was a sinus infection that would not go away.

One day, he loaded the fishing tackle in the car and he and my brother took off for Florida. And they stayed gone for a long time. They went all the way to the Keys, a mythic journey for our homebound family.

There were reports that my father, an abstemious man, had won several hundred dollars on a long shot at the greyhound track in Miami. They fished from bridges and boats. I do not know what else they did there or what my father was thinking. But he came back healed, and not just from the ostensible illness of the sinuses. He had found something in the psychiatry of sun and water that got rid of the black dog that had been walking behind him.

My father was smart to go on his journey and lucky to complete it. I now know there is no guarantee that when a middle-aged man enters the dark forest where this black dog is waiting, he will come out healed. It is possible to be broken there beyond hope of repair.

In 1939, Ernest Hemingway went to Idaho to fish the Big Wood River for trout with his sons. His rods and reels and fly-tying equipment always traveled in a foot locker that was shipped ahead by Railway Express. The three boys regarded the box as a magical container for the totems that defined their father. The railroad lost the box.

"I think it just broke his spirit for trout," Jack Hemingway, the eldest son, recalled years later. "He was stricken. He never really fished streams much after that. You see, his heart could be broken a lot more easily than anybody ever knew."

Ernest Hemingway was forty years old when he lost his gear. We all know the rest of his story. At some point, perhaps the day of which Jack Hemingway spoke, he left the streams he knew and entered a thicket from which he never emerged.

If you contemplate such a trip, I guess it is time to let you in on a tasty little secret. To the degree that the term "midlife crisis" implies brevity, it is a trick. Gail Sheehy was much closer to the truth when she wrote about a "passage." It cranks up somewhere between the ages of thirty-eight and forty-five, and in a really intense midlife crisis, which is the only kind worth having, you should count on five years of steadily intensifying anxiety or depression or some satanic combination of emotional torment.

For some men—men who adore their jobs,

are content in their love lives, do not fear death—
there may be an easier and much briefer adjust-
ment. If you are such a man, count yourself
blessed beyond measure to miss this extremely interesting experience. But it is not for you that I
write.

I address the battalions of lost Rebel boys and
lost Yankee boys, too, thrashing in the Wilderness.
Hear me, my brothers. You know who you are.
Neither the old fathers nor the sons you love can
carry you now. The letters of wives and sweet-
hearts cannot reach you. Your generals have fled
the field. There lies before you a severe journey—
a soul-rending passage that will either heal you or
wreck you. I leave you a note pinned to a tree in
the heart of the forest. It contains all the advice
any man can offer. The black dog is on your trail.
Get ready to meet him.

10
Dick Gives Me the Bug

"My father was a very accomplished fly fisherman. I used to go with him on lakes down in various parts of Oklahoma. My father fished enormous deer-hair bugs for bass."

Dick Blalock is speaking. We are on our second outing. He had called initially, as I said in the first chapter, after I wrote an article about my trip with Mark Kovach on the Potomac River. On that first trip, we had toured the spring creeks in southern Pennsylvania. Today, our destination was Big Hunting Creek near Thurmont, Maryland.

Who can explain what goes into a friendship? Perhaps, having broken with my father and brother, I wanted the support of an older man. But Dick did not look too promising in the support department. He had a cherub face and wispy white hair. He suffered chronic chest pain from the open-heart surgery he had in 1982, and with the weight he was carrying, you had to figure he could go anytime. He was vain about his skill in insulting doctors who suggested he lose weight. Dick viewed any fishing trip as a kind of fat man's progress from one roadside café to the next—a maddening procedure for someone like me who, in those days, was always frantic to get on the water.

Also, when I am in a conversation, I like to say something every now and then. But the only time I got to speak was when Dick paused for breath. If I tried to tell a story, Dick would look bored. If I happened to be talking when he got ready to start again, he would just let fly and keep talking until I shut up.

"So," he said, "my father was a very good fisherman in every respect. He had marvelous hand-eye coordination. He could pick up a fly rod, and on the third cast, his timing would be perfect. The things you and I spend months learning, he would do easily. We would go out on these lakes, and he would throw these hair bugs as big as a hat and catch these enormous bass. They were five or six pounds easily.

"I got my first fly rod either at seven or eight. It was bamboo. It probably cost five or six dollars. It had a single-action reel and a silk line. So I went out and I discovered that I couldn't throw those hair bugs the way Father did. So he took me down on this place called Sheep Creek, and I learned to read the currents. My father tied a rather primitive fly. He called it a Black Gnat, and he fished it with a single-blade spinner, and I learned to throw that because it had less air resistance than the big deer-hair bugs that he used.

"I had this friend whose name escapes me. He was a full-blood Choctaw Indian, and he was just my age. My father's grandmother was part Cherokee, and my father looked Indian, but we did not register as Indians with the government and we did not live as Indians. My friend's name was Glenn something-or-other. He and I would get one of our parents to carry us to Sheep Creek, and we would wear swimming trunks and tennis shoes, and we would wade three or four miles up the stream, casting these Black Gnat flies. We each had a stringer. We might catch one hundred and fifty fish a day—small bass, big bluegills, big goggle-eye perch. We generally would come home with fifteen or twenty fish each, culling them for size. We had a ball, and it was a wonderful, wonderful, wonderful relationship. That was my earliest fly-fishing experience, and that is how I learned to read the water, to spot the eddies and pools and currents that hold fish."

By this time, Dick's Chevy was swaying up the snaky road that runs alongside Hunting Creek. The stream comes down the flanks of a modest mountain range embraced by Catoctin Mountain Park. Even here in northern Maryland, we were still below the Mason-Dixon line and technically still in the South. More to the point, we were in hillbilly territory. In the nineteenth century, these people tended whiskey stills and cheerfully shot government agents. When the Civil War came, they made charcoal to fire the blast furnaces at Thurmont and the weapons plants at Harpers Ferry. Like their brothers farther down the spine of the Appalachians, they were in no great rush to get drafted. Now their descendants still lived back in the hollows of the Catoctins, experienced poachers of deer and turkey and of the fat trout in the fly-fishing-only section of Hunting Creek.

In short, Dick Blalock had brought me to one of the northernmost outposts of the Redneck Way.

"See that pool?" said Dick. "That was Jimmy Carter's favorite pool when he was President. We're only about a mile from Camp David. The Fish and Wildlife boys kept the stream lousy with big brood fish from the hatcheries when he was up here. I knew a guy who used to slip in and give every big trout in the stream a sore lip whenever he heard Carter was coming. Of course, I liked Carter. Charlie Fox and Ben Schley taught him a lot about fishing, and he ties a good fly. Reagan couldn't tie his shoelaces if his life depended on it.

"I tell you, I'm just sort of viscerally liberal on any issue. So I have voted for, fought for, Democrats. I was an admirer of Jimmy Carter. I think he made some mistakes, but I think he was a victim of circumstances. The problem with Republicans is that they would run roughshod over human values in order to protect property values. The good thing about Democrats is they would run roughshod over property values in order to protect human values.

"I've never had strong feelings about property. I was never acquisitive. I suppose it's something I got from my father. It's the American Indian attitude—no one owns the land. No one has a claim on anything or anybody. That's essentially what it is. It is an impossibility to own land. You can *use* it. You can *be* in it. But how can you *have* it?"

And so on. The man could talk, all right, but the political disclosure relaxed me a little. One of the risks you took in fishing with strangers in the Eighties was that you could find yourself in the woods with evangelical Republicans, and if you were in my line of work, that almost always led to them pressing you about whether Reagan wasn't really "a lot smarter than you guys in the press give him credit for." Dick, on the other hand, seemed to have the kind of cheerful hopelessness that was appropriate to the state of his party.

In any event, we parked at a big pull-out where the stream came under the highway through a box culvert tall enough for a man to walk through.

"The pool below the culvert is loaded with trout," Dick said. "They're not shy, either. The tourists feed them bread all the time. Let's string our rods up and I'll show you something."

Dick struggled into a cheap pair of Ranger waders, selected not for quality but because they were cut full and therefore were capable of accommodating his girth. Dick ran his fly line through the guides of a shiny brown rod with red wrappings. His name was written on it in gold.

"This is a Sage blank built by a guy named Dave McNeese in Portland. I saw his ad in *Fly Fisherman,* offering the rod for a hundred thirty-seven dollars, which is seventy-five dollars less than Sage sells it for. It's a nine-for-five, but I throw a six so it will load better."

Fly fisherman in general and Dick in particular talk that way. Acquiring the bits of knowledge needed to translate this jargon is a childishly tedious process that the fishing magazines make as complicated as possible.

Here's the translation. Most of the graphite fly rods in America are made in factories owned by four firms: Sage, Orvis, Fisher and Loomis. These factories turn out "blanks"—that is, rods with no fittings—which are bought by individual rod builders like Dave McNeese or by fishing-tackle companies like L. L. Bean. These buyers then add the guides, cork handles, their own brand names and as much of a markup as they can get by with. But no matter what the name is on the rod or how much you paid, chances are it came from one of these four factories.

The rods are designated by length and by the weight of the line they cast. Thus, Dick's rod was a "nine-for-five," meaning it was nine feet long and designed to cast a five-weight line. The weights of fly lines run from one, for tiny trout and panfish, to fifteen, for tarpon and marlin. The lower the number, the lighter the weight of the line and the smaller its diameter. Most trout and bass fishing is done with rods and lines in the middle of this range—that is, four weight to eight weight.

By "loading" his five-weight rod with a six-weight line, Dick was assuring that the rod would flex more deeply and thereby push his cast out a bit farther with less effort on his part. Accomplished casters may overload their rods by as much as two weights.

Such knowledge is not particularly useful unless you want to become an expert in fly fishing. For my part, I wanted the knowledge because I thought catching more fish with esoteric equipment might bring me a joy so powerful that it would keep the black dog at bay.

It seemed that simple.

Dick put the Sage rod in my hand and said, "Feel that." I did not know much then, but I knew that what I held in my hand made every other fly rod I had held feel like a tree limb. It was a lovely thing. Dick took it back and led me to the pool. We peered into its depths.

"You see anything?"

"No," I said.

"It's loaded with trout. If a tourist came along and threw in some bread, they would come zooming from every direction. That is sad, because the behavior of these fish has been debased by close contact with humans. Since we can't change that, we can use them for teaching purposes."

He gave me a small ball of bread and bade me throw it upon the water. When I did, big coppery fish with rosy sides came boiling to the surface.

"Hatchery rainbows," he said with contempt. "A hatchery rainbow is to a wild brown trout as a bald eagle is to one of Frank Perdue's chickens."

Personally, I thought the fish looked pretty good, and I wanted to catch one.

Dick had a rectangular box strapped to his chest. It was composed of hinged shelves that swung out and down to reveal a half-dozen foam-lined trays full of row upon row of tiny flies.

"Now," he said, "I will show you the dirty little secret of trout fishing in America."

He pulled out a fluorescent fuzzball about the size of an English pea. "More trout are caught on this than on any other wet fly."

"What is it?" I said.

"It's a Glo Bug. Just a little yarn wrapped around a small hook. It is meant to imitate a salmon egg. Trout love fish eggs.

"To a great extent, it was the use of the Glo Bug that really got me into trout fishing. I fished with this fellow Ken Miyata. He's a herpetologist at the Smithsonian. Most intense fisherman I've ever known, and one of the best. He wrote a piece for *Fly Fisherman* called 'Fishing Like a Predator.' It was about putting yourself into the mind-set of a predatory animal and stalking trout the way, say, an osprey would. Pretty spooky stuff. Anyway, Ken introduced me to Glo Bugs and suddenly I was able to go out and catch fish where I hadn't been able to catch fish before."

I tied a Glo Bug on my leader. Dick produced a thumbnail-sized piece of foam rubber with an adhesive backing. He stuck it on my leader about two feet above the Glo Bug.

"That's a strike indicator," Dick said. "When a fish hits your Glo Bug, the strike indicator will twitch and you set the hook."

I made a cast into the pool. Whango-bango, I caught a trout. It dashed back and forth in the dark water and wore itself out. I released it.

"You could catch every one in this pool, if you kept chumming them up with bread," Dick said. "But you wouldn't want to do that. Let's go down to the Green Drake Pool."

The Green Drake Pool turned out to be a shaded, sylvan spot where it was possible to see the dark shapes of big fish moving over a stony bottom.

Dick lowered himself onto a boulder and announced that he would fish there because he was having trouble getting around. I should push on upstream to the pools above us.

"Biggest brown trout ever caught in Maryland came out of this pool," Dick said. "A guide named Art Lee was out here with a client and he sees this huge fish cruising in the pool. Lee figures the client will never raise or land this kind of fish.

So he ties a big olive-green Wooly Bugger right there on the hood of his car and then he catches the fish with it. Over eight pounds. That was back when you could keep one fish a day on this stream. All the locals still want it that way. They fought us like hell on making it catch-and-release."

I went upstream with my Glo Bug to a place called the Elbow Pool. When I plopped the Glo Bug into the middle, a big rainbow came boiling out on the lower end of the pool, racing for my fly as if it wanted to mate with it. The fish grabbed the fly, made three wild leaps and spit it out. I was stunned. I remember saying to myself: "This shit really works."

I was talking about fly fishing in general. It seemed so easy and the fish so cooperative. I felt pretty good.

A funny thing happened on the way back to Washington. Dick started talking about a reporter I knew who had been in North Africa when Dick was stationed there. Now this particular reporter was someone that friends of mine suspected of being too cozy with the CIA. Then Dick said, "I got listed as a CIA agent once in this book of supposed American agents that the East Germans published. It caused a stir at the time. A lot of the people in the book were Agency, but a lot of them were just Foreign Service officers like me. Since I had been an Army officer and was stationed in Yemen, where the Agency had a lot of operations, the author just assumed I was CIA."

I wondered why he was telling me this. In my line of work, it is a reflex to wonder why people tell you things—or, for that matter, why they ring you up out of the blue to become your friend.

"Pretty amazing to see a stream like that only one hour from the White House, isn't it?" Dick said.

I said I thought so, too.

"I'll show you something even more amazing someday," he said. "There's a stream with wild brown trout just outside the Beltway, only twelve miles from the North Portico of the White House. The State of Maryland has been trying to pave it over for years. I've pestered the governor so much about it, he and I have a personal vendetta.

"You mean he actually knows who you are?"

"Oh, yes. When he's on a call-in show and I ask him a question, he says, 'Dick, I can hear the hate in your voice.' Makes me feel kind of special."

Thus began my Glo Bug phase.

11
The Redneck Way of Fly Fishing

When I decided to get serious about fly fishing, I outfitted the boys and me with inexpensive Lamiglass graphite rods from the Hook and Hackle Company in Plattsburgh, New York. Together, these three homely, serviceable rods cost about what I could have spent on a first-rate Orvis or Sage rod for myself. But I did not count it a sacrifice, because I despise cheapness in a man, especially when it comes to fishing tackle. I hate to see kids fishing with junk tackle while their old man hogs the good stuff. There are a lot of things you cannot control about what kind of man you become. But one you can control is whether or not you are cheap.

I will not drag you through the tedious process of how Ben, Jeff and I gradually built our stock of fly boxes, waders and vests. So many packages made their way to Chevy Chase from Orvis, Cabela's and my old friends at L. L. Bean that

Pat Tyler pronounced me a "gear hog." I came by this passion for gear honestly. It is a family trait, reaching its most extreme form in me, a tackle addict, and in my brother, who has been for all his life a compulsive buyer of boats. In my experience, this lust for gear is widespread among American men. We think that if we have the right equipment, we will acquire expertise and that expertise will bring us happiness. At least, that's what I thought.

In those days, I found myself quoting Dick so often that the boys ribbed me about all the sentences that began "Dick Blalock says . . ."

"Who is this Dick Blalock?" Susan said. "You make him sound like God."

"He is, Mom. He is," said Ben.

"Dick rules," said Jeff.

Even though the boys teased me, they always wanted to know "What does Dick say?" whenever we were heading for new waters or trying to choose a fly. So they were game when I announced one day, "Dick says we should go to Jeremy's Run up on the Blue Ridge Parkway. He says that's the best place he knows for beginners."

Actually, you leave the car on the parkway and hike a half mile down into a canyon that lies in the heart of the Shenandoah National Park. It's a rough, twisting path that starts out innocently enough. For a few hundred yards, we strolled along the Appalachian Trail itself, which is easy going over hard-packed clay.

Then the dimmer trail to Jeremy's Run angled off toward a creek we could not yet see or hear. Down we went, but at a gentle slope through the laurels and greening dogwoods. These were open, parklike woods where deer grazed as placidly as cows. I remember one doe, in particular, that raised her head to watch us while she made water in the steaming leaves.

The slope steepened and the trail zigzagged through a tiring series of switchbacks. Soon we found ourselves hobbling down the watercourse of a wet-weather branch, and the backpacks containing our waders, lunches and water bottles felt less friendly on our backs.

"I can't believe Dick hiked down this," said Ben. "He'd never get out."

"Maybe he was thinner then," I said.

Finally, we were in the green world of the floor of a mountain hollow. We waded a feeder stream that went through a tangle of alder and birch, and there under an arching canopy of tulip poplars was Jeremy's Run. Its long glides and the frothing plunge pools were the emerald color you see only in streams fed by water that has never touched asphalt.

Somewhere in a fishing log, I wrote down the number of fish we caught that day. Ben, as was his habit, caught the most. They were small fish, four to eight inches, I suppose. These were native brook trout, country fish made innocent by their distance from town.

We cast big, fluffy flies, White Wulffs and Humpies that I had bought at the Eddie Bauer store on M Street in Washington because they "looked about right."

Jeremy's Run became our kindergarten. But one night during the two-hour ride back to Washington, Jeffrey said something that had been on all our minds. "That's a lot of walking for such tiny fish."

"Yeah," said Ben. "Can't we go somewhere that has big fish?"

I asked Ben to dig my fly box out of my fishing vest, which was on the back floorboard. As I drove, I opened the box and pulled out the Glo Bug that Dick had given me at Big Hunting Creek.

"Dick Blalock says these are deadly on the Yellow Breeches," I said.

So it happened that the boys and I became the Glo Bug scourges of Boiling Springs, Pennsylvania, where you could see big trout cruising like torpedoes and scores of dandy-looking fellows in outfits that put to shame our rough rods and cheap waders.

We exploited the biology of bread. That is to say that on certain streams like the Yellow Breeches, there is a mixture of trout born in the stream and trout placed there from hatcheries. At the point where the Yellow Breeches flows from the big spring-fed lake at the quaint little town of Boiling Springs, the big hatchery trout gather under a bridge where the tourists and antique shoppers stop to throw bread in the stream.

Trout, some of them monstrous, come zooming out of the current to strike this bread in a savage way, and if you drift a Glo Bug through this area when the bread is on the water, you can catch a fish on every cast. It's a pretty spot, too.

The boys will not like me telling this. But there were times when things were slow that we actually cast a little bread onto the water ourselves. We salved our consciences by saying that it did not matter, since we were releasing the fish.

A little farther downstream is a house with a deck that hangs over the water. The boys and I labeled it the Bread House, because the big rainbows that cruised back and forth under the deck were fools for Glo Bugs.

I think it was Ben who first noticed the obvious. If you put a Glo Bug on the end of your leader and attach a lead shot to the leader and use a strike indicator that disappears when a fish takes the Glo Bug, you are doing something very similar to bait fishing with a cane pole.

"Dick Blalock says it's all right," I said, a little defensively.

"It just doesn't seem much like the fly fishing you see on television," Ben said.

I had to admit that. Still, on many outings, it was Glo Bugs or nothing, especially if I wanted fish like my first two big trout. I got them on a drizzly December day when I skipped work and went by myself to the Yellow Breeches. A slow rain had begun to soak through my parka. The creek was so cold I was shaking in my waders when I got myself in position to cast toward the Bread House. No sooner had the Glo Bug settled into the water than my strike indicator sank slowly, as if waterlogged. I set the hook on the heaviest fish I had ever felt on a fly rod, and it began a long run downstream. The drag sang loudly, and I played the fish patiently. It was a rainbow trout of eighteen inches. Before long, I caught another just like it.

I entered these fish proudly in my log and reported my accomplishment to Dick.

"What did they take?" he said.

"Glo Bugs."

"Oh," he said.

"What does that mean?" I said.

"Nothing. Glo Bugs are fine. A lot of people take a lot of fish on them."

"So do you," I said.

"No. I thought I mentioned that. I quit using them after I went up to Alaska and saw rainbow trout sucking the eggs out of spawning salmon. I decided right then never to use Glo Bugs again. I lost a lot of respect for rainbows on that trip."

"What's that got to do with not using Glo Bugs down here?"

"Nothing, really. I just decided it was too much like bait fishing. I don't need to catch a fish that badly anymore."

"Then why did you start me on Glo Bugs?"

"I thought you did need to," he said. "It's a necessary phase."

It was then that I knew I was in the hands of a tricky bastard.

12
Easy for You to Say

In 1986, *The New York Times* assigned me to London. It did not occur to me nor, I am sure, to my employers that I was being offered a chance to peer even deeper into the gene pool of the Redneck Way, an experience that profoundly affected my ideas about killing fish.

Britain truly is the home of American fly fishing and American field sports in general. As Americans, we are heir to two stereotypes—the Tweedy Gentleman and the Poacher—that are deeply rooted in the British class system. The gent was the protector of forest and stream. The poacher of the British Isles, sometimes actually called by the name "redneck," was the remorseless fish killer who snagged the salmon from its spawning redd or netted the tame trout from the garden stream. Imagine my surprise to discover that a class inversion had taken place.

We got a glimpse of this when on one of our

first nights in London, Jeff and I settled in front of the television to watch a program about fly fishing for rainbow trout in a pretty lake outside London. A Tweedy Gent caught a fish of about three pounds, held it up the camera to admire, then reached into his satchel, produced a small club, and smacked the fish smartly on the head. The whole business was over in a wink.

Jeffrey leapt from the sofa as if he had seen a murder. He had, in fact, never witnessed the killing of a trout, because at fourteen, he had done all of his fishing on catch-and-release waters back home.

"Dad, he killed that fish," he said, pointing at the television. "Did you see that? He just hit it on the head and killed it.'

The club that the Tweedy Gentleman used is called a "priest," and it is a rare British fly fisherman who does not have one on his person. No-kill streams are almost unheard-of in Britain and still rare on the Continent. From the Royal Family right on down, the gentry are still avid killers of Britain's dwindling supply of Atlantic salmon, the most endangered members of the salmonid family, which includes the majority of our cold-water game fish. Indeed, a cultural anthropologist would conclude that killing salmon is one of the ways by which Britons determine social rank and those within the higher ranks prove their importance to themselves.

As evidence, consider that one of the few honeymoon pictures of the Prince and Princess of Wales released by Buckingham Palace shows Diana posing in front of four large dead salmon. The 1981 photograph was taken on the Scottish estate of the Duke of Westminster, the wealthiest landlord in London. Diana, clad in country clothes, stands casually, one lanky leg crossed over the other, like a dancer at rest. She has linked her arm through that of her gillie, a stout man in a tweed suit, matching cap and dark tie. As the Princess leans against him, the gray-haired man beams with fatherly pride. In a society attuned to interpreting the signals of rank, the intended message from the Palace was clear. Here is the queen-to-be, able to reap fish from the streams of the wealthiest and command the service and adoration of the hoi polloi.

Among affluent Britons, the link between social rank and the right to harvest fish and game is so fundamental that they find themselves going to ridiculous lengths to preserve it. The legendary chalk streams of Hampshire, the Itchen and the Test, offer fishing for flaccid hatchery trout.

The gap between style and substance is even more striking when it comes to hunting. On shooting preserves near London, mallard ducks and pheasants that are stocked each summer stroll around tame as chickens, and it takes an ingenious gamekeeper to get them ready for the fall gunning season.

The ducks are a particularly sad lot, as they must go into a training program. They are made to sleep at night in towers, then released every morning so they can glide down toward a nearby lake, where they soon learn that food awaits them. Once the season starts, of course, people with shotguns will be waiting along their glide path. It is nothing like shooting at a wild duck, but at least these mallards are flying after a fashion when they are sacrificed to sports who pay around $1,500 a day for this shooting.

All the participants in the gentrified sports of British "country life" look down on "coarse fishermen." These are, for the most part, working-class men who use live bait for carp and other less exalted species. Barred from the free-flowing streams of the private estates, they fish Britain's sluggish tidal rivers, lakes and canals. They are the most militant catch-and-release fishermen in the world. The distance they have advanced beyond the Tweedy Gents in environmental consciousness would have to be measured in light-years. But their place in the pecking order of British sports is symbolized by the layout at Farlow's, the excellent store at 5 Pall Mall in London, where the fly-fishing gear is on the main floor and the tackle for "coarse fishing" is kept upstairs, out of sight.

On one of our first weekends in Britain, Derek Seymour, a true Cockney and the driver in the London bureau of the *Times,* invited the boys and me to come to a contest between his club and another on a canal out beyond Regent's Park. We wandered for several hours in the greener suburbs before we found his crowd along a slack canal of gray water flowing through a canyon formed by the red-brick walls of industrial warehouses.

It was quite a sight. Fifty or so fishermen were strung out along the canal at assigned spots or "pegs." Each of them had a big black net hanging into the water to hold the catch. They fished with long, whippy poles and tiny maggots for bait.

The members of these clubs, of which there are hundreds in Britain and Europe, are by all odds the most honorable fishermen I've ever encountered. All quit fishing on the stroke of an assigned hour, and a man with a portable scale passed along the canal weighing the catch from each net and writing down the figure. Then the fish went back into the canal.

I once asked Derek what would happen when these fellows were out fishing on their own and one of their number caught a nice pike. Would he take it home to eat?

"It's just not done," he said. "Anybody who did that would get a lot of aggro from his mates. If he kept it up, he'd likely get a bit of the old fisticuff."

Derek, about the most extreme fishing addict I have ever met, became my guide to coarse fishing. We actually went fishing only a couple of times, because he was involved in "matches with my mates" almost every weekend. But he began bringing me publications like *Carp World,* which outlined the rigorous conservationist approach of serious coarse fishermen. Such publications, among other things, report the state of health of individual fish. A typical entry might read: "Tom Parker of the Midlands Club caught Old Copper on a trip to Rudman Water on Nov. 20. Tom reports he weighed 37 pounds, 6 ounces. That's up from the 36 pounds even reported when he was caught last summer, which means this fishery maintains a good growth rate."

There were also less happy news items, including a rash of electrocutions. Of fishermen, not fish. It seems that the new graphite poles are excellent conductors of electricity. Every so often, some fellow would raise his eighteen-foot pole, for which he might have paid as much as $2,000, and contact a power line. Bingo, fried to a crisp right there at the peg.

This is one of the hazards of fishing in an

industrial landscape. There are more sylvan settings, too, but the point is that coarse fishermen use every inch of Britain's fairly limited network of canals, rivers and lakes. And because they have so few places to fish in comparison to a large country like the United States, these fisherman have long since figured out that unrestricted killing would soon clean out the carp, roach, tench, bream, chub, pike and barbel from every last ditch and puddle in the "green and pleasant land."

I was struck by the reverence of these fishermen for even the most unenchanting species. One day Derek happily reported that he had "sacked up the gudgeon" in a weekend match. A gudgeon, it turns out, is a minnow that must be taken on an almost microscopic hook. But in a contest that depends on total weight, it is possible that a sack containing one hundred gudgeon will beat the one-pound carp taken by the fellow on the next peg.

British clubs travel all over Europe to compete. Derek's club, a championship outfit called Trev's Browning Fishing Club of Walthamstow, made annual trips to Holland and Germany and then hosted those clubs on return matches to Britain. The fishing conditions on the canals near Amsterdam were very difficult, Derek observed. It seems prostitutes in hotels overlooking the tournament's waters like to call to the fishermen with lewd suggestions about what they could do with their poles. It is very bad form to leave your peg before the fishing is over, even in Amsterdam on a slow day. "It's just not done," Derek said. "Period. End-of."

I did not find the competitive aspect of this fishing attractive. In that respect, the ethos of the clubs seemed a lot like that of the American bowling league or bass-fishing tournament. But one thing was obvious. These lads and I had a common descent. We were all children of the Redneck Way of Fishing. Yet they had moved on to higher ground, quietly establishing catch-and-release fishing decades before their American cousins, not to mention the priest-wielding Tweedy Gents who club their trout and look down their noses at "coarse fishermen."

I took an elegant new Sage fly rod, nine feet long for five-weight line, to London. The rod stayed in the closet in the hallway of the equally elegant flat that the *Times* owns in Belgravia. I think the black dog lived in that closet, too.

It was the longest period of my life without fishing. It was a happy time for Ben and Jeff, who were fourteen and sixteen when we arrived and really came of age there. They crawled the pubs and played in bands and pursued their interests. When we left, a blond girl named Samantha wrote in Ben's yearbook: "Thank you for lending me your little brother for my experiments."

It was not a happy time for me or for Susan. One day I was browsing in the psychobabble section of a bookstore on King's Road and I ran across a badly written book that included ten rules for avoiding anxiety and depression.

One rule leapt out at me. It was: Figure out what you really want to do and do it.

Easy for you to say, I thought.

13
A Meditation on the Midlife Crisis and the Literature, Psychology and Mystique of Fly Fishing

The most widely read American fishing writer of the mid-nineteenth century was Henry W. Herbert, who was singled out by Edgar Allan Poe as a finalist in the category of having "written more trash than any man living." Herbert was born into a titled English family, but shortly after he finished Cambridge, he was given a small trust fund and exiled permanently to New York by his father for a breach of manners so profound that its exact nature has been scrubbed from the family history. The trust fund proved inadequate for the full support of Herbert's interests, which included womanizing, horse racing and perfecting "the skill exerted in casting and managing a fly."

Herbert thought of himself as a serious novelist, but it was his fishing writing, under the pen name Frank Forester, that the public craved. Around 1845, when he was thirty-eight years old, Herbert fell into a notable funk. It lasted for thirteen years, culminating when a younger woman, who married him for his money, got a look at his bank book and took off. "This desertion seems to have broken his will," notes one of his biographers.

In 1858, Herbert invited all his friends to a banquet to be served on May 15, but only one person showed up, perhaps because Herbert did not send the invitations until May 14. The solitary guest spent the entire evening trying to talk Herbert out of his threatened suicide and thought he had just about succeeded when his host left the table and went into an adjoining room. There was a gunshot, and Herbert came back into the room, bleeding from a mortal chest wound, and said, "I told you I would do it."

I was intrigued, even relieved, when I ran across this tale in *McClane's New Standard Fishing Encyclopedia.* Clearly, I was not the first writer to see—or at least experience—a confluence between fly fishing and masculine angst in life's middle passage. Poor Henry W. Herbert had long ago explored the aesthetics of the sport and stumbled down the dark tunnels of midlife. Never mind that Poe said the man could not write. Like most geniuses, Poe was intolerant of those with lesser gifts, and besides, Edgar was not exactly a model of stability himself. In any event, Herbert's importance for our purposes is that he was one of a claque of propagandists who by the time of the Civil War had established the artistic and psychic superiority of fly fishing. Herbert's editor at the *Turf Register* in the 1830s, William Trotter Porter, put it this way: "Fly fishing has been designated the royal and aristrocratic branch of the angler's art . . . the most difficult, the most elegant, and to men of taste, by myriads of degrees the most exciting and pleasant mode of angling."

There are over five thousand books on fishing in the English language, and in a fair number of them, the authors wrestle with the question of why some people like to pull fish out of the water. Since this is the most extensive literature of any sport, we can conclude that the question is (1) not easy to answer and (2) capable of holding the interest of at least a fair portion of literate humankind.

The standard explanation is that people are drawn to fishing as a way of reenacting and presumably calming the "atavisic impulses" inherited from our hunter-gatherer ancestors. But this explanation does not answer what is really being asked by the person who turns to you at a cocktail party in New York upon hearing that you've just paid $800 to be flown to Jackson Hole and another $350 to have someone float you down the Snake River while you wave a $300 rod in the air and says, "Why do you like to fish?"

In my view, the people who fish do so because it seems like magic to them, and it is hard to find things in life that seem magical. Partly this magic resides in the physical sensation. Hitting a line drive or a tennis forehand or a golf shot produces the species of pleasure I'm trying to describe. Another way of thinking of this feeling is to imagine that cells scattered throughout the bone marrow—and particularly in the area of the elbows—are having subtle but prolonged orgasms and sending out little neural whispers about these events.

For some people, including me, pulling on a fish generates a physical pleasure on the order of what I've described above. I think that's part of why I like to catch fish. But what is there about catching a fish that seems magical in the psychological sense? The appeal is the same as that which resides in pulling a rabbit out of a hat. We have reached into a realm over which we have no explainable mastery and by supernatural craft or mere trickery created a moment that is as phenomenal on the hundredth performance as on the first.

Fish in the water represent pure potential. If the water is not clear, we do not know if they exist at all. To get them to bite something connected to a line and pull them into our world is managing a birth that brings these creatures from the realm of mystery into the world of reality. It's a kind of creation.

Then there are the fish themselves. When I see fish coming through the water, they seem as sovereign and self-contained as beings from another planet, and beholding them engenders the same kind of fascination that I imagine I might feel if a spacecraft opened and I was able to look inside and see beings of a profoundly different sort swimming in light.

In an essay for *Trout* magazine, Kitty Pearson-Vincent, a photographer, was trying to convey the quality of this visual experience in declaring that "the fish is otherworldly." She added: "Trout are like dreams hovering in the elusive unconscious. In capturing one, if ever so briefly, before release, there is that sense of revelation occurring when one awakens in the night, snatching a dream from the dark portals of sleep."

There is also the shape of fish. There are certain people to whom the shape of fish is extremely satisfying to behold. If you do not think so, start looking at the number of fish you see in sculpture and paintings. It is one of the most satisfying and seminal shapes in creation, and there are some of us who need to see it a lot. My house is chockablock with fish drawings, fish ceramics and fish carvings from India, Africa, the Caribbean and, of course, Minnesota, where the production of antique fish decoys is a thriving new industry. I have had to get more selective in my collecting because of the recent explosion in fish fashions. These days there is hardly a boutique or catalog without its array of fish earrings and fish T-shirts. The Kellogg Collection, a trendy furniture store in Washington, is offering a chest of drawers with a hand-painted fly-fishing scene. From Tiffany to the lowliest pottery shed, vast schools of trout, bass, sunfish, sharks and sting rays swim across our dinner plates.

I am drawn to the more primitive kinds of fish art. But whether we are talking about a hand-carved decoy from the North Woods or an Art Deco marlin on a Miami Beach hotel, it is important to remember that such objects exist because this shape swims eternally in the Anima Mundi, the oceanic common memory of mankind. For my part, as I reflect more deeply on the fish's history as a mythic symbol and religious icon, I begin to wonder if having fish shapes around me is a way to stay in touch with the ideas of Jesus without having to go near the people who do business in his name. Anyway, those are some of my guesses about why people fish.

Moving from the realm of speculation to that of fact, we know that New Stone Age Man invented the fishhook sometime around 8000 B.C. It was a hard thing to invent, if you ask me, which probably explains why Old Stone Age Man did not invent the fishhook in the 640,000 or so years he had to work on inventing tools. Let's face it, the club is easy compared to the fishhook.

The metal hook with a barb and an eye existed in Crete about 3400 B.C., and it was the Macedonians on the Astraeus River who invented the fly. They tied red wool and cock feathers to a hook to imitate an "impudent" buzzing insect favored by brown trout there, according to Aelian, a writer in the third century A.D. He said: "When the fish spies one of these insects on the top of the water, it swims quietly underneath it . . . [A]pproaching it, as it were, under the shadow, it opens its mouth and gulps it down, just as a wolf seizes a sheep, or an eagle a goose, and having done this it swims away beneath the ripple."

Observing this, the Macedonian fishermen dangled their flies at the end of six-foot lines affixed to sticks of equal length. "The fish being attracted by the color becomes extremely excited," Aelian wrote, "proceeds to meet it, anticipating from its beautiful appearance a most delicious repast; but, as with extended mouth it seizes the lure, it is held fast by the hook, and being captured, meets with a very sorry entertainment."

By the late Middle Ages, flies on the same principle were being tied in the British Isles and dangled over trout there with long poles. In the earliest British fishing writing, we see an emphasis on aesthetics, using light tackle and conducting oneself in an elevated style. That is clear in the chapter on fishing with flies that Charles Cotton, a London layabout, contributed to the 1676 edition of *The Compleat Angler,* a book first published in 1653 by his friend, the noted bait fisherman Izaak Walton.

The younger man properly honored Walton as a better writer and as his "father" as a fisherman. But Cotton is a far more important figure than Walton in developing the aesthetic sense that has dominated British and American fishing ever since. Cotton wrote that the most elegant way to catch trout was to fish "fine and far off" with a long pole, a light line of one to four horsehairs, and virtually weightless flies that drifted naturally on the surface. Ever since, fly fishermen have looked down on live-bait fishermen like Walton and their heavy lines. "He that cannot kill a trout on two [hairs], deserves not the name of angler," Cotton said.

With Cotton originated the idea that this kind of fishing had to involve physical grace, utilizing motions that blended with the gentle movements of breeze and current. But with a pole of fifteen to eighteen feet, Cotton could not make the elegant casting motion that developed with the shorter, highly flexible rods that began to appear in the early nineteenth century, along with reels and lines of greased silk. These made possible the distinctive buggy-whip effect gained from a rhythmic waving of the rod and the airy extension of a gradually lengthened line that settles to the water like a falling strand from a spider's web.

For over a century, the great breakthroughs in fly-fishing technology have occurred in the United States. In 1846, Samuel Phillippe of Easton, Pennsylvania, perfected the hexagonal rod, made by gluing together six long, triangular-shaped splinters of Asian bamboo. In cross section, Phillippe's rod looked like this:

Because of the difficulty of shaving, fitting and gluing these long pieces of bamboo or cane, such rods are still the most expensive. But they were surpassed as casting and fish-fighting instruments, although not as art objects, by the next round of innovations. These came with the perfecting of fiberglass rods by Dr. A. M. Howald, a chemist from Perrysburg, Ohio, in 1948 and with the manufacture of graphite rods in the 1980s. Also, the introduction of a new coating material for fly lines, polyvinyl chloride, in 1949 made greased silk lines obsolete and ended the sinking problems that plagued my uncle Erskine.

As far as equipment goes, we are living in the Golden Age of Fly Fishing. Where there used to be only a couple of hundred truly expert fly fishermen in the United States, there are now thousands who could match the best practitioners in the history of the sport. Naturally, as in any group so large, some are jerks. All are snobs when it comes to what they really think about other forms of fishing.

That is because of the aesthetic principle at the core of fly fishing. It is the most beautiful way of trying to catch a fish, not the most efficient, just as ballet is the most beautiful way of moving the body between two points, not the most direct.

Fly fishing is to fishing as ballet is to walking. It is interesting that many men come to fly fishing after they have been through other kinds of fishing, usually forms that involve powerful boats, heavy rods and brutally strong fish.

Perhaps this is because they are getting wiser and less hormonal. Or perhaps it is that as men get older, some of them develop holes in their souls, and they think this disciplined, beautiful and unessential activity might close those holes.

14
Among the Maymaygwayshi

Sometimes we need to be close to the earth and feel its true age and contemplate its real history. We need to contemplate, as well, the history of man's imaginings about the earth and to remind ourselves that truth has many tellings, only one of which we call science.

The earth, for example, is about 4.5 billion years old. Around 3.5 billion years ago, a vast carapace of stone was formed over an area that straddles the border between the middle part of the United States and Canada. This stone covering, shaped like a turtle's back and currently known as the Canadian Shield, was scoured by glaciers in the several ice ages. Lakes were created, and as the granite resolved itself into soil, trees grew.

Once there was enough vegetation to feed them, moose appeared—really big moose actually, around the size of small elephants. About ten thousand years ago, bands of Paleo-Indians formed a social order based on the fact that it took several people working together to bring down one of these elephantine moose. By more recent antiquity, the moose had diminished in size, and the Dakota, Assiniboin and the eventually dominant Ojibway had arrived.

At some point in all this, the Maymaygwayshi moved into the sheer rock cliffs that rise straight up a hundred feet from the waters of some of the Canadian Shield lakes. The Maymaygwayshi were small men, about three feet tall, with hairy faces, mischievous fellows who emerged at night to cut fish from the nets of the Ojibway and leave the nets in shreds. They actually lived inside the cliffs. The knowledge that they were in there came from the reports of Ojibway shamans, who claimed the power to enter the cliffs, speak to the Maymaygwayshi and trade tobacco for rock medicine, which was the drug of last resort for a sick Ojibway. The exact facial appearance of the Maymaygwayshi is difficult to determine, because they were ashamed of their hairy faces and thieving ways and when encountered in daylight would cover their faces with their hands and duck below the gunnels of their canoes.

The best surviving picture of a Maymaygwayshi is on a cliff in the south bay of Darky Lake in the Quetico Provincial Park in Ontario. He appears to be dancing with upraised hands. Each hand has only three fingers, but these digits look long and serviceable. This Maymaygwayshi also has a large, erect penis, although the organ has been airbrushed from the illustration that you will find in the booklet *Pictographs of Quetico,* published by the Ontario Ministry of Natural Resources.

Some people do not believe in the Maymaygwayshi, but personally I find it about as easy as believing in giant moose and the Virgin Birth, particularly when the cliffs with their distinctive yellow streakings and red-ocher pictographs lie in the blue shadows of late afternoon and the waves are marching down the lake. Was it not Einstein, our greatest modern theologian, who said, "The mysterious is the most beautiful thing in life"?

This is how I came to be among the Maymaygwayshi. I had been calling outfitters in Ely, Minnesota, in the summer of 1989 because I wanted to fish the lakes in the Boundary Waters Canoe Area in northern Minnesota and the adjoining Quetico Provincial Park in Ontario.

Outfitters kept saying, "Just come on up. The fishing's great everywhere."

After four decades of fishing, you learn to recognize this as the most fundamental of all statements of ignorance. The fishing is never great everywhere.

Finally, I reached an outfitter named John Schiefelbein. He said, "Tell me exactly what kind of fishing you want to do."

"That's easy," I said. "I want to catch very large smallmouth bass on a fly rod."

"Do you mind working a little to get to your fishing?" John asked.

I said I did not.

"Then I will send you to the best place in the world," he said.

Maybe he did. The trip there, like the day at South Sauty so many years ago, lingers in my memory, as clear and intact as a movie that can be unreeled and replayed in rich and specific detail. For one thing, my sons and I regarded ourselves as fly fishers now. That is not to say we were purists. We still had our spinning gear. But we thought of ourselves as *going fly fishing,* and looking back, I can see that we were in the very beginning stages of getting good at it.

This was the summer after Jeff's junior year in high school and Ben's freshman year at college. We had moved back to Washington from Britain by this time, but Ben was away for the summer, living in London with his girlfriend and working as the compost man at a tony gardening shop near Sloane Square.

So Jeff and I went to Quetico alone. The Boundary Waters–Quetico parks make up the third-largest roadless area touching on U.S. soil. The area comprises 2.75 million acres and fifteen hundred lakes. At the rim of the wilderness, the lakes are connected by leisurely streams of leaf-stained water. But as you press inward toward the higher lakes at the center of the park, these streams become impassable torrents, and the only way to get from lake to lake is to portage over rough or muddy pathways, with one person carrying the canoe over his head like a cumbersome hat and the other staggering along behind with heavy packs as big as steamer trunks.

This was what John Schiefelbein meant when he asked if we minded working for our fishing. This was true wilderness of a type neither Jeff nor I had experienced. We had lakes as big as the reservoir at South Sauty totally to ourselves. We came to understand the nature of true wilderness silence. It is not just an absence of broadcast or recorded noises. It is, fundamentally, the absence of the sounds of internal combustion engines. Even at the most remote places back home, it is hard to find a place where you cannot hear tires crunching gravel or, far off somewhere, the whine of an expressway.

From the time the float plane dropped us at the Hilly Isle Ranger Station on Lac La Croix, we were on our own. It was a foggy day when we set out, the air heavy with water that sometimes congealed into a slow rain. We clamped rod holders to the sides of the canoe and trolled deep-running lures as we paddled for several hours to get off the big lake and into the network of streams branching from the Maligne River.

"Maligne" means "evil," and for me, the river turned out to be aptly named. Fish were at the lures constantly. I had stopped paddling to remove a small northern pike when, with a flick of its head, it drove one point of a treble hook deep into the flesh at the first joint of my thumb. I managed to get the fish off and then tested to see how soundly I was hooked. I felt the point of the hook scraping bone. In forty years of fishing I had never hooked myself. Now it came in the most remote place I had ever been.

"Jeff," I said, "you're going to have to try to get this hook out."

"How?" he said.

"That's what we have to figure out."

Hook removal is a messy business. The traditional method is to push the hook on through the flesh until the point reemerges. Then the barb is clipped off and the hook is backed out. One day, forty miles out in the Gulf of Mexico, I had held the arm of my friend Don Marion while Jerry wove a big snapper hook through the palm of his hand and Don danced passionately on the deck of our boat.

Once you've seen that operation, it does not have a lot of appeal.

Jeff and I were in a swampy stretch of river, but we found one boulder big enough for the two of us to perch on. He looked at the silver Fat Rap dangling from my bloody thumb. "How'd you do that, Dad?" he said in a tone that caused me to flash on that time when the parental role reverses and the grown-up child appears at the nursing home to ask exactly how the old man managed to break his hip.

Before leaving home, I had ordered a hook removal kit for $4.95 from a fishing catalog. It seemed a good time to see what was inside the kit. That turned out to be a red plastic handle of the sort that could be used to crank a lawn mower. Attached to this handle was a loop of thick monofilament. The idea, obviously, was to loop the monofilament around the lure and snatch it out.

Jeff, who is not one to take his time, looped the monofilament around the lure.

"Wait," I said. "Read the directions."

The printed instructions did, indeed, contain some useful tips on aligning the hook so it could be pulled out along its entry path. The principle here was that one short, sharp pain was better than the longer agony of pushing the hook through. The directions assured us that while this method might seem primitive, it really produced less "tissue damage."

Something about the term "tissue damage" raised an image of myself, with a balloon-sized thumb, being flown back to an emergency room in Ely.

"Let's do it," I said.

Jeff looped the mono around the hook, aligned it as per the instructions, and gave a little tug.

"You're going to have to really snatch it," I said.

"Get ready," he said.

He really snatched it.

It worked, and with very little pain at that. Everyone gets cute after a crisis. As Jeff dribbled Merthiolate over the unimpressive hole in my thumb, I allowed as how the hook removal kit was underpriced by about $195.05.

After a series of hard portages, we made Minn Lake just at nightfall and took the first campsite that offered itself. The mosquitoes came in hordes, big repellent-proof fellows that had us twisting in agony by the time we got the tents up. There was no question of grilling the steaks that John had packed for our first night. We ate peanut butter sandwiches in the tent and drank our daily ration of Jack Daniel's, and I fell asleep thinking that eleven days of this would be torment.

Things looked better in the morning. We could see immediately that in our race with darkness we had selected an island that stood at the rim of a huge marsh. We had invaded the homeland of the mosquitoes, rather than vice versa. On the other side of our island lay open water, where a loon was diving for fish. These waters formed themselves around a low, verdant point where later that day, after we had moved our campsite to higher ground, I would catch a fish that I remember as the beginning of my education in catching heavy fish on the fly rod.

In the three-billion-year history of the Canadian Shield and on the surface of this ten-thousand-year-old body of water called Minn Lake, this fish and I represented newcomers of the rankest sort. As a representative of male Caucasians who first appeared about two centuries ago, I had seniority. The ancestors of the smallmouth bass I was about to meet arrived in Minn Lake courtesy of a stocking program undertaken in 1901 by the Ontario provincial government.

The lakes already contained northern pike, walleyes, lake trout, brook trout and a few muskellunge, not to mention crappies, bluegills, suckers and ciscos. It is still possible to find North Woods purists who grouse about the introduction of smallmouth bass into these waters. Why they do beats the hell out of me. I say that as one who labors to be an environmental absolutist. But I figure if we have to put up with transoceanic visitors like starlings, English sparrows and fire ants, we ought to be able to take a little pleasure in a species that has strayed only a few hundred miles from its original home in the Ohio River watershed. In their ninety-odd years in Canada, smallmouth bass have not competed for spawning sites or food with any of the original residents. They fill an unoccupied ecological niche so perfectly that today it is sometimes possible to catch two-to-four-pound bass as rapidly as one can catch spawning bluegills in an Alabama farm pond.

The individual bass that I have in mind was swimming near the aforementioned low-lying, verdant point on Minn Lake on the afternoon of July 31, 1989. For two hours, Jeff and I had cast large, bushy popping bugs—deer-hair flies like those used by Dick Blalock's father—and taken only one small fish. As we neared the point, there popped into my memory a television program I had seen about Roland Martin, a leading tournament fisherman for largemouth bass. In this program, Martin had put aside his usual pursuits to fly fish for smallmouth on Crooked Lake, not far from where we were.

When it came to form, Martin's fly fishing was nothing to aspire to, even for a novice like me. Upon hooking a fish, he played it in the old down-home style, dropping retrieved line onto the floor of the boat rather than cranking it onto the reel as the fish was pulled in. I already knew from Dick that putting a fish "on the reel" was a matter of near-theological importance to some fishermen, including his friend, the legendary Ben Schley of Shepherdstown, West Virginia. Schley, the former head of fish hatcheries for the Department of the Interior and a fishing coach to Dwight Eisenhower and Jimmy Carter, could barely stand to be on the stream with anyone who failed to put every fish on the reel. According to Dick, Schley regarded this as a matter of respect and discipline, of art and in the end a way of measuring the knowledge and seriousness of an individual. To tell the truth, this sounded like a lot of fuss about whether or not you wound line on a reel. But I knew one thing. If I ever got on a stream with Ben Schley, I intended not to embarrass myself.

I suppose that all this was on my mind when Roland Martin, the famous bass predator, flashed across my memory as we paddled our canoe into a small cove formed by an indentation along the southwestern side of that low-lying point on Lake Minn. What Roland Martin said was that smallmouth bass in the Canadian Shield lakes sometimes prefer tiny popping bugs to the large poppers commonly used for bass. So, on a hunch, I tied to my leader a frog-colored bluegill popper dressed on a number 8 hook and cast it into the open water in the middle of the cove. In bass fishing, the standard tactic is to cast a topwater fly toward the rocks and weeds along the shoreline, but earlier in the day, Jeff and I had gotten strikes out in the open water while trolling past the same point. Creativity, in the form of remembering small incidents and following hunches based on them, is a mark of good fishermen. I have never been particularly good at this. But this time I got it right.

No sooner had my bug settled on the still water than a fish came up behind the bug, showing its dorsal fin and then sinking from sight. In saltwater fishing, big fish like marlin or sailfish may show themselves in this manner, sometimes even swimming along behind a trolled lure while they inspect it. Such behavior is rare among bass. Even rarer was my own response.

Perhaps the peace of the wilderness was already settling over me. In any event, I somehow overcame my natural inclination to strike as soon as I saw the fish, or when it refused the fly, to cast frantically in the vain hope of luring it back. Instead, I left my fly on the water as if the fish's behavior had not rattled me. Once the surface was still again, I gently pulled in about six inches of line, swimming my bug forward by a like distance.

For just a bit, the circle of water, sky and light in which I found myself seemed to have slipped the bonds of sidereal time, and this fish, my fly and I converged according to the elongated beats of dreamtime. A whorl opened in the slick top of Minn Lake. A glossy, perfect snout appeared in this hole and my fly entered the snout. I raised my rod and the fly line leapt from the water. It became as tight as the string of an archer's bow and described a straight line between the tip of my rod and the point on the surface where the line entered the water. My fly rod defined a parabola against the Canadian sky, and the sky contained along its lower, western border a tall bank of cumulus clouds, which were backlit in a religious way.

There is a photograph of a particular instant in the necklace of long, slow-beating moments in which this fish and I held two ends of a string and danced together. All that I have described is visible in this picture, plus an element of magic. Jeffrey snapped it when the fish was in the air, its tail pointed toward the sky and its head toward the middle of the earth. When the catching of this fish was done, I knew it was the best bit of fishing that I had ever been part of.

It was with this fish that I began to relax. It was a state, as we shall see, that was not permanent, not for a long time. But for an instant, I glimpsed the way I had to go, the road to Blalock's Way. In all the years after South Sauty, I fished with a formless passion, not for a single fish, but for many fish, *all* fish. My brother and I had a chant that we used when we were cranking up snapper and grouper on heavy tackle off Panama City or Caminada Pass in Louisiana: "Got to get them out of there. Got to catch them all." If I was near water that contained fish I had not caught, I could not rest. And this often led me to fish frantically, clumsily and, in the end, badly.

But this fish I had hooked by moving slowly, almost indifferently, by casting fewer times, not more, by letting the bass come if it was going to come, bite if it was going to bite. I had deftly put this fish on the reel and played it firmly, but delicately, so that if either Ben Schley or Dick had been watching, I would not have embarrassed myself. I had entered a new knowledge or allowed it to enter me, a circumstance that requires an act of relaxation, a surrender, a submission to the knowledge one wishes to possess. Walt Whitman was speaking of art, not fish, in "Song of Myself," but he was getting at the same idea: "Have you practis'd so long to learn to read?/ Have you felt so proud to get at the meanings of poems?/ Stop this day and night with me and you shall possess the origin of all poems."

In any event, I caught the fish, which was something over three pounds and up to that time the largest smallmouth bass I had caught, and for a creature that possesses an IQ of, say, six, it taught me a lot. This fish and others that followed it were punctuating moments in a skein of days that Jeff and I shared in a spirit of profound companionability.

I was not in top condition for the hard traveling we were doing as we pressed toward the inner wilderness, and without a word, Jeffrey took the hardest job, that of carrying the canoe, at every portage. We camped the second night on a grassy point graced by an elegant pine tree. Beside this point ran a torrent of fast water called the Darky River, which had its source miles away in the lake of the same name. I knew I was still swimming in the aura of my earlier fish when, while unloading the canoe in the darkness, I casually flipped a popping bug into the torrent and caught a two-pound bass.

That night I handed Jeff a copy of *Huckleberry Finn* that I had slipped into the book bag. He had been on a teenager's tear through Vonnegut and Tolkien, but it was not long before Sam Clemens had worked a mightier spell on him. In our tent, on that evening and on many to follow, his flashlight shone far into the night.

I allowed myself a moment of congratulation for giving Jeff the chance to discover this book in a place where it was still possible to glimpse the untamed continent that young Sam Clemens knew. In all this—our nation's great yarn, the drawings upon the rocks, the moose among the lily pads, the brown fish falling from our fingers into the darkness of their home waters—I felt that Jeffrey might encounter memories to carry at the center of his heart for years, for a lifetime, perhaps. I know I did.

At this moment, many adventures lay before us. We were in a landscape that changed me and changes me still every time I return. Before us lay the water paths and the very campsites packed hard by the moose-hunting bands of the Paleo-Indians, by the Ojibway and by the voyageurs led by the old French fur men, Jacques de Noyan and Pierre de La Vérendrye. And at the center lay Darky and the clifty home of the Maymaygwayshi and the ghosts of South Sauty.

15
Backsliding Down the Redneck Way

"What if Dick could see this?" Jeff said.

He spoke these words from a perch on a rocky bank at the foot of the series of rapids that brings the Darky River into Darky Lake. I cannot remember my exact answer, for at that moment, I was in the throes of a powerful ancestral lust. I suppose if I said anything it was in the neighborhood of "a man's got to do what a man's got to do."

Where the river entered the larger body of water, the force of its current pushed long, thready swirls of water out into the lake. Gathered in that moving water was the largest concentration of sizable smallmouth bass I have ever seen.

In our hands were ultralight spinning rods spooled with four- and six-pound-test monofilament. At the end of those lines were small jigs with rubber tails of purple and fluorescent red.

Impaled on the hooks of those jigs were black, eely-looking creatures. Leeches. Live bait.

Only forty-eight hours after my epiphany at Minn Lake, we had fallen off the fly-fishing wagon in a big way. We were having a fine time.

Actually, it was John Schiefelbein's fault. He had put a container of the foul-looking creatures in our gear, with the advice to try them if the fishing got slow. And it did get slow once we left Minn Lake with its shallow, grassy bays. Darky is a deep lake with steep sides, and we could find few of the flats and rubble-strewn shorelines that are best for fly fishing with surface bugs and streamer flies.

And besides, every damn bass in the lake was stacked up in this one spot. It is true that we had streamer flies that imitate a live leech, and now I regret not trying them, because the fly fishing would probably have been as good as the spinning. That is exactly what I would do today. But I did not know much about fly fishing then, and it did not occur to me, as it would now in an instant, to look inside my box for the leechlike streamers.

In any event, once we got started with the leeches, we just lost control of the situation. Besides, we had stumbled onto leech magic in an innocent way. At least, that is my alibi, and I am sticking with it. It happened during the long, grinding passage up another section of the Darky River to reach the lake. This involved a succession of portages along steep grades, loading and then reloading the canoe six times in a single day. In this kind of rough going, the fly rods have to stay in their cases or they will be crushed. But the shorter, tougher spinning rods could stay out for fishing during the rest stops. And it was at one of these that I idly hooked a leech to the jig I was using and tossed it into a pool at the foot of a small cascade of rapids. Instantly I had a fish. We stayed there for several hours, and we discovered that these fish could not get enough of the leeches.

But nowhere did we find so many large fish as at Darky. You might as well know the whole sorry story. I also discovered that if you attached a bobber about three feet above the line, you could just let your bait drift with the current and get a strike almost every time. Ever since that day at South Sauty, I have had imprinted on my inner eye the picture of a red-and-white bobber. After a hard day of staring at my float, this visual memory gets recharged, and when I close my eyes at night, I can see quite clearly the persistence-of-vision image of a fishing bobber. Sometimes it floats on the surface, and sometimes it is going under the way a bobber does when a fish takes the bait. It is not a bad way to go to sleep. Later, I was reminded of that in my tent at Darky, for we saw our bobbers go under many times that first evening.

Even with live bait, catching heavy fish on light line requires a touch. There was a routine to catching these big fish at Darky. It involved a light drag and a precisely timed strike. There is an exciting moment when the float swoops under and you know that a fish has taken.

You aim your rod toward the fish and bow toward it, trying to get your arm, rod, line and fish in a precise line. With the reel hand, you crank in slack until there is such a tight connection that you clearly feel the muscular thumping of a swimming fish, and with big fish, it is a formidable thump, for you are hooked to a wild energy.

But you have only an instant—like a held note in a piece of music—before you must set the hook with an upward sweeping of the rod, firm, but gentle and above all smooth.

When the hook bit them, these big bass would then streak away downcurrent, peeling line from the reel. At this point, everything surrenders to the strength of the fish. Any attempt to snub or turn it will break the line. I like this feeling, which I compare in my imagination to trying to stop a really powerful fullback by grabbing his belt.

At the end of this long run, the fish at Darky would head up, climbing into the air with a muscular twisting leap, and it was at this point that you would see the real size of these fish, which ran between three and four and one-half pounds.

We released them every one. Let the record show that. Even in our backslid condition, we recognized that to eat a fish that had been tricked by live bait would be an unendurable affront to the teachings of Dick Blalock. But there is no question that Jeff and I were hungry for fish.

The hunger that we felt was hereditary. I have two such hungers, bred into me in the bosom of my family or, perhaps, passed along as genetic tracery from the countrymen who saw the wilderness days in "the old Southwest," as Alabama was known in their time. In any event, one of these hungers is for barbecue—specifically, pork cooked over hickory—and the other is for fried fish.

So the next day we went to different water and caught two bass on flies and, deeming them honorably captured, put them on a stringer. This was just at nightfall. Perhaps it was our moral hair-splitting about the conditions under which these fish would die that stirred the archaic spirits of the Ojibwayan dark.

Did I mention that this can be spooky country? Ever since Étienne Brulé became the first European to cruise Lake Superior in 1623, so-journers here have talked about "the mist people," whose voices rise from the rapids at night. Sigurd Olson, the author of *The Singing Wilderness* and other books on the North Woods, has written of the haunted quality of the woods and waters he knew better than any other white man of this century. Olson wrote often of the "the horses of mist" that rose each night and morning from the waters of Quetico. They were galloping every which way through the inky darkness by the time Jeffrey and I reached our campsite.

As we prepared the fire and began to heat our grease, there was a ferocious splashing down by the canoe, and when Jeff and I went down with a flashlight, we found a snapping turtle chewing away on the nylon rope that held the fish. The bass, still alive, were bucking frantically, and their struggle was pitiful in contrast to the purposeful mastications of the mossy creature that regarded us with red-eyed, primordial indifference.

This turtle looked at us and kept right on gnashing the rope. Its confidence was rooted in the strength of its mighty home, which was a shell that looked as creviced and impenetrable as rock, as the very granite of the Canadian Shield itself. Suddenly I understood the Ojibway riddle. Here was the Maymaygwayshi! Here was the little fellow who lives inside a rock and comes in the night and steals your fish by cutting the strings that hold them.

The Maymaygwayshi, like turtles, had the power of disappearance, vanishing into the clifts or into the shells of their canoes. The Ojibway believed the Maymaygwayshi to be so ashamed of their appearance and the way they got their fish that they hid their faces in their hands when confronted. Indeed, this turtle had handlike, prehensile paws, each with distinct digits and long nails, and when it grasped the rope with these paws and brought it up to its jaws, the turtle seemed to be hiding its snout, or praying.

But if there was any shame in this Maymaygwayshi, it flew out of him and into us. We killed the fish and ate them, and I feel guilty about those fish to this day. I have killed other fish since then, but I can no longer do it with the aplomb I possessed when I walked on the Redneck Way. The experience also damaged my taste for bass fillets, and I find it hard to enjoy them now, even when I am camping and there are no other fish to be had.

If I wanted to stretch things, I could say that I became so generally high-minded on that night that I am also ashamed about using the live leeches. I would like to say that, but I cannot. Perhaps Jeff and I would have felt that way if Dick had actually seen us in the act of using live bait. But he did not, and on this score, we—like the turtle in the beam of our light, like the Maymaygwayshi crouched in their canoes, like the seven-year-old boy who caught the twenty crappies on the bridge at South Sauty—had no repentance in us.

16
A Digression:
Fried Fish

As I mentioned, I acquired specific, periodic hungers for barbecue and fried fish as a child. When I became a man, I thought it important to learn to cook these things properly—or at least to my taste—and I did. I do not barbecue much anymore. It takes so long to do it right that there is too much risk of either losing your appetite or getting drunk before it is done. Besides, it is possible to buy excellent barbecue in the South and passable barbecue in the East, so why bother?

But fried fish is another matter. Few people can fry fish in the classic way, and almost none of them work in restaurants, other than John's in Birmingham, Captain Anderson's and the Sunset in Panama City, Florida, Miss Isiah's Busy Bee in Oxford, Mississippi, and another place in Mississippi that I do not wish to name because it would ruin it. It is also possible to luck into a decent meal of fried fish in small or medium-sized towns, but the search for such places is full of disappointments because the average mom-and-pop restaurant is too cheap to buy quality fresh fish from local waters when their wholesaler is pushing a bargain in frozen "ocean perch" from the Georges Bank in the North Atlantic. So when the hunger hits me—which is usually in the spring about the time that the crappies and bluegills are stirring back in Alabama—getting good fried fish is mostly a do-it-yourself proposition.

The menu for my favorite fried-fish meal is as follows:

Fresh tomatoes of the kind not found in supermarkets, peeled and sliced.

Fresh corn on the cob, preferably Silver Queen picked on the day it is cooked.

Fresh, baby green onions with the tops trimmed and the outer skin peeled off or quartered Vidalia onions from Georgia or quartered Bermuda onions from Texas.

Corn bread, made according to the recipe on the Indian Head cornmeal bag. (Do not use any recipe that calls for sugar. Corn bread with sugar is an abomination and demeans the death of any fish with which it is served.)

Quartered lemons.

Hellman's Tartar Sauce. (You can make your own. Frankly, I never figured I could top Hellman's, a noble product in my book.)

Some of these items are seasonal, and if you substitute, do so with something like fresh spinach or collard greens or okra that is not going to compete with the fish. If you lay on too many side dishes, you lessen the impact of the fish, and the meal will leave you feeling both heavy and with your central craving unfulfilled. In a good fried-fish feast, the fish is the star, and that is where you have to put your work.

As for the fish, first get some boneless fillets. For years, I favored fillets from largemouth bass of one and one half pounds that have been caught in the spring or early summer before the water turns warm.

Lately, I have been taken with northern pike. In any event, it is important to reduce these creatures to boneless fillets. With bass, this is easy to do according to the standard filleting method to be found in any basic cookbook.

Northern pike are another matter, because their flanks are laced with tiny, Y-shaped bones that anchor the pike's swimming muscles and help produce the killing speed with which the freshwater barracuda falls upon its prey. These bones are such devils to get rid of that many people simply pronounce the pike inedible and let it go at that or else grind its flesh into the little fish sausages that the French call *quenelles*.

Luckily, modern American life has been enriched by the publication of *A Boundary Waters Fishing Guide* by Michael Furtman. No one will ever accuse Furtman of being a poet, but his name will live forever in the pike-cleaning business because of the diagrams and instructions on the following pages.

Among freshwater fish suitable for frying, the most delicately flavored are crappie and walleyed pike. Bluegills, which are generally too small to fillet and must be cooked whole, were favored by the late Euell Gibbons, the naturalist who specialized in eating wild plants. Gibbons had a high tolerance for inconvenience and therefore was not bothered by the problem of picking through the bones of bluegills and other small sunfish. It is not my favorite pastime, but as I've become more reluctant about eating bass, I find myself eating more bluegills when the fried-fish hunger hits me.

The secret to ameliorating the bone problem is to be wasteful. Once the fish is cooked, carefully pull away the dorsal and anal fins. This frees the meat from the backbone. Then use a knife and fork—or your fingers if the fish is not too hot—to pull free the large chunks of meat on each side of the backbone. This is the part that you eat. Leave the rib cage and any meat around it attached to the backbone and discard all this. The process is not unlike picking a crab, and as with crabs, you must start with a large pile of fish. But bluegills are plentiful and prolific, and so far I can eat them with minimal guilt.

The same technique will work with white or yellow perch or with small saltwater fish such as mangrove snappers. Among saltwater fish, my favorites for frying, in ascending order, are speckled trout, redfish, red grouper, black grouper, scamp, yellowtail snapper, mutton snapper and the Atlantic red snapper. In fish over a pound and a half, I prefer to cut the fillets into slices about the size of the index finger.

The red snapper is the best frying fish in the known universe. A fresh-caught red snapper has a bloom to its flavor that is encountered in no other fish that I have tasted. This is partly a matter of the way it feels on the tongue, a texture that I can only describe as slightly mealy. This quality, however you describe it, is not encountered in frozen snapper or, in my experience, any snapper that passes through the Fulton Fish Market in New York City. However, you can get very decent fresh snapper at Cannon's Sea Food in the Georgetown

Fig. 1

Fig. 2

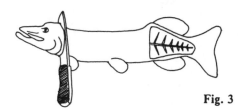

Fig. 3

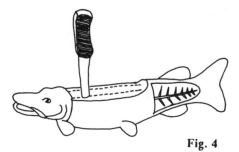

Fig. 4

Fig. 5

Northern Pike Filleting

Fig. 1 *To fillet a northern pike, first lay it on its belly, not its side. If you are right-handed its head should face toward your left. Hold it by the head and make your first cut just behind it down until you hit the spine. Do not cut through the spine. Now turn the blade toward the tail and slide it along the backbone until you get to the back (dorsal) fin, which is set far back on a pike's body. At that point cut upwards and remove the first fillet.*

Fig. 2 *Turn the fish on its side now and look toward the tail. Just below the point where you ended the top cut is where you will make the next incision. This area of a pike does not contain "Y" bones, so its removal is straightforward. Cut down to the backbone at a point just in front of the dorsal fin. When you reach the spine, do not cut through but turn the blade toward the tail. Slide the knife along the spine and slice through the skin at the tail just like you would for any species. Flip the fish over and do this same step on the other side. You should now have three fillets.*

Fig. 3 *Now for the fun part. On both sides of the fish make a cut just behind the head, stopping at the backbone.*

Fig. 4 *Now put the pike back up on its belly. Looking down, you should see the spine and a row of small bones running parallel on either side. If you can't see them, run your fingertip along the flesh and you will feel them. Take the very tip of your knife and insert it on the outside of one of these rows. Cut along this row back toward the tail with the tip of the knife angling slightly toward the center of the fish. Remember, these bones are not called "Y" bones for nothing. You are trying to run the knife along the outside edge of one of the arms of the "Y" while at the same time working to the tail.*

Fig. 5 *After you've cut a little way down toward the belly you can gently begin to peel the flesh away while cutting. Soon you will reach the outside of the ribs. Using your knife tip, follow the ribs down toward the belly and back toward the tail. When you've reached both the bottom and the back edge of the ribs, you can cut the fillet away from the carcass. Repeat this procedure on the other side and you should end up with a total of five fillets.*

These can then be skinned as you would any fillet, although that top cut fillet may be a bit difficult because of its rounded shape. By following the knife blade closely with your hand and forcing the skin flat as you separate it from the flesh (the fish's, not your hand's) you should be able to remove the skin in one piece. If you have problems with this step, first swear (it helps relieve tension), then scale this piece and cook with the skin on.

section of Washington, D.C., and Cannon's does not charge as much as I would if I were sitting on the best red snapper supply north of Morehead City, North Carolina.

Since a keen awareness of what you have missed is part of catching fish and of eating them, I'd like to say that the best fried snapper and the best hush puppies that I have ever encountered were served at Mattie's Tavern in St. Andrews, Florida, but Mattie's closed about forty years ago. The second-best was probably at Jess Cook's Seafood at the old Tarpon Docks in Panama City. There you could sometimes see Jess himself dining on snapper center cuts. These are the unmarketable backbone sections from which the fillets have been cut. But you missed that, too, by twenty-odd years. So be it.

Fortunately, you have this recipe. Frying fish is not passive cooking. You have to stand over the skillet, jockeying the heat up and down to keep the cooking oil at exactly 375 degrees. That is the key to frying fish. If you are not willing to buy a candy thermometer and learn how to do this, spare yourself the trouble of going through the rest of the exercise.

Preparation of the boneless fillets or fingers is simple but important. I like to soak them in milk for a few minutes. Meanwhile, take a brown grocery bag and pour one to two cups of cornmeal into it. Add salt and pepper to taste. I like the meal to look speckled from the pepper and to be able to taste the salt when I sample a pinch of the mixture.

Take one large fillet or three or four small pieces of fish from the milk. Shake off the excess moisture and drop the fish into the meal, one piece at a time. Close the top of the bag and shake it vigorously for a half minute or so. Do not try to do all your fillets or pieces of fish at once, or you will wind up with a gummy ball of fish and wet meal. It is important to shake your fish in a dry mixture. If, after a few shakings, the meal gets wet enough to start balling up, throw it away and make a fresh batch. Cornmeal is cheap.

Coat your fish with cornmeal just before cooking. You do not want to leave mealed fish sitting around because the coating will get gummy.

At this point, you have one to two inches of cooking oil heated to 375 degrees, preferably in a black skillet. Drop in the fish pieces one at a time. This will immediately knock down the temperature of the oil. Keep it as near 375 as you can by adjusting the heat upward. But remember that once you have a few pieces in the skillet and they start cooking vigorously, the temperature of the oil will start to climb and you will have to turn down the burner. Frying fish at this point is largely a matter of twisting a knob on your stove back and forth.

Once the bottom of a piece of fish looks golden brown, turn it over. When the second side looks golden brown, too, take it out. With small pieces this takes only three or four minutes. This is not like frying chicken, where you put the chicken in the skillet, cover it and walk away for a while. I prefer tongs for turning these pieces and removing them from the grease. Drain the cooked pieces on paper towels, and do all your frying as fast as you can and serve immediately. I like my fried fish hot, but I have had bad luck putting it in an oven to keep it hot. That tends to make it soggy. On camping trips, I let everyone start eating while I am still frying, and if there is a large group, I simply eat while standing at the stove.

Do not be discouraged if your first batches of fried fish are less than perfect. It takes practice to get the touch. If the cornmeal coating gives you indigestion, stir in some flour. You can whip an egg or two into the milk in which you dip the fish.

This is part of what I have learned about frying fish, and all you need to know to get started.

17
Dick Drops
the Count

Catching that big bass on a fly rod in Canada did wonders for my confidence. In times past, I had never been a confident fisherman. I was easily discouraged. Where other fishermen would become more determined, more inventive, more dedicated in the face of adversity, I simply assumed that there were *no fish here* or they were *not biting*.

But now I was fishing with more patience and precision. Sometimes I even felt a sense of certainty—that I was *destined* to catch fish—especially when it came to fly fishing. In times past, I always carried my spinning rod as a backup. Now I stuck to the fly rod, content to practice my casting if the fish were not showing. As my indifference about catching fish increased, I was catching more fish than I ever had. Sometimes I felt that fish were flocking to me.

Alas, as my confidence increased, so did my

vanity. I became, in a word, cocky. I acquired a fishing log in which I kept count of the fish I caught on each trip.

"I don't believe in keeping count," Dick said one day. He mumbled something about "that goddam counter" that Mark Kovach kept on his raft to tally the catch for his clients. "That's a kind of a game they play," he said. "It's keeping score. If you're going to keep score you might as well be on a golf course."

Naturally, we were headed toward the Rapidan when Dick said this. The trip always seemed to make him feel pontifical.

This part of the conversation I've re-created from memory. But generally I know exactly what Dick said, because I started tape-recording our conversations when we were on the road. I had it in the back of my mind that I might want to write something about the sport of fly fishing someday, and I knew that Dick had read a lot of tedious, obscure books that I could avoid by picking his brain.

Dick certainly took to being interviewed. It reminded him of his favorite diversion, which was calling radio talk shows. The only time he clammed up was when I pressed him about a remark I thought I remembered him making about doing intelligence work in the Army. He said I must have him confused with someone else. He also seemed by turns forthcoming and evasive about contacts he had with the CIA when he was working in Middle Eastern hot spots.

Generally, the man would talk, as talk he could. I had hoped to get a short course in the history of fly fishing. The joke was on me. What

I got, mostly, was the World According to Dick Blalock.

The subject of counting fish reminded Dick of Ken Miyata, his fishing companion who wrote "Fishing Like a Predator." Ken had drowned in 1983 at the age of thirty-two while fishing alone on the Big Horn River. The obituaries described Ken Miyata as one of the best young fly fishermen on the East Coast, but in Dick's telling, his approach to fishing sounded a lot like work.

"My friend Ken Miyata, when you stopped him on the stream after he jumped out of your car two hours ago and raced away, and you say, 'Had any luck?' a simple yes or no would suffice. But he would say, 'Yeah, I caught sixty-three.'

"That's when he pulls his scorecard out and looks at it. The reason for a scorecard is that he uses it to enter that info into his computer. I've fished with a fair number of people who keep a stream log. The idea of keeping a stream log! I just don't understand it.

"Yet I know people who say, 'How many did you catch?' I like to be able to say I caught none, two, twenty, forty, sixty—some number, you know—not exactly. And I don't ever have any idea of whether I'm exaggerating or underestimating.

"I'm very much opposed to any kind of competition in fishing. I think that fishing should not be a competitive sport. Or if it's competitive, it should be competitive only in the sense that it's between you and the stream, rather than you and the fish, and certainly, I'm not out in competition with you—ever, ever, ever."

In those days there were many trips to the Rapidan. Sometimes Ben and Jeff went, and sometimes Eva Hughes, Jeff's half-Comanche girl-friend, did, too. Eva looked the way Indian prin-cesses in the movies used to look, and Dick was fond of her and her father, Bobby, a slow-talking government economist who seldom caught a fish. Once, Eva Otterbeck, the Swedish girl Ben had met in London, came along, too. Dick referred to that as the "two-Evas trip."

One soft spring day, Jeff and Eva Hughes had been rambling up and down the dirt road beside the river in my new Trooper, which had only two hundred miles on the odometer and which Jeff was not allowed to drive at home. When they got back, Jeff thanked me for use of the car with such fervor that I was immediately suspicious. Later, Eva revealed that Jeff had failed to set the brake when they got out to fish one of his favorite pools, and he had barely chased down the vehicle before it parked itself in the Rapidan. Later, Eva clipped off the tip of Jeff's first expensive fly rod in the electric window of the same car. He handled the loss of his rod tip with more equanimity than had my brother. On the other hand, when you looked at Eva you understood that he had more incentive to be forgiving.

Unlike some older men, Dick was capable of paying attention to young women without seem-ing to leer. Usually. Bill Dunlap and his sporty-looking wife, Linda Burgess, had taken up fly fishing in a semi-serious way. Once we were using a big cabin with dormitory-style sleeping, and just before lights-out, Linda came dashing across the room in a T-shirt and bikini panties and dived into the sleeping bag with Bill. Darkness fell across the room, and after a few moments, we heard Dick say, "If you decide during the night that you don't like that sleeping bag, you can share mine."

More silence. Then I answered softly, "All right, Dick."

There was an explosion of laughter. It kept building when everyone realized that for once Dick was at a loss for words.

Dick was the chief cook at the Rapidan, and despite his heart problem, he quit counting calories as well as fish. Heretofore he had made a show of watching his weight in an erratic, slightly comical way. He was the sort of fellow who would use Sweet'n Low and then plan his itinerary so that it would take him past a place that had particularly good coconut cream pies.

One of Dick's closest friends was Carl Geyer, a radiologist at Walter Reed Army Hospital. The two of them went to the Rapidan one weekend, and later Carl told me that he had taken the opportunity to warn Dick about his weight. The resulting argument was so disagreeable that Carl abandoned the cabin to Dick and slept in the car. Carl said he did not intend to broach the subject again. Neither did I. Along about this time, Dick announced that to the dismay of his wife, Sigrid, he had decided that he had a "fat persona" and he might as well go with it.

"Does Dick ever fish?" Ben said one day. "Every time I come by the cabin he's cooking." Actually, Dick would usually toddle off to the stream in midday to fish some easily accessible pool. Ben and Jeff began to raise their eyebrows at the reports of ten-, eleven- or twelve-inch fish that Dick brought back from his brief forays.

Meanwhile, his menus grew more formidable. Dolmas and Lebanese lamb stews. Bouillabaisse. Chicken paprikash. I remember one rainy night when Dick, Bill Dunlap and I were in a cabin at the Rapidan. Dick served up rare sirloins, seared in a heavily salted skillet, along with fresh spinach cooked in olive oil and some variation of Potatoes Anna in which he had managed to involve a pint of heavy cream. We had champagne. There was dessert, but I've forgotten what it was.

Meanwhile, the Rapidan was teaching the boys and me to be trout fishermen. We were learning from the same water that educated Datus C. Proper, a friend of Dick's from the Foreign Service and the author of *What the Trout Said*, a highly technical treatise on fly design.

"The man who becomes a good fisherman on the Rapidan will probably be competent on any small freestone stream," Proper wrote in *Trout* magazine. "The brookies here are wary, stream-bred fish, and the brook trout in his own habitat can be demanding—especially if protected from the indiscretions he likes to commit with worms when the water is high. These brookies rise to dry flies as readily as browns, but they disappear at the first glimpse of a fisherman, and a dragging fly will cause them to stop feeding."

This, of course, was Proper's statement of Blalock's Paradox. By this time, Ben had mastered it so soundly that he was taking fifty or more fish a day and emerging as an inveterate fish counter. Such competitiveness, Dick allowed, was an understandable failing of youth, and he took considerable pride in the boys' growing skill and my emergence as a zealous buyer of fly rods.

For my part, I was hot on the trail of the elusive twelve-inch brook trout. Not even the great

Datus Proper claimed to have taken a brook trout over twelve and a quarter inches. I interviewed Harry Murray, the author of *Trout Fishing in the Shenandoah National Park*, and he said there were probably not a half-dozen fish as long as twelve inches in the entire park.

I had named the place where I got the eleven-and-a-half-incher Humility Pool, and I was convinced that this was where my foot-long fish was living. It never failed to turn up at least one nice fish if I could get there before anyone else had hit it. The river came spilling over a shoulder of dark stone into a basin of deep blue water. On the right-hand bank, the current had cut a deep path at the base of a maple tree, and just where its roots entered the river, there was a clean gravel bar that made an ideal feeding lie for a sizable fish.

I took a series of nice fish from this pool, and I learned to fish it well. One day I floated a dry fly called the Mr. Rapidan across the gravel bar at the foot of the maple tree, and a big fish came up, opened its mouth like an alligator and came churning across the surface toward my fly. It was a very unusual kind of rise, and an ostentatious one, to say the least. Rattled, I snatched the fly right out of the fish's mouth.

Sometimes a brook trout that has not felt the hook will strike again, but this one did not, and that was the last good fish I ever saw in Humility Pool. After a while, I gave up on this water and started fishing a half mile or so downstream. It was there, bushwhacking through new territory, that I found the most glamorous pool on the Rapidan.

It was long and narrow, with a deep green hole in the middle. The water tailed out into a shallow flat that offered a platform of low, irregular boulders from which to cast. In the utmost depth of the pool, I could see the flash of moving fish.

It was the kind of water Datus Proper had in mind in his brief section on the Rapidan in *What the Trout Said:* "With luck, you might get one of the rare twelve-inch brook trout. They are as big as the stream produces, and they are present only in good years."

If the fish cruising in the depths of this pool were the twelve-inch giants, it would be hard to tempt them to the surface with a dry fly. I started to change to a nymph right away, but I figured that I could make a drift or two with my dry fly without spooking so large a pool. I made a long, careful cast and put my Elk Hair Caddis over the deepest part of the hole.

A shape moved off the bottom, and it became a large brook trout, levitating upward into clearer water, its long body striking a forty-five-degree angle if you can imagine the green pool as a kind of movie or television screen, which it resembled. It rose without hesitancy and ate my fly matter-of-factly.

Of brook trout in this size, Datus Proper wrote: "If you hook them and fail to treat them with the respect due old men, they can even break your tippet."

The fish did not break my tippet, because I bowed to its opening dash toward the far end of the pool, letting it pull line from my reel. Then it was simply a matter of working the trout carefully back down and into my hand. It was one of the old men, all right, but this old man measured out at eleven and three-quarters inches.

Dick fixed crab cakes that night, and I told him that I was closing in on him. Not being competitive about his fishing, he took this calmly. But the next morning, when we were climbing from our sleeping bags and scratching and stretching, Dick brought up brook trout again. And as he slipped his feet into his house shoes and padded off to start the coffee, he said this:

"You know, I was thinking about it last night just before I went to sleep, and I believe I caught a thirteen-inch trout up there one time. In fact, I'm pretty sure I did."

18
Throwing Slack, or Seeming Not to Care

There is a motion that is central to the Redneck Way of Fishing. I saw it demonstrated in its purest form one day in Buck's Pocket, the mountain gorge that was flooded by South Sauty Creek when Guntersville Dam was completed in 1939. The fishing at the bridge on South Sauty had played out by the mid-Fifties, but there were still plenty of big fish within reach of the outboard boat that my father kept at the South Sauty Fish Camp. Whenever someone told you he had been "back in the Pocket," you knew he had made the long run to the spot where South Sauty Creek entered the lake. The steep mountainsides were covered with beech, hickory and oak, and wherever one of these trees had toppled into the lake, crappie were apt to gang up around the submerged treetop.

On the day I had in mind, my father and his first cousin, Hartley Best, and I were "fishing the tops" when a lanky countryman emerged from the forest. He wore overalls and carried a pole and a large tin can which, it soon became apparent, was serving as his minnow bucket. He baited up and made a whistling cast that plunked his bobber down near our boat. He set the butt of his pole in the bank, and paying us no attention, he hunkered, in true, old-time hillbilly fashion, with his feet flat on the ground, his butt on his heels and his forearms resting loosely on his knees.

Presently, his bobber dipped under. With a mighty heave, he lifted a large crappie into the air. Held at the utmost end of the line by centrifugal force, this fish described an arc that carried it thirty feet in the air. The man never stopped accelerating the pole until it extended behind him in the forest, and we could hear the fish flopping in the leaves far back in the woods. He dashed into the trees and fell upon it.

For years, just about everybody I fished with was a devotee of the South Sauty heave. My brother, in particular, thought it was a sin to lose a fish because of a broken line or to waste any time playing a fish. He was a believer in the old saw "First you get the fish in the boat, *then* you play with it." The heave, in short, was bred deeply into me.

I mention this here because I wish to discuss an essential stage of any fly-fishing career. In Canada, as I mentioned, I began learning to play heavy fish on a fly rod. After practicing on the three-pound bass that took the tiny popper on Minn Lake, I later landed and released a smallmouth of almost six pounds on Lac La Croix. But I was using strong leaders on those fish. Catching large trout on the almost invisible leaders, or tippets, required in very clear water is a more difficult matter.

Just how difficult I was to discover at an elbow-shaped pool on the Neshobe River near Brandon, Vermont. There for the first time I raised a sizable trout on a dry fly. It was a rainbow that darted from a deep whirl of current and gobbled the fly without ceremony. I set the hook sharply, and the fine tippet parted immediately. To say that this gave me a sinking feeling is accurate but does not capture exactly the quality of the moment.

When you are a beginner at fishing for trout in fast, clear water, you do not get many strikes like that. Most often, the fish see you because of your bad casting and clumsy wading, and they will not bite. Or your line gets caught in the current and jerks the fly along in a way that announces its fraudulent nature, and they do not bite because you have failed to achieve what the instructional booklets call "drag-free float." In any event, the uninhibited, get-hooked-or-be-damned strike of a substantial trout is a rare—indeed, for me at this stage, an unprecedented—event.

I am trying to communicate the profound feeling of stupidity that settled over me as I paced the gravel bar beside the pool and hurled curses into the genial summer sky. In psychological terms, I was contemplating the vast gap that lay between my knowledge and my behavior.

I knew, for example, that a trout will not strike a dry fly unless it is fished on a very fine tippet. I had tied my fly to such a tippet. I therefore knew that this tippet, by virtue of being thin to the point of near invisibility, was subject to the physical laws that govern our life on this planet.

That is, I *knew* that it was not strong enough to drag a trout through the water against its will, much less lift it out onto the bank. All the same, I had given this fish the South Sauty heave.

The heave, of course, depends on those very same physical laws. That is, if you hook a large crappie—say, three pounds—and you are fishing with twenty-pound line, you can do what you like with that fish. You can, as my brother travelers on the Redneck Way are wont to say, "set the hook hard enough to cross his eyes."

But if you are after a three-pound trout on a two-pound line, *this will not work*. The fish in question punctuated this leap of cognition for me by dashing about the pool for a few moments, my fly clearly visible in the gristly joint of its jaw. This fish was well hooked, but it was not connected to me or, more precisely, to my several hundred dollars' worth of tackle that was *not capable of heaving a trout*.

That is how I came to understand the relationship between heavy fish and light lines. The act of setting the hook must contain within it an almost simultaneous act of surrender. Upon seeing or feeling the strike, the fly fisherman is required to pull back with precisely enough force to slide the point of the hook into the tissue of the fish's mouth. Then he must release all pressure and let the fish go where it wants to go. It is an act of physical discipline and of hope—the hope being that by and by when the fish is tired of going where it wants to go, it and the fisherman will still be connected by a thread that leads them to the same place.

This act of sliding home the hook and then bowing to the energy of the fish is easier to describe than to execute. It defines the difference between breaking rocks and cleaving diamonds. Mastery of this skill marks the line between those who are good at casting with a fly rod and those who are good at catching trout with a fly rod.

That day on the Neshobe, where the purple loosestrife bloomed in the meadow and tasseling corn whispered in the field, I was not optimistic about traversing that line. The eye-crossing hook set seemed embedded in the muscle memory of my right arm. I could feel it there when Ben and Jeff came hiking in from their beats on the Neshobe, fishless but full of teenage certainty that if that fish had hit *their* flies, it would have gotten defter play.

As it turned out, they were to break off their fair share of fish before we began to understand that the way to catch big trout was to give up in advance on the possibility of catching them. It was a matter of attitude, according to *A Modern Dry Fly Code*, published in 1950 by Vincent C. Marinaro, the arch-guru of Pennsylvania fly fishing. Forget about the actual landing of fish as a way of measuring your "luck," Marinaro advised, "for in the lexicon of the fly-fisherman, the words 'rise' and 'hooked' connote the successful and desirable climax; landing a fish is purely anticlimax."

A beautiful sentiment, I thought. But there was a self-evident flaw in the Higher Consciousness as defined by Marinaro. If you break off every good fish that rises to your fly, it leaves you feeling like a klutz. I had by this time begun to overcome my lust for fish, but I still lusted for expertise, for the feeling of artistry, for some control over the line-snapping reflex that lay coiled in my wrist, forearm and biceps.

Dick, as it turned out, knew quite a lot about Vince Marinaro. He made his living as a corporation-tax specialist for the State of Pennsylvania. The jacket photo on his book showed a wavy-haired, sharp-featured man in a tweed coat. He was looking, with a slightly sour expression, through a magnifying glass at a tiny fly. Marinaro's book, with its emphasis on fishing with impossibly small flies on the wispiest of leaders, had truly revolutionized American fly fishing, Dick said. But there were rumors that Marinaro died in 1986 an embittered man, feeling he never got the recognition he deserved. He left orders for his handmade bamboo fly rods to be burned.

"We ought to ask Charlie Fox about that the next time we go up to Cumberland County," he said, referring to the old man we had met on the banks of the Letort Spring Run on the day I caught my first trout.

It was on the Letort in the early 1950s that Marinaro and Fox had coached a young architect named Ernest Schwiebert in the learning that went into *Matching the Hatch*. The books by Marinaro and Schwiebert, Dick said, established the superiority of American fly fishing over its British antecedent. Fox himself had written a book, *The Wonderful World of Trout*, that also showed up occasionally on the outdoor magazines' lists of the ten best books about American fly fishing. In short, in Marinaro, Schwiebert and Fox on the Letort, you had something like the fly-fishing equivalent of Hemingway, Fitzgerald and Dos Passos in Paris.

"The one quantum leap I made last year was on the Letort. I describe it as 'beyond barbless,' " Dick said. "I went up last February and I was fishing for these big browns with Shenk's Sculpins, and I tell you I was knocking them dead. I finally decided that the fun was not in landing the fish. The fun was in seeing the fish take. So I began cutting my Sculpins right at the bend of the hook, and they would grab it, and I would just jerk it out of their mouth, except that one time a fish grabbed it, and I pulled him up on the bank. He wouldn't let go. I guess I decided that in a number of situations as long as I can see the fish take, I'd just as soon not have the hook on. I could go out here on a blue-ribbon trout stream, and I could do that with a dry fly because it would be the take that would give me the thrill."

I was not ready for "beyond barbless," nor for the abnegation of Vince Marinaro. But as a political reporter, I had learned to be patient when being lectured or lied to and to look for the lesson lurking beneath the bombast. What would happen, for example, if upon raising a trout one immediately feigned indifference to its capture? What if one set out not to land the fish, but simply to prevent it from breaking the line?

I had plenty of time to contemplate that question, for it seemed that after I broke off that fish on the Neshobe I had hit a kind of plateau. I no longer enjoyed Glo Bug fishing, but I was not very good at anything else. The confidence that had bloomed in Canada and among the innocent wild brookies of the Rapidan began to wither. One hot Sunday afternoon, Ben and I went to Big Hunting Creek. I was making my way from pool to pool with clumsy perfunctory casts, feeling neither confidence nor hope, when I threw an Elk Hair Caddis into a dark pool at the foot of a small waterfall.

A trout came up instantly, and something

happened there that I did not will or control. It was if a kind of synaptic switch had flopped over in my brain and I experienced the strike of this trout in slow motion, just as on the less demanding water in Canada. Instead of setting the hook with a furious jerk of my rod, I raised it smoothly, and once I had put the hook home, I relented and let the fish go where it liked, exerting just enough pressure to make the line tight and to pull a nice bow in my rod.

The fish zoomed upstream, making my drag sing. Reaching the limit of the pool, it came back down toward me until it reached the tail of the pool. Then it took off again toward the upper end, again making my reel sing its mechanical song. Next the fish dove to the bottom of the pool, and I could feel the biggest brown trout I had ever hooked butting its head against the rocks, and I thought certainly it would rub the leader in two. But all I could do was choose between breaking the line or letting the fish have its way for a while. So I let the fish go where it wanted to go until it was so tired that it had to go where my rod and line wanted it to go, which was into my hand.

I laid it on the wet gravel and photographed it, a brown trout of astonishing beauty. I had just released the fish when Ben came bursting through the trees.

"Was that your drag I heard?" he said.

I said it was, and for once, I understood what it was saying. It was telling me that the only way to land a big fish is to submit to its power, especially at the strike and in the early moments of the hookup when it is throwing raw energy every which way.

Later, I learned there was a name for what

I had done. It is called "throwing slack." As Lefty
Kreh explains in *Lefty's Little Library of Fly Fishing*,
"It's the jerk of the leader that breaks the line. So
after I set the hook, I always throw a little bit of
slack."

Being an English major, I knew that Mr.
Yeats had said it better in "The Three Beggars":

> It's certain there are trout somewhere
> And maybe I shall take a trout
> If but I do not seem to care.

19
Fathers and Sons, Nerds, Dweebs and Wonks

In the town of Boiling Springs, Pennsylvania, there is a lake of about eight acres. It was created by artesian wells substantial enough to generate a constant flow of cold, crashing water over a spillway at one end of the lake, and between this spillway and the nearby Yellow Breeches Creek, there is a channel of fast water called Boiling Springs Run. The run is about two hundred yards long, and it is usually loaded with trout. Some are big, stream-hardened fish that have seen, and refused, every fly in the catalog, and some are naive hatchery fish. Boiling Springs Run is where Dick brought me to catch my first trout. During our Glo Bug period, it was also where the boys and I went to fish the "bread hatch," when tourists would touch off feeding frenzies by throwing crumbs to the half-tame trout in the deep pool at the upper end of the run.

The boys and I caught our first dose of fly-fishing hubris there, as well. At the time, Dick was president of the National Capital Chapter of Trout Unlimited. In fact, he was in his second or third consecutive term, and in true Blalockian style, he was conducting himself as President-for-Life and having a fine time doing it. Dick wrote a column called "Leader's Lines" in *Riffles*, the chapter newsletter, and his favorite theme was why more members did not volunteer to do jobs for TU. The reason, of course, was that Dick was doing all the jobs. One guy actually resigned over the issue of whether he or Dick ought to invite a popular fishing writer to speak at the chapter's annual fishing show. Dick won. This was my introduction to the Fly-Fishing Ego Wars, of which more later.

You would think anyone who belonged to an organization with a name as stupid as Trout Unlimited would have a sense of humor about it. I certainly felt amused—well, actually embarrassed—when I sent in $20 for a family membership for me and the boys, but Dick said we had to be members to get invited on the semiannual fishing trips. It did not take long to discover that if you were going to rename Trout Unlimited, you might go for Nerds, Dweebs and Wonks. It combines the dorkiness of the Audubon Society, the moral indignation of Greenpeace and the political self-congratulation of the Sierra Club. The social ambiance is a schizoid mix of Woodstock Nation and Skull & Bones.

Every fall Dick led an expedition of twenty-five or thirty people on a "chapter outing" to the Allenberry Inn, a resort on the catch-and-release section of the Yellow Breeches. On Saturday nights, there was a communal cocktail party and dinner, with menu planned and cooking done by Chairman Dick. The boys looked forward to these occasions with the demonic satirical glee of adolescents who know they are being given ringside seats at a festival of adult pomposity.

There were borderline trout bums, shaggy lads who revered the memory of Ken Miyata (who had a doctorate in zoology from Harvard) for telling an interviewer shortly before his death that "having a steady job really interferes with fishing."

There were a few truly proficient fishermen, like Dick's friend Carl Geyer, the power-casting radiologist from Walter Reed Army Hospital; Ron Ashmore, a carpenter, house husband and latter-day hippie whose waders had more patches than an Amish quilt; and Rick Duffield, a bearish-looking entomologist who stomach-pumped his trout so he could classify the bug carcasses.

There were government bureaucrats like the charmless little rooster who was a Reagan appointee in the Interior Department. Dick, with his usual contempt for Republicans, said that working for an environmental criminal was what made this guy so unpleasant. For my part, I figured you could blame Reagan for a lot of things, but making someone else act like a twit was not one of them.

There seemed to be a small, shifting claque of gay fly fishers. They were very precise about tackle and technique and cordial if approached, but they were understandably remote, being surrounded by so much overblown and ofttimes oafish masculinity.

This flowed from the chapter's complement of tedious Wasps. If you think of the Bush administration, you can picture the type. With their Orvis tweeds, L. L. Bean camp moccasins and vaguely giraffelike social manner, they provided the controlling ambiance. Ben and Jeff loved to embarrass these guys, especially in front of their wives or girlfriends. Ben, in particular, was adept at playing the earnest adolescent at the cocktail hour, sipping a Coke and waiting patiently until one of the tyros would sidle up to him and say, "I got three trout this afternoon, son. How did you do?"

"I got fifteen," Ben would say, truthfully. "My brother only got nine."

Ron Ashmore took particular pleasure in this and wrote us up in *Riffles:* "The Chapter's annual visit to the Allenberry Inn on the Yellow Breeches River in Boiling Springs, Pa., was its usual success the weekend of Oct. 11, 12 and 13. There had not been a hard freeze in the area and the fall colors were just beginning to change. The fish were plentiful and active and there were numerous hatches coming off the water all three days. Saturday night we all congregated in the Eisenhower Cottage for a communal dinner prepared by Chef Blalock which lived up to its reputation. The accompanying wines and spirits caused much cheer to be promulgated. The prize for the most fish goes to the Raines Family. Between Howell and his two sons, they caught upwards of 50 to 60 fish. Congratulations."

I remember that weekend. I remember particularly the cold blue light that fell across the Yellow Breeches late on Saturday afternoon. I had been down on the main river, trying for some rising fish that required more skill than I possessed. In this section of the Breeches, a grassy lane runs alongside the stream for a mile or so, making a pleasant parklike space. I gave up on

the fish, feeling frustrated, and sat on the grass.
I had the stream to myself, alone among the
golden leaves and the blue light, and a heavy feeling of oppression and hopelessness enveloped me,
palpable as a blanket.

I can remember little about its cause or content, except that it involved a strong sense of time
being wasted, my life itself wasting away or, more
properly, being piddled away, by me, in the grind
of daily newspapering. I was a supervising editor
now, with the number two job in the Washington
bureau. I assigned stories to reporters and edited
what they had written, and at the end of the day,
I had produced nothing that would last. I also
knew that like millions of American men my age,
I was a hamster who would not be allowed to step
off the wheel. Too many mortgages, bank notes
and college tuitions for sums not yet imaginable
depended on my diligently bartering my days for
dollars.

I got up and waded the Yellow Breeches at
a shallow riffle that has built up just where the
run enters the larger stream. It was almost dark
now, and I found Ben at the big pool, making
long casts and fishing them carefully down the
current. On the high, flat ground beside this pool
was a parking area used in the daytime by fly
fishers and picnickers. It was deserted now except
for an old man who stood on the bank watching
Ben fish.

The man said something complimentary
about Ben's casting. I revealed that he was my son,
and said, "He's really a better fisherman than I
am." I had never said it before, and I do not know
why I said it to this man, or what I expected him
to say. But it was an idle observation on my part,

and I am pretty sure that whatever response I expected, it was not the one that I got.

"Of course he's a better fisherman," the old man said. "He's younger than you are, so he's got better eyes. That means he can see his fly better and spot more fish than you can. He's got quicker reflexes, so he's going to miss fewer strikes. And he's taller than you are, so he can cast farther than you can."

He was a bony old man, a little bent, and neither his face nor his voice was very pleasant. I had never seen him before, nor have I seen him since that afternoon, but I am pretty sure that if my life were a movie directed by Ingmar Bergman, I would know what he represented.

Later, Dick and I discussed this experience. He said that it pointed up a little-discussed aspect of fatherhood. Inextricably braided into the joy of having sons is the fact that their growth is a reminder of our mortality. Contained in every hour of fatherly instruction is the seed of that moment when the son's skill surpasses the father's. I told Dick of a tennis-playing friend who, realizing that his fifteen-year-old son was now the stronger player, began calling foot faults on the boy to throw him off his game and delay his own inevitable defeat. It was not such an unusual story, Dick said. Suddenly, he was talking in a new vein about his own father, a man he had formerly praised for his skill as a fisher and hunter.

"One of the first times my father ever took me down to Sheep Creek, he said, 'Figure out where you want to fish,'" Dick recalled. "I was smart enough to know that the stream came down, and it hit a kind of a bluff and there was a lot of drift there, and I said, 'I'm sure there are some fish there.'

"He said, 'You picked a damn good spot. I'm proud of you.'

"I'm sure we were fishing with worms. We would dig worms in the back garden. After a while, I said, 'I've got to go to the bathroom.' He said, 'Well, go over there behind a bush.'

"I said, 'No, I've got to do number two.'

"He said, 'Well, do something then.'

"There was some gravel there of the bed of the stream and I dug out a little hole and I defecated into it. Then I pushed the rocks back in.

"And he said, 'Well, just like a goddam cat. You scratch a hole and you shit in it and then you cover it up.' And he said, 'Right next to the goddam fishing hole.'

"Well, it wasn't really right next to it. Then when I caught a fish, he said what he would say if he were alive today: 'Well, that damn fish is no bigger than your pecker.'

"He had the consummate capacity to belittle. He was a put-down artist of the first order," Dick concluded.

For me, Dick's story illustrated the quality that kept him from being just another blowhard: He had an unusual capacity to reveal himself. Also, notwithstanding his fondness for the frat-house politics of Trout Unlimited, he was a man of broad interests who cared about things that mattered. He cared, for example, about the health of rivers, the fate of the Arabs and Jews, the emotional lives of himself and others.

Yet, on the personal side, he brought things into very tight focus, with an interest in the tiny details of memory and experience. He saw his life in novelistic terms, as a story to be told and pondered, a story driven by character and action, characters with distinct traits, actions with consequences that stretched over generations, all occurring in episodes, each episode having somewhere within it a moral point waiting for discovery. In this case, the story of Dick and his father seemed to open a deep well of anger that I had never sensed in his reminiscences about the man who gave him his first fly rod.

"My father tended to be a buffoon around older people," Dick continued. "People used to always make jokes about Jess, old Jess, Jess Blalock. My father tended to be the typical underdog who always has to have somebody he can beat on. That was it, if you want to go into the psychology of it, I'm sure. I was available and I was vulnerable and I wasn't going to fight back, not for a while at least."

In Dick's account, his father seemed torn between an instinct to tutor his son in the masculine arts and the need to maintain dominance over the boy. The family was living in Seminole, Oklahoma, when Dick's father, an oil field contractor who had lost his business in the Depression, found a new job with Phillips 66. "With some of his newfound money, he purchased a twenty-gauge automatic shotgun, a Browning as I recall. He used to take me down to the lake and let me fire that shotgun and I would shoot at cattails. He would try to get me to not flinch, and my tendency was, by God, to flinch."

This, he said, would occur on weekends, after his father returned from a week of travel with the oil company. During the week, Dick discovered the local library.

"I had a compelling, compelling curiosity about books. This was before I started school, mind you. I used to go to the public library in Seminole, Oklahoma, and read books. It would be very hard to describe my father's capacity to deal with the written word. He wrote and he read, but he didn't write well and he didn't read very much. I don't remember there being very many books in our house. I started going to the library and reading books. You can't say 'reading'—looking at books. Maybe just looking at pictures. I don't even remember that part of it. But one day the librarian said, 'Would you like to take some of these books home?' And I said, 'But I don't have any money.' She said, 'Do you know that you can take books home from the library?' Well, I thought that was the greatest damn thing I ever heard of.

"I would get three books every day. I soon discovered that by getting three books every day I could get the approval of all of these librarians. They would say, 'My goodness, here's that little boy just like clockwork. Here he is to get his three books.'

"I discovered this was like getting a piece of candy every day. In fact, they probably gave me a piece of candy. One day, I went in there and they said, 'What time will you be here tomorrow?' I said, 'Three o'clock,' or something like that. The next day I went in there and here is this young man, and they said, 'This is Mr. So-and-so from the Seminole newspaper and he wants to write a little story about you and all these books.'

"When he interviewed me he asked me a lot

of questions. He said, 'Is there anything else you like to do?' and I said, 'My daddy lets me go out with him, and he lets me shoot his rifle.' This article came out on the front page, mind you, of this little newspaper, and boy, when that article came out my mother said, 'Oh, you're going to get in trouble with your daddy.'

"And I said, 'Well, I told the truth.' She says, 'Yeah, but that doesn't make any difference. You're going to get into bad trouble with him,' without saying anything further.

"When my father came home he was livid. He was outraged. There were two things. I'm sure he said a lot. He may have slapped me around and beat up on me and spanked me or something. But there were two things that he said. He said, first of all, 'You didn't read those goddam books.' And he must have said that a thousand times. 'You didn't read those goddam books.'

"And the second thing was, 'You're a goddam liar. You never fired a rifle in your life. That was a shotgun.' Now think about that. Here I am, I'm five years old and 'You're a goddam liar. You didn't read those goddam books.'

"I had a lot of psychotherapy, and I probably had the most sympathetic therapist in the world, because he and I had gone through a lot of similar experiences. And when I would talk about some strange thing that would happen, he would say, 'Come on, you didn't read those goddam books.' He spoke of this as a 'mirror experience' because it's one of those half-dozen experiences that you can remember from your childhood. They may not come to mind immediately, but they're the things that forge your psychological makeup. They determine your psychological blueprint."

Dick's story illustrated something no father should forget. In the arsenal of familial emotions, fatherly condemnation is a nuclear weapon. Yet none of us is perfect. After Dick told about his own father, he told me, with no sense of irony, about an argument at Christmas dinner with his younger son, a government economist who differed with Dick on politics. For months, the two of them hardly spoke.

In the movement from sonhood to fatherhood, few of us are able to chasten our inherited flaws. I was reminded of this when I heard John Maclean, the son of the author of *A River Runs Through It*, interviewed during the publicity buildup for the movie based on his father's book. Even before the movie made him known to the general public, Norman Maclean was regarded by fly fishers as a secular saint, an example of the ennobling influences of their sport.

But listen to the memory of his son. "A lot of people, I think, go through their lives never knowing what heaven and hell are. I knew what heaven and hell were at a very early age. Hell was when I lost a big fish in front of my father. And my father would just be devastating. 'What did I bring you here for?' You know. 'How could you have muffed him? You muffed him.'

"And heaven was when I caught a big fish in front of my father," John Maclean continued. "And he became part of it, literally. I mean, I remember I caught a big one on the Swan River near our cabin . . . about a two-pound rainbow, and he put up an enormous battle, and my father literally went into the water after him to kind of shoo him up toward me so that he wouldn't get away from me. And even despite that, I landed him, and my father became rapturous—I mean, just rapturous and smiled at me the way God must smile on people coming into heaven."

I guess such experiences are part of what they are talking about in the men's movement when they go on about "forgiving the father." And no doubt John Maclean had forgiven his old man for his hellish outbursts and learned to treasure the rapturous moments of paternal approval by the time Norman Maclean died in 1990. But why should all the burden be on the sons? It is a lucky father who gets a chance to clean up his act before death reduces him to fodder for therapy sessions.

I got lucky in that way, and I have tried to do something with the opportunity. As it happened, I had always been proud of spending a lot of time with my sons. So I was stung by what Susan said to me one Saturday when Ben and I were about to leave on a fishing trip.

"Now don't be too hard on Ben today," she said. "He's been looking forward to this. Try to let him have a good time."

"What are you talking about?" I said.

"He says that sometimes you criticize him a lot when you're fishing. It spoils it for him."

Her words afflicted me with guilt. She was right. Even as his skills improved, I was always at Ben for making too much noise or fishing my water or losing too many flies. Was I nagging him about how he fished because I sensed that he was, indeed, surpassing me as a fisherman? I'll never know for sure. But I do know that after hearing from Susan and Dick and John Maclean and the old man who spoke to me in the blue afternoon beside the Yellow Breeches, I quit doing it for good.

20
Rerouting the Redneck Way, or A Cracker Shall Lead Them

On *The New York Times*, we have a bias against superlatives. There is a handsomely paid editor in charge of keeping superlatives and other grammatical gambles out of the news pages. Our view is that it is hard to know what is really "the greatest" or "the most," since history is long and our vision is finite and one person's medicine is another's poison.

But this is not the *Times*, so I can let you in on a piece of history you can take to the bank. In 1938, Lee Wulff, who was probably the greatest all-round fly fisherman who ever lived, published what is certainly the most important single sentence written about angling ethics in the twentieth century. It was: "Gamefish are too valuable to be caught only once."

Through no fault of Mr. Wulff's, a great injustice has flowed from that sentence. Scores of angling writers, many of them Mr. Wulff's cronies, have given him credit for establishing catch-and-release fishing as the nationally accepted practice that it is today. And there is no question that catch-and-release was Wulff's *idea*.

But it took a slip-sliding, fast-talking apostle of the Redneck Way to put catch-and-release into the head of every potbellied Texas bassin' man and every worm-slinging Vermont trout murderer. To find this man, you must leave such storied waters as the Restigouche and the Little Codroy of Newfoundland, the Laxa of Iceland and the Dee of Scotland—this last being where, according to the British sporting press, Wulff in 1962 caused "something like a sensation" among the bloodthirsty natives by releasing his salmon unharmed.

You must travel into the heart of deep Alabama, down below Montgomery, crossing the slack, catfish-blessed waters of Catoma Creek and passing through the sun-blasted hamlet of Pintlala, before you find the lakeside home of Ray Scott.

It is hard to imagine two men more different than Ray Scott, born in 1933 in Montgomery and founder of the tournament-fishing movement that brought us the red-metal-flake bass boat, and Lee Wulff, who was born in 1905 in Valdez, Alaska, and spent his last years trying to protect the Atlantic salmon from extinction.

Lee Wulff graduated from Stanford University in engineering. He studied art in Paris, invented the modern fishing vest, created an important family of dry flies, pioneered light-rod fly fishing for salmon and wrote several elegant books.

Ray Scott set out at nineteen to emulate the

success of a Montgomery insurance salesman whom he admired as a "classy dude" who "strutted when he walked." He wrote possibly the worst book ever written by a major figure in American sport fishing, *Prospecting and Selling: From a Fishing Hole to a Pot of Gold.* It is devoted only in passing to fishing, but deals mainly with popularizing Scott's "Wheel of Fortune" concept of salesmanship, which rests on such key principles as "Definitizing Appointment." The book also contains the breathtaking—and, thankfully, shamefaced—revelation that Scott's own sales techniques include telling "bald-faced lies to poor unfortunate [black] people" in order to collect on their twenty-cents-a-week burial policies.

Still, Ray Scott *is* a major figure in American sport fishing. His decision in 1972 to impose catch-and-release rules in the tournaments of his Bass Anglers Sportsman Society (BASS) has probably saved the lives of more fish than any other regulatory step since state governments first began putting legal limits on catches in the 1870s.

This step popularized "catch-and-release fishing for the vast majority of American freshwater anglers," according to Gene Mueller, a veteran outdoor writer in Washington, D.C. "Sure, trout purists have turned fish loose for centuries, paying more attention to outsmarting the wily critter than frying it later in the day, but it was Scott's BASS group that made live releasing of fish truly popular. Now there isn't a backwoods kid in the U.S. that doesn't practice it at least part of the time."

Catch-and-release swept the South in the 1980s, and it seemed to gain its biggest boost during the period when I was in London. I was surprised, upon my return, to find my brother Southerners were becoming as ardent about conservation as the Cockney live-release purists in Derek Seymour's fishing club. The sharpest moment of enlightenment came to me in Cajun country, when I saw Louisianans, traditionally the most bloodthirsty of Southern fishermen, obeying a four-fish limit on redfish. This was not pure catch-and-release, I'll admit. But in the consciousness-raising department, the mass observance of a fish limit in south Louisiana definitely gets you into Great Leap Forward territory.

I went to see Ray Scott at his big house overlooking a heavily stocked fifty-acre lake where stumps, tree limbs and rocks had been professionally installed to make the best possible habitat for largemouth bass. Scott had sold his interest in BASS to a group of Montgomery investors in 1986 for a rumored $17 million. He didn't seem to care much for fishing anymore, but he doted on his role as a personal friend and fund-raiser for President Bush and took an almost childlike joy in Bush's semiannual fishing visits. As for what inspired him to try catch-and-release, there was a short answer: "It was good business. I am first and foremost a businessman. I work for money."

By 1972, Scott was making a lot of money from the tournaments he started in 1967 and from *Bass Master Magazine*, started in 1968 to plug the tournaments and the products made by the tackle companies that bought space in the magazine. But he ran into "a gnawing problem."

While the motel owners and fish camps were always glad to have a bass tournament on the big lakes that dot the South and Southwest, local fishermen and sportswriters were infuriated by the bass carnage that was on view when Scott would turn up in his cowboy hat to preside over the weigh-in.

"We were catching these fish and putting them in a johnboat behind the weigh-in, and after they all flopped themselves to death, we'd give them to a children's home or an old ladies' home or whatever."

At first, Scott relied on scientific quotations to calm the yokels. He cited biologists who "tell me that when you've got twenty-five thousand acres and you take a ton of bass out, that's like a grain of sand. They can show me on paper that the lake could regenerate that much poundage before you could weigh them in."

This did not work. "I can still picture those chubby old men with the gray hair with their hands tucked down in the bib of their overalls, looking down on those fish, mumbling to each other, 'By God, that's why we ain't catching no more fish.'"

So Scott told the highly skeptical "tour fishermen" that if they wanted to participate for tournament dollars they had to install aerated live wells in their boats. Scott himself built a giant aquarium where the captured bass were displayed before being weighed and released into the lakes from whence they came.

Two years later, in 1974, Scott noticed that what began as a public-relations tactic was altering the attitudes of the fishermen themselves. This happened when a burly, sunburned contestant appeared at the weigh-in with four live fish and one dead one.

"He said, 'Ray, I'm sorry, I don't know why that fish died. I did everything I could to keep him alive.' And he got a big tear in the corner of each eye. I thought, 'My God, I just wanted to give the guy a little religion. I didn't mean for him to become a priest.' "

The catch-and-release gospel spread quickly enough among warm-water fishermen to force makers of bass tackle to drop their historical practice of advertising lures by showing a stringer of dead fish. Editors of saltwater publications got angry letters for pictures of fish being landed with a killing stroke of the gaff. All up and down the East Coast, guides like Mark Kovach on the Potomac and Bob Clouser on the Susquehanna altered their policies of allowing a customer to keep one or two trophy fish and went to complete no-kill fishing.

What caused this tidal wave of acceptance? No one, including Ray Scott, had counted on the proliferation of cable television shows starring tournament fishermen. Each Saturday, viewers could see a Jack Nicklaus lookalike named Roland Martin, or Jimmy Houston, an Oklahoma hustler with a hyena laugh, or Rick Clunn, the most radical environmentalist on the tournament trail, throwing fish back right and left.

"The same thing happened with fishing that happened with golf," Scott said. "A golfer sees Jack Nicklaus on television and when he goes out to the course, he wants to wear the same kind of clothes and use the same clubs and try to hit the ball the way he saw Nicklaus do it. A fisherman sees Roland Martin throwing back a seven-pound bass and he decides that's what you do if you're a real fisherman."

Scott's explanation was interesting as far as it went, and disarming in that he did not claim to put a philosophical polish on what he had done for money. But I wanted to know more than the how and why. I wanted to know where the spark of the idea had come from in the first place. I was pretty sure the author of *Prospecting and Selling* had never read the foundation text of catch-and-release, Wulff's 1938 *Handbook of Freshwater Fishing*.

But as it turned out, the circuitry of Ray Scott's inspiration did loop around to touch on fly fishing and an organization that Wulff helped found, the Federation of Fly Fishers. In 1970, Scott was invited to be a guest speaker at the annual conclave of the federation in Aspen, Colorado.

"One thing they promised me was to take me fly fishing for trout on one of these little old rivers, and it turns out a cow could make a bigger stream than we were fishing on," Scott said, recalling how he eagerly claimed the role of bumpkin among the tweedy gents. "They gave me one of those jackets with all of those fuzzy patches and a thousand pockets, and I became a fly fisherman.

"This guy just a couple of clicks up from me on the stream, he set the hook on his fly, and he's got this roaring fish—he broke the water once in a savage rage. It looked like it might have weighed three-quarters of a pound if it had lead in its pocket.

"And man, you've never seen such whooping and hollering and all the guys threw their rods down and ran over there and it was like an Auburn-Alabama game, with the cheerleaders. Man, they're cheering for this guy, and every time he would bow to this little old fish, they would just go into some kind of orgasmic spasm, and just carry on like you can't believe.

"And I'm standing there with my blue jeans on and my borrowed fly jacket, and I'm watching these guys have a big kick out of this guy catching this fish. But that was only half the fun. The big fun was when he beached this trout, and he got down there and wet his arms up to the crotch of his body, and he got everything he could wet, and he reached out and he pulled that little fish over there to him and with more hardware and more hand finesse than a surgeon. From nowhere he pulls out what looked like scissors. It turned out to be a device with which you disgorge a hook.

"And he carefully held that fish under the belly and he released it from that hook. I'm thinking he's going to put him in his pocket and eat him. He turned it loose, and the little fish swam off. Well, when he swam off, those five or six men that were standing on the shore went absolutely nuts. I mean, I have never seen such cheering and clapping and patting backs and high fives and low fives and shaking hands and congratulations.

"I'm standing back there thinking what in the world is going on. Well, that was it, and I found out that that's the way they fish. I went on and caught me a trout, and I turned him loose, and somehow, slow as I am, I got to thinking, perhaps on the way home, you know, there's an application for that idea and that philosophy in my business."

Do not let the Andy-from-Mayberry tone of Ray Scott's narrative fool you about the importance of that moment. I am convinced that without the mass acceptance of catch-and-release, the best bass and trout fishing in the country would have been wiped out by the next century. I speak as a person who has seen the great and seemingly inexhaustible snapper, grouper, sea trout and mackerel fishery of the northern Gulf of Mexico decimated in his own lifetime. A charter captain along the "Redneck Riviera" summed it up perfectly when asked what happened to the red snapper that used to inhabit the reefs off Panama City, Destin and Pensacola. "They all went to Birmingham and Atlanta in ice chests," he said.

To a person who does not follow fishing, it seems impossible that our vast lakes, rivers, streams, bays, estuaries and bordering oceans could be picked clean. But remember that in the seemingly inexhaustible plains of Montana, a handful of hunters using primitive weapons reduced the buffalo herd from 13 million to two hundred in only five years between 1876 and 1881.

Conservationists have known for decades what was happening in American waters. Today, there are 36 million fishermen and 18 million fisherwomen in the United States, using startlingly effective lures and fast boats to fish an ever diminishing area of water that is clean enough to support the spawning and growth of fish. We could pick those waters clean in ten years easily. "The day of the great catches is passing," Lee Wulff wrote in 1938 in his *Handbook of Freshwater Fishing*. But it took decades for public awareness to catch up with his vision.

The prophet of catch-and-release and its popularizer never met. But their luck went sour at about the same time. Wulff flew his airplane into a hill near Hancock, New York, on April 28, 1991. Almost exactly a year later, Ray Scott flew his foot into his own fast-moving mouth. A Georgia newspaper carried an interview in which Scott spoke this paragraph in describing the guesthouse beside the lake where George Bush often came to fish:

"You ever been to an old nigger house? Smell that kinda old ashen kind of smell coming from the fireplace? You know, you've got that smell in the house. Bush walked in there the first time like this [sniffing]. He said, 'Man, I could stand some of this.'"

Ray Scott's public—particularly the black members of BASS—proved more interested in his racist language than in his accounts of President Bush's fondness for the smell of wood smoke. Scott issued a forlorn statement of the sort that white Southerners and politicians of every region issue when they get caught talking that way: "I am not a racist," he said. "I am ashamed to have carelessly made reference to a racial epithet." The presidents of two black fishing clubs—the Original East Atlanta Bass Anglers and the Golden Rod Bassmasters of Birmingham—came forward to say that they were satisfied with Scott's apology. But you will not be surprised to know that in the dashing to and fro of the 1992 campaign, President Bush did not stop off again at Ray Scott's pond. Late in the campaign, Scott was allowed to stand near the President on the speakers' platform at an outdoor rally in Montgomery. He managed to get hold of a microphone and assure the crowd that, having once seen Bill Clinton in a men's room, he could attest that the Democratic nominee was not a manly man. Even the seasoned slur-meisters of the Bush campaign thought this public discussion of penis size went a tiny bit too far.

So, as I said, Ray Scott is hardly in Lee Wulff's league when it comes to eloquence or, for that matter, minimally civil behavior. Moreover, as one who lived his boyhood surrounded by the ugliness of a racist society, I have made it a policy never to feel sorry for people who get caught using "nigger" or "Jap" or "kike" or any other word designed to wound people in their identities.

Still, when I think of old motor-mouth Ray sitting down there in his big house beside the pond where George Bush used to fish, I cannot help feeling a twinge of pity. I say, all hail the elegant Mr. Wulff for his role as prophet. Long may we remember him in our prayers. But don't forget to say a few for Ray Scott, too. In fishing, at least, he rerouted his people from the Redneck Way.

21
Another Culinary Digression: McClane's Pensacola Fish Stew

Willie Stark, the redneck dictator in *All the King's Men*, said it best when he was assured that his political enemy, Judge Irwin, was a person of such towering virtue that an investigation of his life would reveal nothing venal or corrupt. "Man is conceived in sin and born in corruption and he passeth from the stink of the didie to the stench of the shroud," he said. "There is always something." What Willie meant is, we are slaves to our appetites. That is about as far as I can go in justifying the inclusion of this recipe in the same book in which I bemoan the decimation of the great redfish schools of the northern Gulf Coast. Why, indeed, did our fellow Americans kill the aforementioned 13 million buffalo in Montana in five years? The answer, I fear, is that we are full of lust, and some of it has got to get out.

Viewed in this light, it seems clear, our problem is the management of these appetites. It is better to be the kind of person who kills one nice redfish on a hook and line than the kind who traps a ton of them in a purse seine. It is possible to argue that it is better to be the kind of person who does not kill even a single redfish. But let us assume that you are not that kind of person and find yourself with a dead four-pound redfish on your hands. Or two dead two-and-a-half-pound redfish. Then it would be a good idea to follow these instructions from the late A. J. McClane.

PENSACOLA FISH CHOWDER

One 4-pound red drum,
or two 2½-pound fish
Salt
Ground white pepper
2 large baking potatoes
1 large yellow onion
2 large garlic cloves
6 scallions
⅔ cup celery leaves
2 medium fresh tomatoes
1 medium green pepper
¾ cup tomato paste
2 teaspoons Worcestershire sauce
8 black peppercorns
2 tablespoons minced fresh parsley
2 pinches of dried basil
2 pinches of dried oregano
2 large bay leaves
2 lemons
⅔ cup dry red wine
2 slices of bacon, or 4 tablespoons bacon drippings
4 tablespoons flour

4 cups canned tomatoes
Cayenne or crushed pepper to taste
(optional)

When you dress the fish save the head (or heads) with the gills pulled out. If you have an extra fish head or two, so much the better. Cut fish crosswise into steaks about 1¼ inches thick. Sprinkle with salt and pepper and set aside. Put the fish heads in cheesecloth and tie with twine, leaving a loose end for a handle.

Peel potatoes and cut into 1-inch cubes. Peel and chop onion and garlic. Chop scallions, including 2 to 3 inches of the green tops, the celery leaves, fresh tomatoes and green pepper. Put these last four ingredients in a large bowl and add tomato paste, Worcestershire sauce, peppercorns, herbs, ½ lemon, unpeeled and unsliced, ⅓ cup wine.

If using bacon slices, put them in a Dutch oven or large cast-iron pot and heat until all fat is rendered and bacon is crisp. Remove bacon, pat dry, crumble and set aside. Gradually sprinkle the flour into the fat or bacon drippings, stirring all the time. Cook and stir until roux is the color of strong coffee with cream, being careful not to scorch it. Add chopped onion and garlic and continue to cook until onion is translucent. Add canned tomatoes and heat and stir until well mixed with the roux. Add boiling water to within 4 inches of the top of the pot. Add the bowl of chopped ingredients and seasonings and the crumbled bacon, if any. Tie the bag of fish heads to the pot handle and drop them into the chowder. Bring to a boil, cover and simmer about 2 hours. Stir occasionally, and add hot water if liquid is reduced too much.

Remove fish heads and let the sack drip into a bowl to save all the juices; add juices to the chowder and discard the sack. Add cubed potatoes and cook for 5 to 7 minutes. Add fish steaks and cook until potatoes and fish are just done—the potatoes should be somewhat crisp and the fish still firm. Add remaining ⅓ cup wine.

Cut the remaining 1½ lemons into slices, and place a slice in each soup or gumbo bowl. Ladle chowder into bowls, giving everyone some fish and potatoes. Add cayenne pepper or crushed hot pepper to taste.

Serves 8.

That is the best recipe I know for fish stew. I had another good one from the North Woods for a sour stew made with northern pike, but I lost it. You can come pretty close to it by boiling potatoes and onions until done, adding vinegar to taste to make it sour and black pepper to make it hot. Then add boneless pieces of northern pike at the last minute and eat as soon as the fish are done. If anyone has a more precise recipe I'd like to see it.

22
Cutthroat Business

If you like fly fishing, there will come a time when you want to penetrate to the heart of the sport. Then you are likely to find yourself landing at an airport in Montana or Wyoming. In our case, it was Butte, the birthplace of Evel Knievel, the site of the world's largest open-pit copper mine and the best place to rent a car that will take you to the Big Hole River, which was where Susan, the boys and I found ourselves headed one day in August.

How Susan came to be on that trip is an interesting question, and I'm not sure I know the entire answer. She ordered waders, boots and a fishing vest from L. L. Bean and signed up for Mark Kovach's one-day class. Mark ridiculed me for sending her out with a battered Orvis rod and tried to turn her head with a Powell rod he happened to have for sale. Then Dick produced a Teton five-weight from his vast collection of seldom-used rods and announced that Susan should take it west. Teton is a small rod company, then located in Idaho, and its advertising projected a kind of latter-day hippie irreverence. That particular Teton was finished in surfboard purple, and it was about the sexiest-looking fly rod you ever saw. Susan said it would do.

This was the summer of 1990. Ben had finished his sophomore year in the film school at NYU, and Jeff had graduated from high school and was getting ready to go off to Colorado State in the fall. I remember Susan saying at some point that this would probably be our last vacation together as a family. I think we both believed that, and not just because our sons were leaving home.

Selectivity is a problem in the West. It is big, and it is full of rivers that are legendary in the sport. In Montana alone, there are the Big Hole, the Big Horn, the Missouri and the Blackfoot, which is no longer what it was but has a kind of holy status as the setting of *A River Runs Through It*. Then, in Wyoming, you have the Yellowstone, the Madison, the Gallatin and the glorious Snake, which actually becomes better when you cross into Idaho and get two Snakes, the South Fork and the Henry's Fork. What the best of these streams have in common is that they have more fish in a mile than you'll find in an entire county back East.

The boys and I had the typical Easterner's response. We wanted to eat the whole thing. Susan, being lower on the fanaticism curve, prevailed on us to accept an itinerary that called for concentrating on a few pieces of quality water. We would hit the Big Hole, the Yellowstone and Madison in Yellowstone Park, the Snake at Jackson Hole, and then wind up with a week of wilderness fishing at a guest ranch on the Gros Ventre River.

On the Big Hole, our guides were a couple of *Rancho Deluxe* types named Wayne Clayton and Stuart Decker, who work out of the Complete Fly Fisher, a fly shop and lodge at Wise River Junction. From their headquarters in an Airstream trailer they called "The Aluminum Love Tube," they played the Western wildman game very hard. On their days off, they went fishing. As soon as the tourist season ended on the Big Hole, they took off for British Columbia for steelhead. They liked to fly fish. "I'd better. I gave up a wife, a house and a car to do it," said Wayne.

He, in particular, was full of arcane social strategies and droll information. His response to the AIDS crisis was to date nurses on the theory that they got a lot of blood tests. He said he won a lot of money playing golf with his boyhood friend Evel Knievel, because Knievel played poorly and had never learned not to bet against a sure thing. In other words, Wayne said, Knievel was no better at hitting golf balls than he was at staying on motorcycles. Wayne specialized in fishing small dry flies for big brown trout in shallow water that most of the other guides passed up, and I remember him for guiding me to one of the most memorable fish I've ever caught. It was an eighteen-inch brown that was bigger than anything I had ever raised on a dry fly, and I resisted the South Sauty heave and struck the hook perfectly. Just perfectly. I knew it and so did the guide, and Wayne punctuated the moment by shouting "El grande marrón"—Spanish for "big brown"—as the fish boiled out into the current and took off.

That was the day I began to understand the

kind of fishermen Ben and Jeff were becoming.

"We're going to have fun today," whooped Stuart as soon as he got them into his raft. "These guys can cast."

Wayne, who was in the boat with me, looked across the water at Jeff. "That boy has a beautiful backcast," he said. "Of course, the front end doesn't look so good."

It did after a day of Stuart's coaching on long-distance casting. He taught both Ben and Jeff to double-haul, a technique of pulling, or "hauling," on the line in midcast, so as to increase the velocity with which it moves through the air, thereby increasing the distance that the line can travel on the cast. By the end of the day with Stuart, they were carving the air with long powerful strokes that looked like scenes from instructional films. Both boys now speak reverently of that day as a watershed experience in their fishing careers. For the next three weeks, we heard an astonishing number of sentences beginning with "Stuart says . . ."

In one particularly productive stretch of the Big Hole, I was indulging my weakness for watching birds rather than my fly when I heard Wayne shout, "Set the hook!" I obeyed on reflex and was fast to my biggest fish of the trip, a brown trout of nineteen inches. After releasing this beautiful and totally undeserved fish, I said to Wayne, "Now I can ask the question I was about to ask when that fish struck. Is that a water ouzel over there?"

In Western fishing, I found the birdlife a constant threat to my concentration. I developed a particular fondness for ouzels, humble robin-sized birds that make their living by walking on stream bottoms. In the category of magisterial birds of prey, we saw plenty of ospreys and bald eagles. But nothing beat the sight of white pelicans, summer visitors who rode the rapids of the turbulent Yellowstone with a goofy aplomb.

It had been over twenty years since I had driven through the Rockies, and I had forgotten how fully they confirm the saying that the true joy of pursuing trout is that they live in such beautiful places. That is doubly true of the area where the borders of Montana, Idaho and Wyoming come together in a slightly cockeyed intersection.

The views along the twenty-mile section of the Snake that runs beside the Tetons are simply supernal. Like the Big Sur coast, this is one of those American spots of such intensely concentrated beauty as to make one say, "Yes, this is it. Bury me here." Elsewhere, the routine beauty of lodgepole pines, granite escarpments and red rock canyons inspires the happy feeling of being time-warped onto the set of a John Ford western.

We certainly owe U. S. Grant our thanks for preserving the Union, but for my money, his best single day's work took place on March 1, 1872, when he created Yellowstone National Park. There are 3,472 square miles in the park, and if you get out while the RV owners are still snug in their bunks, the old gods still rule.

That was underscored for me one morning when my sons and I were casting for cutthroat— the handsome coppery trout that is indigenous to the Rockies—at a spot on the Yellowstone River called Buffalo Ford. This area, near the Yellowstone Lake Lodge, is one of the most popular fly-fishing areas in the park, yet that morning might have been the one the world began.

We had the entire stream to ourselves except for a brown beast that lumbered out of the lodgepole pines, waded into the deep main channel and then swam like a huge dog until it reached the eastern shore about fifty yards below Ben's fishing spot.

"Well, I guess we know why they call it Buffalo Ford," he said.

Rapids-shooting pelicans and swimming buffalo add spice to a fly-fishing outing. Even so, it's hard to upstage the Yellowstone cutthroat, whose original Latin name, *Salmo clarki lewisi*, honored the two explorers who brought their "corps of discovery" here in 1806.

The six miles of catch-and-release water immediately north of Yellowstone Lake is teeming with these handsome fish. I know of no better spot for building the ego of the beginning fly fisher or making the middling fly fisher feel like an expert. Get there just after the mid-July opening, cast a number 16 Parachute Adams or Caddis with reasonable delicacy, and something stimulating will happen.

Later in the season, the fish get smarter, but cutthroat are the innocents of the trout world. So much so that many accomplished anglers denigrate them. Indeed, the Yellowstone cutts can be pushovers. One day, I had three strikes from the same fish, pricking it sharply each time with the hook, before I finally got it on the fourth take.

But for those who think all cutthroat are dumb, there is Flat Creek, just outside Jackson in the vast meadow at the National Elk Refuge. Flat Creek is noteworthy for several reasons. One, it is the only catch-and-release stream in Wyoming, a state that has been unconscionably slow to protect its trout from people who regard a frying pan as an essential part of their gear.

Secondly, it is good for one's humility, after the pushover fishing on the Yellowstone, to meet the smarter cousins of *Salmo clarki lewisi*. The Snake River finespot cutthroat who live in Flat Creek are as spooky as any Eastern brown trout, and it is good for one's humility to watch them streak away in fits of survivalist terror the moment a fly touches the water. This is what serious fly casters call "highly technical fishing," and a little of it goes a long way.

By the time we set out from Jackson for the South Fork of the Snake River just across the border in Idaho, Susan was beginning to feel that all the fishing was a little too technical. She had been content to practice her casting and laugh about missed strikes on the Big Hole and Yellowstone. Now she wanted to catch a fish. Luckily, she and Ben were guided on the South Fork by Tom Montgomery, a Massachusetts man who got the fly-fishing bug at Middlebury College and went west to find acclaim as a wildlife photographer, fishing writer and, by most accounts, the best fisherman in Jackson Hole.

It was a superb day for dry fly fishing from the locally made boats marketed as South Fork Skiffs, and under Tom's tutelage Susan brought three fish to hand, including one legitimate trophy of over sixteen inches. "By the end of that day, I was beginning to feel like a fisherman," she recalled later.

Meanwhile, Jeffrey and I were being guided by Paul Bruun, a former Jackson Hole city councilman who is the godfather of the local fishing industry. If they gave doctorates in reading the water and selecting flies, Paul would have one.

Paul's technique with people who are serious about their fishing involves relentless coaching. "Put a cast in that slick spot behind the boulder. Leave it. Leave it. Now strip in line. Strip, strip, strip. Your fly is dragging. Pick it up and go again. Just in front of that willow. Strip, strip, strip." And so on.

Either the person in the front seat of Paul's boat will learn a hell of a lot about reading the water and getting a drag-free float, or he or she will have a strong desire to throttle the guide. At midday, after Jeff had been in the front seat for a few hours banging casts into every target, Paul Brunn said, "How old are you?"

"Eighteen," said Jeff.

"If I had been able to cast like that at your age, I would be a world-class fisherman today," Paul said.

Paul did not get so worked up about my skills. Still, the high point of my day came when he spotted a big cutthroat that was "lit up." That is to say, the fish was literally glowing—a phenomenon that occurs frequently with saltwater fish such as marlin, but is rarer in freshwater species. The luminescence signals that the fish is in a feeding frenzy.

Indeed, this particular fish was rising regularly. But it was tucked in behind a willow along a sheer bank in a way that made it almost impossible to reach with a delicate cast. Anyway, it rejected all our standard mayfly and grasshopper imitations. Finally, Paul concluded that the fish was taking nymphs so tiny as to be invisible to the naked eye. He tied a fly no larger than a pinhead to my tippet, and with one clean cast, I had the trout.

"Your old man is a pretty good fisherman," he said to Jeff by way of congratulating me on the accuracy of my casting. I swelled with pride, but we all knew that I would never have taken that trout on my own. But I did not argue with the man. He was an expert at the business of catching cutthroats. I figured he ought to have his say.

23
Flying Out of the Mountains

The Jesuits complicated the final week of our family fly-fishing vacation. Jeffrey, as I mentioned, was all set to go to Colorado State, a relaxed institution where they seemed more interested in his casting and canoeing ability than his grades. But late in the summer, Loyola University in New Orleans, which had been his first choice, sent word that it would take him. The problem was that Jeffrey was required to be in New Orleans in the middle of the week we planned to spend at the most remote guest ranch in Wyoming, a place reachable only by single-engine plane or a ride of several hours over a bone-jarring dirt road.

I urged Jeffrey to stick to his original plan, both because I thought he would be happy in Colorado and because I worried about his readiness for the academic rigors of a strict Roman Catholic institution. At eighteen, Jeffrey was an accomplished guitarist who had already spent a fair amount of time in the back-alley jazz clubs of New Orleans, hence his devotion to the city. He was much better read than I had been at his age. But his grades and study habits had broken the heart of every teacher he met. The Jesuits, I warned him, ran a strict liberal arts curriculum that required a kind of diligence he had always avoided.

"You don't know anything about the Jesuit order," I told him. "They're not playing. These are the people who conquered Central America."

"Don't worry, Dad," he said. "I can handle them."

"They're going to love you," I said.

So it came to pass that we chartered a plane to come one August morning and pick up Jeffrey at a rocky airstrip high in the Gros Ventre Mountains. He and I fished together on the day before his departure. We abandoned our usual practice of splitting up and fishing different sections of the stream. Instead, we stayed together and took turns on the best pools as we moved up the narrow canyon of soft red rock that brings the Gros Ventre down from its headwaters above Ouzel Falls.

Although we had the stream to ourselves, we failed to move a trout. I wanted Jeff to make a memorable catch on what was, in a sense, the last fishing trip of his boyhood. When we came out of the canyon into the big meadow below Ouzel Falls, I quit fishing altogether and let him take all the good water. Finally, where the river had cut a deep narrow channel into the face of a grassy bank, Jeffrey hooked a fish, and it was memorable enough for our purposes, running wildly upstream with the speed and zeal of a bonefish.

The day was going fast, and in the cool afternoon, we hiked on up to Ouzel Falls, which is not a vertical waterfall, but rather a place where the river descends at a sixty-degree angle down a long slide of smooth rock. We tried for the brook trout that live in the plunge pool at the foot at the falls, and perhaps we caught a few. I don't remember. What I remember is leaving the stream and climbing up to a piney hummock and watching the water come down and saying something I wanted Jeffrey to hear before he flew out of the mountains to New Orleans.

I told him I wanted him to know how much fun it had been to be his father and what a deep joy it had brought me to watch him grow up. I told him about the confidence I had that he would succeed in college, because he would get there having read, at his own pace and of his own volition, more about music and more important novels than most people have read by the time they graduate. Finally, I told him that notwithstanding the fact that he was my son, he was a man whose company I would choose on any day, on any stream.

In the days that remained, Susan and I spent one day fishing down the Gros Ventre into another, wider canyon where the slopes stood back from the stream and sagebrush and small trees covered the red rock. We were looking for the home territory of the osprey we often saw hunting its way upriver past the ranch in the afternoon. I did not see a fish in this new water, but Susan went off by herself and caught one. "It was more fun without you and the boys shouting, 'Keep the line tight, keep the line tight!' " she said.

It was a companionable day, bound as we were by the pride that we had raised sons who were good company. But it was also a time freighted with a largely unspoken sense of finality and divergence. The winding down of any long marriage is a complicated story and a sad one, too, if the marriage has been a very good one for a very long time. I am not going to tell the entire history of that marriage, because the story does not belong to me alone. Suffice it to say that over the course of a few years Susan and I realized that what had started between us in the green springtime of Alabama had run its course. We did the reading and talking and hiring of experts that serious, caring people do at such moments. But by the time we reached the mountains that summer we knew that this salvage operation had run its course, as well.

One day, Ben and I took horses, strapped our rod cases to the saddles and went up past nine thousand feet to fish a remote creek. Coming back, we rode slowly through a lush stretch of bottomland where pathless thickets of red willows came up to the withers of the horses, so that you had the sensation of forging through a whispering green sea. Just as Jeff had become a person whose company I would seek even if he were not my son, Ben had grown into a man whose advice I would seek—and trust—even if we did not share the same blood. I've always felt Ben would wind up as a writer of some kind, because from the start of his life, he has had the writer's gift of being able to care passionately and analyze coldly.

So as the horses moved through the whispering willows, we spoke of our family's past and its future, and I asked him how he would feel if his mother and I divorced, and he said, "I think you both might be happier."

And so that, too, came to pass.

24
It Is a Good Day
to Die

Dick and Sigrid went on a vacation to Florida, and when he called me at work after a week or so, I did not at first hear the new thing in his voice.

"Dick, how's it going?" I said, when I picked up the telephone, and he started off heartily.

"Well, I am here in the intensive care unit of the Indian River Memorial Hospital in Vero Beach . . ." Then his voice caught, and I could hear him weeping.

He was being treated for congestive heart failure, and only now, following several days of interventions by a round-the-clock team of doctors and nurses, was he strong enough to call his friends. Dick's report had a kind of charm for anyone inclined to think of life as a joke. After all those years of doing what no man in his shape should do—wrestling canoes into and out of the water, wading in fierce currents where he had no hope of surviving if he fell—Dick had almost bought it while strolling through Disney World on a hot afternoon.

Dick Blalock was frightened when he called that afternoon. Fear was the new thing I heard in his voice. Yet on balance he was more calm in the face of death than any other man I know. This was notable to me, because I come from a death-denying family that regarded dying as an intrusion, rather than a completion of the natural cycle of a life.

As I navigated through the final shoals of the passage to middle age, I came to see that the acceptance of my own mortality was the final and indispensable issue for me, that indeed it was hardly worth going to the trouble of having a mid-life crisis equal to the name if you were not going to figure out how to be comfortable in the embrace of what Mr. Hemingway called "that old whore death." Given his sexist, fatalistic worldview, Hemingway never figured out that the presence he called an "old whore" was, in fact, Skeleton Woman, the Native American figure whose death and rebirth signified the way in which death is braided inextricably into the process of living.

It took me an embarrassingly long time to understand that, but I comfort myself with the knowledge that one of the wisest and calmest men I have ever known, the Reverend Martin Luther King, Sr., thought of the education of the emotions as a lifelong task in which we learn mainly by observing others. The Reverend Mr. King was a very old man when I interviewed him, and he spoke in a suprising way of his lifelong struggle against hatred. As a boy witnessing the routine brutality to blacks in rural Georgia, he said, "I promised to hate every white face I ever saw when

I got to be a man." He conquered this hatred, in part, by reading the Bible.

"But nobody helped me more than Martin Luther King, Jr. He helped me to rid myself totally of hate, and just before he left and after he left, I wrote all hate off for anybody anyway. And I don't—I say, I just do not hate. Hate is like sin. When it is finished it brings death. No man can hate and live."

I think it is equally true that no one can fear death and fully live, and nobody helped me more in coming to grips with my own mortality than Dick. I do not mean that he was fearless. Certainly he was scared the morning he called from the hospital in Florida, and there is no such thing in a sane person as being fearless in the face of death. But for me the key to the midlife passage turned out to be a calm acceptance of one's mortality and of the inevitability of death and, beyond that, of its naturalness as the completion of the biological journey that each human life represents.

Perhaps because Dick had left home at sixteen and been faced with death as a teenage infantryman in Korea, he had more chances to develop a balanced attitude about death. Even at his most ill, he never whined. He had ignored tons of medical advice to live as he wished, and he was calm about the consequences of that. His attitude reminded me of the old frontiersman Thomas S. Woodward, who had lived among the Creeks in Alabama before the future President they called Old Mad Jackson defeated them in 1814 and deported them to Oklahoma. In 1858, Woodward wrote a series of letters to journalists, historians and other old soldiers who were attempting to compile a record of that time.

"You say you reckon I am now an old man; you are right," Woodward said in a letter to a fellow he had known on the frontier. "Time, the common leveler of our race, has not passed me unnoticed, and according to the course of things it will not be a great while before I am turned over to the terror of kings. If you see Jack or Thacker Howard, tell them I am living. May you live as long as suits your convenience."

In my family, we lacked that calmness in the face of death, partly because people lived for such a long time that the end always seemed untoward, no matter how tardily it arrived. In 1914, my grandfather and namesake, Hiram Howell Raines, was buried in the graveyard of the Methodist church in Curry, Alabama. In 1967, that man's wife, Mary Martha Jane Best Raines, was buried beside him. In the half century separating those two events, there was not a death in either my mother's or my father's family, save for that of one stillborn infant. As a child and even as a young adult, I had no experience with hospitals, funeral homes or any of the other way stations of modern morbidity. I do not know whether it is more accurate to say we were a death-fearing family or simply a family that refused to accept death for lack of practice. But I remember when my maternal grandfather, Robert Cyle Walker, died in 1972 at the age of ninety-one, my mother was grumpy because she felt the doctors had let him down.

For years, not thinking about death was a family tradition that suited me. In midlife, there is plenty of psychic pick-and-shovel work to do that has nothing directly to do with mortality. There is the business of being married or not, of accepting the independence of one's children, of shedding the baggage of old grievances against parents and siblings. But at the end of the day, none of it is worth the work it takes if you cannot turn and face the black dog.

For me, the negotiation of this final stage of the midlife crisis began in a cinema on King's Road in London and ended in Wyoming. I was watching *Moonstruck*, in which a woman played by Olympia Dukakis discovers that her husband is having an affair. She turns to her daughter's dunderheaded suitor, played by Danny Aiello, for advice on male psychology.

"There's a question I want to ask. I want you to tell me the truth, if you can. Why do men chase women?"

Danny Aiello gives an evasive answer about men trying to replace the rib taken by God to create woman. His interrogator, spotting the flaw in this logic, persists. "Why would a man need more than one woman?"

"I don't know," says the bewildered guy. "Maybe because he fears death."

"That's it," says Olympia Dukakis. "That's the reason."

"I don't know," he says, alarmed that he has been believed.

"No, that's it! Thank you. Thank you for answering my question."

They were talking about the motivation for adultery, but the exchange seemed to me to have a much broader application in the behavior of middle-aged males. Goofy male behavior is often seen as a case of a "middle-aged crazy" trying to prolong youth. But another, darker way of describing the same behavior is that men act wild because they are trying to run away from death.

I remember feeling sheepish about finding a pearl of wisdom in a movie that was being promoted as an opportunity to regard Cher as a serious actress. But this was the first time I remember explicitly admitting to myself how profoundly fearful I was of dying, how intolerable I found it to contemplate ceasing to exist. This fear felt childish to me, and it was, but it was real.

Something else happened a bit later that was connected to these events, although I am not sure I can explain precisely how. Back in Washington, I discovered that I was fearful of one of my superiors, a man with whom I had had conflict in the past but was now on a friendly basis. Indeed, he had played a central role in promoting me to run the Washington bureau and was supportive, even solicitous, in every way. Yet I feared his condemnation.

It made me embarrassed to be in my late forties and to be fearful of another man. I did not share this with anyone. But I fell into a habit. Every morning when I got to the office, I took a piece of adhesive note paper and wrote on it this sentence: "It is a good day to die." I then stuck this piece of paper beside the intercom through which I talked each day with this person.

"It is a good day to die" is, of course, the battle cry of the Dog Soldiers, the warrior class of the Cheyenne Indians and the most feared fighters among the Plains Indians.

One day, Ferne Horner, the office manager in the *Times* Washington bureau and the only woman I know personally who has been a paratrooper in the Israeli army, came in and pointed to the note. "I know what you're doing," she said.

She remarked that Crazy Horse, the greatest war chief of the Oglala Sioux, had borrowed this cry from the Cheyenne and used it to prepare the confederated armies of the Plains Indians for the battle at Little Big Horn. "It works," she said.

"I know," I said.

And it had. I was not only free of the specific fear I wanted to remedy. Somehow when that fear left, other anxieties began following it out the door. The last thing that I wish to tell in this regard happened in the days after Jeffrey went away to college from the airstrip in the Gros Ventre Mountains.

I went back to the canyon where he and I had fished, and I stayed in the canyon all day, hiking carefully up the rock-boned shore and casting carefully into each promising eddy. I fished alone from morning until great shards of black shadow lay across the walls and the Gros Ventre in its rushing down became opaque, in-different and a little dangerous-looking. Beside those waters, the death song of the Cheyenne entered me, filled me up, and I knew that it *was* a good day to die. And I understood, on the stroke of that moment, that the cry of the Dog Soldier is not about fatality but about freedom.

25
And Now, This
Report from the
Ego Wars

Having contemplated death and divorce, I began the next phase of my fishing career, which consisted of an inquiry into the true nature of expertise.

This is not a simple subject. In her novel *The Way Men Act*, Elinor Lipman gives us Dennis Vaughan, a television newsman and fly fisherman who goes in front of his own camera to demonstrate how to tie a gray nymph. The demonstration is part of a feature story that is kept on the shelf in case his show, *Newsbreak New England*, ever needs an emergency filler. As it happens, the "eternal filler" is never aired. "But it didn't matter. It gave Dennis ideas. He wanted to be an expert at something, and he wanted to do it in a place where people knew him. . . ." Before long, Dennis has quit his job at a Boston television station and returned to his Massachusetts hometown on the fictional Starkfield River to open a fly-fishing shop.

Lipman is on to something. Yearning for expertise in a field that is, by the standards of the mundane world, unessential and uneconomical is a powerful force among middle-aged men. This yearning breeds fantasies—the fly shop on the Starkfield, the dive shop in Key West, the historical novel about the settling of Carbondale, Illinois.

In her novel, Elinor Lipman made Dennis twenty-seven, an age at which it is still possible to achieve commanding expertise in most pursuits, including fly fishing. But in my case, the desire to explore the territory of the expert came at a time when one ought to be understanding one's limits. As an Alabamian, I knew the chastening tale of Zelda Fitzgerald, who decided to become a prima ballerina at thirty-five and danced herself all the way to a mental institution in Asheville, North Carolina.

I knew that I was now a fair fly fisherman and that by the end of my life I could be a very good one. But I knew that I would never be as skilled as my sons were going to become. I lacked the pure athletic ability to be a great caster for distance. I lacked the patience needed to become a great caster for accuracy. I lacked that indefinable gift—a mystical sense of where fish abide and what they want to take into their mouths—that is needed to become a great stalker and catcher of fish. A younger man in the throes of a powerful obsession might navigate around one or perhaps two of these obstacles. But as a man approaching fifty, I knew that I would hit a ceiling, and I thought: So be it.

Still, I wanted to explore the world of the expert fly fisher, to go among the living legends of the sport, and frankly, I felt worthy to be a part of that world. What I knew about fishing had not come cheaply, in expenditure of effort, time or dollars. Moreover, as a newly single man whose children were away at school, I now had the time and appetite and, perhaps, the need for a journey of exploration.

Dick, of course, was my guide. In the course of two decades of fishing on a government pension, he had attended dozens of fishing shows, seminars and Trout Unlimited banquets. He had met virtually all the living legends of fly fishing, and being Dick, he was not short of opinions about them. Of this group, Dick acknowledged Lee Wulff and Ernie Schwiebert as the most dazzling all-round experts. Both were well educated, urbane, widely traveled and, in Dick's view, "vain as peacocks."

"One thing that characterizes all these people is that they thrive on recognition," Dick said. "I look upon fly fishing as a great individual activity. I can go out and do it all by myself and have a marvelous time, and I'd say a good percentage of the people that I fish with feel the same way. I think probably these fellows could go out and fish by themselves and have a wonderful time. But they would want the world to know that they were out there fishing and having a wonderful time. And they would want the world to know their accomplishments."

Dick had singled out two lesser legends as his special heroes. One was Bernard "Lefty" Kreh, the retired fishing writer of the *Baltimore Sun* and by most accounts, including his own, the greatest living fly caster. The other was Ed Shenk, whom I had dubbed The Troll of the Letort because of his gnomish appearance and his fondess for fishing under bridges.

Ed had won a measure of fame as the designer of two important flies on Pennsylvania waters, the Letort Cricket and the Letort Hopper. But he found his real calling as an evangelical promoter of short rods in the sporting magazines. He had used his excellent little book *Ed Shenk's Fly Rod Trouting* to condemn "long-rod advocates" for their "broken-record recitations" about the superiority of rods of eight or nine feet. As Ed's fame grew in the angling community, he had developed a business sideline, making and selling dainty little rods between five and six feet in length. Naturally, Dick Blalock owned one of these rods, and he was very proud of it.

In fact, he was so proud of it he took it along to Trout Unlimited's annual fishing show in Bethesda, Maryland, where he had been accorded the honor of introducing Lefty Kreh for a casting demonstration. As soon as he came onstage, Lefty grabbed the Shenk rod and began making long, graceful casts with it. According to Dick, he kept extending his casts until the entire ninety-foot fly line was in the air. This is fairly hard to do with a standard rod and damn near impossible with one of Shenk's toothpicks.

Then Lefty turned to Dick, who was smiling proudly, and held the rod out to him, saying, "Here, Dick, take this piece of crap."

Dick told me this story by way of introducing me to the animosity between the short-rod tribe and the long-rod tribe. This particular blood feud had heated up when one of the outdoor magazines carried a photograph of Lefty breaking a bundle of short rods over his knee. Fishing insiders knew that the picture was a rivalrous gesture aimed at Ed Shenk.

There are similar animosities between the graphite-rod crowd and the bamboo-rod crowd. Also between the dry fly fishermen and the nymph fishermen. Similarly between the dry fly fishermen who favor mayfly imitations and those who favor terrestrials. And so on.

The one thing "that I find almost kind of distasteful about fishing is the enormous egos," Dick said. "I don't find very many people who enjoy having a joke at their own expense. They love to tell jokes about their fishing buddies, but they don't tell many jokes about themselves and particularly if there's even the slightest suggestion that they aren't God's gift to the fly-fishing fraternity. Boy, that's what really turns them off."

There was another trait that the experts had in common, Dick added. They were driven by the need to solve any problem that seemed too difficult for their style of fishing. "I kind of take my style of fishing and I sort of superimpose it upon the situation, and if the fish cooperate, that's wonderful. I'm not a great accommodationist. I think that one of the things that characterize these fellows, they had to, by God, catch fish. It wasn't enough to be out on the stream and fishing over fish. They measured the quality of their experience by the number of fish they caught. They measured the quality of *their existence* by the number of fish they caught, their egos were so wrapped into it."

Dick followed the ego wars by reading virtually everything written by or about the big names in the sport. He had an extensive fly-fishing library. He was an amused and skeptical reader of outdoor magazines. The skepticism arose from the blatant commercialism and conflict of interest in many articles on fishing. Mainstream newspapers and broadcasters have long since banned freebies, but the world of outdoor journalism often seems a throwback to the days of payola. Well-known writers serve as paid consultants to tackle companies. Magazines plug the products of their advertisers. The "writer's discount" and other gifts, which have disappeared in other fields of journalism, have been enshrined by the Outdoor Writers Association of America in its flagrantly misnamed code of ethics. "A member may accept accommodations, travel, meals or other related services," the code says, "if there is a reasonable expectation of a saleable story/stories resulting."

Dick took a more relaxed view of these matters than did I. He figured that nobody except the folks at Orvis was getting rich on fly fishing. Anyway, Dick said, the history of fishing was rife with penny-ante promotion.

A little research proved him right. Consider the case of John Conroy, a New York rod maker. He rose to fame and commercial success on the strength of what the historian Paul Schullery called "more or less constant" plugging in the leading fishing magazine of the 1840s.

"It is always difficult to judge statements in the sporting periodicals (of any day) about the quality of one manufacturer's tackle compared to that of another," Schullery wrote in *American Fly Fishing: A History*. "Friendships and commercial arrangements often interfere with objectivity, leaving the reader unsure of how much to believe."

But vanity and back scratching are only part of the reason you can't always believe what you read in fishing publications. In some writers, the mission of journalism, which is to share information, collides with the core instinct of the fishermen, which is to keep secrets. Of course, virtually all fishermen practice recreational lying among themselves. It is part of the bonding ritual of the sport. A guide once told me I had caught a nineteen-inch trout. He spoke those words as I watched him put a tape to the fish, which was just a shade over eighteen inches long. But I now believe I caught a nineteen-inch trout and have so reported the catch to friends.

Talking is one thing. Writing is another. Dick and I were struck by the number of articles in which the writers seemed to be disguising the exact locations of their best spots. Dick said this was not exactly lying, but more like the reality warping that the government calls disinformation. For my part, I came to think of it as deception by greed. In this case, greed refers not to money, but to the desire to consume the best fishing for ourselves before anyone else can get to it, somewhat in the manner of old Herbert Hoover turning the Rapidan into his private preserve.

It is surprisingly common to find articles that endeavor to lead their readers away from the best places, although few writers are as innocently candid about their intentions as the aforementioned Harry Murray. "Red" Murray owns a drugstore and fly shop in the tiny Shenandoah Valley town of Edinburg. He is the author of *Trout Fishing in the Shenandoah National Park* and another ranking member of Dick's pantheon of experts. Inside the small circle of truly knowledgeable fishing professionals, there are some who say he is the best all-round fly fisherman in the world.

He is also the inventor of the Mr. Rapidan dry fly, which takes its name from the stream where he teaches fishing classes at the rate of $125 per person per day. Yet in his 124-page book on fishing in the national park, the Rapidan gets only six paragraphs. Two of them are devoted to exaggerating how bad the roads are and warning that "you are a long way from civilization and telephones if you get stuck."

"I really have mixed emotions about attracting a lot of people to the Rapidan," Harry said when I told him I was writing about the stream. "I'm going to come down on you. We're playing down the publicity on the Rapidan River. That is why the [National] Park [Service] wanted me to do that book. The Rapidan is getting so much pressure that it was getting to be elbow to elbow. Actually I did not want to write the book at all, but the Park kept saying it's getting too crowded, so they wanted to show people where the other streams were."

When I told Dick about this conversation, he was tickled. The only time either of us had ever seen crowds on the Rapidan was when Harry was in there with his fishing classes. In almost thirty years of journalism and a somewhat longer fishing career, I have seen many curiosities. But I think Harry Murray enjoys a footnote in the history of both fields for asking $9.95 for a guide book specifically designed to lead the buyer away from the best destination. Then again, this is but one of many paradoxes from the land of the living legends.

26
Living Legends I: The Master of the Redneck Way

A benefit of having Jeffrey in school in New Orleans was that it gave me an excuse to go back to the bayou country of south Louisiana, where I had fished often in my twenties and early thirties. It was there that I met the man I regard as the greatest living Master of the Redneck Way. I speak of Mr. Bobby Edward Bryan of Downsville, Louisiana.

My friends in Louisiana told me about Bobby Bryan's skills as a fish finder. Even so, I was not prepared for the dazzling display I witnessed in the muddy waters off Timbalier Island.

We were cruising in a small outboard boat along a beach of gray sand when Bobby throttled back the outboard and pointed toward an indentation in the shoreline where the waves washed against a clump of driftwood that was half buried in the sand. The wind was down. The sea nudged the beach with the amiable push-and-pull that you see on still afternoons.

"Make a cast into that little nook," Bobby said.

He indicated a spot of water about the size of a kitchen sink. It was a small slick tucked into a slight indentation in the beach that had been created by the suction of the waves against the driftwood.

I lobbed my bait, a minnow known locally as a cockahoe, and was almost instantly hooked to a redfish.

A second cast and a second strike were enough to convince Bobby that we should anchor about seventy-five feet off the beach. Jeffrey and I were plunged anew into one of our episodes of live-bait recidivism. From midafternoon until the red autumnal sun crashed into the marsh grass, we had a ferocious time with redfish up to eight pounds.

Once we got plenty of bait in the water, the school spread out, so that we were catching them all across a broad area that extended from the shore to within three or four feet of our boat. These fish were "rallying," as the old saying goes among Gulf charter fishermen. That meant the more we caught, the more competitive the remaining fish became in their feeding.

Bobby called to two men in a nearby boat and invited them to join us. These amiable fellows, a businessman and a lawyer who had fished with Bobby earlier in the year, announced that they had lost their anchor. Somewhat testily, Bobby instructed them to tie on to our boat, which they did. The fish smashed their baits obligingly, but they had a hard time hooking up. When one of them did finally snag a fish, he managed to play it so roughly that it got off.

I left my place on the bow and moved back to where Bobby sat at the steering console.

"Bobby," I said, "there is something I have to tell you, but I'll have to whisper it in your ear."

"What's that?" he said, grumpy over the spectacle in the next boat.

I leaned close to his ear and said, "These suckers cannot fish."

Bobby laughed so hard I thought he was going to fall overboard. Finally, he managed to hiss, "You're right. They can't fish a lick."

I was in the grip of hubris. But of course, I was riding the coattails of Bobby Bryan's expertise, as I have on many days since. I have spoken elsewhere of what I call "the gift of knowing." I realized after that first day off Timbalier that Bobby had it in the purest and most powerful form I had ever encountered.

Later I pressed him about what attracted him to the spot. He shrugged and said, "It just looked like a place that would have fish."

On subsequent trips, he and I talked about whether some people possess an innate sense that enables them to find fish where others fail.

"I don't know," he said. "You just ride along, and all of a sudden, something says, 'Stop. Right here.' It's not superior knowledge. It's not anything like that. It's just that something tells you that this is the right place. It's a funny thing. You can do it sometimes almost in the wide-open water. Just something tells you, 'This is it right here.' Whether it be that you're looking at a certain ripple in the water—it might not be enough ripple to even be noticeable if you're not really looking for it. A certain change. I don't know.

"It's hard to describe. You just see it in your mind, and your mind tells you that's it. Whether you know what your mind is talking about or not, you know that's it."

Dick developed a scientific theory about why certain people seem to have a preternatural gift for finding fish. He contended that world-class fish finders have a biological advantage in the form of super-acute vision. He said that Ken Miyata, the young scientist who drowned while fishing the Big Horn, seemed to have naturally polarized vision that enabled him to see through the water and spot trout where other people, equipped with the best polarized sunglasses, saw only slick currents and barren rocks.

There is no denying the role of superior eye-sight, memory and observational skills. This is true in any kind of fishing and especially true in fly fishing. Yet this is one of the few debates in which I come down on the side of mysticism rather than rationality. What Bobby calls "seeing it in your mind" happens to other world-class fishermen, too. If you think of the mind as a computer, the sixth sense in fishing can be explained as cramming that computer with so many fish facts that it suddenly produces an insight that depends on those facts but leaps beyond them. In this analysis, the gift of knowing functions like the Romantic poets' "creative imagination"—their term for the intuitive leap that carries the literary scholar to the higher ground of truly inspired creation.

The experiences described to me by Rick Clunn fit this pattern. I met Clunn after telling

Ann Lewis, the public relations director at the headquarters of the Bass Anglers Sportsman Society, Inc., in Montgomery, that I wanted to spend some time with the smartest and most thoughtful of the professional fishermen. Without hesitation, she picked Rick Clunn, a Texan who had chucked a career with Exxon to fish full-time.

Besides winning the BASS organization's major annual tournament in 1976, 1977, 1984 and 1990, Rick is widely regarded as both the finest technician and the most ardent environmentalist on the professional tour. As we fished the shoreline of the Potomac River near Mount Vernon one day, he told me of two experiences that fit my theory of the intuitive leap. For Rick Clunn, these took the form of "pictures" or "visions" that would come when his mind was at rest.

"I first had those visions in 1976. At first I tried to disregard them. On Lake Mead, Nevada, I saw the fish that won the tournament for me on the next day," he said.

As he recalled the episode, he was in his motel room after a fruitless day on Lake Mead, that surreal reservoir created by Hoover Dam in the middle of the desert outside Las Vegas. In this lake, clear water of nuclear blue laps against sheer red cliffs. It is a barren-looking impoundment having little in common with the swampy, stump-studded Southern waters where bass fishing got its start. As he lay on his motel bed, listening to the sigh of the air conditioner, Rick saw two fish suspended in the water in a specific location.

The next morning, he fired up his outboard and zoomed away on a trip that exhausted much of the allotted fishing time. "I went one hundred and five miles, and I caught two five-pound bass.

Normally in Lake Mead, you're lucky if you catch one five-pounder in a month. I got two in one day."

He remembered thinking that "something's going on here, and I don't recognize it. I started looking for something that would explain what was happening to me."

For Rick, that meant digging into New Age books about mental imaging and going on retreats with a sage from New Jersey who studied Native American mysticism. Rick found that he could not force his fish visions, but he learned to take them when they came, as they did in another tournament.

"I was lying in bed, totally drained, and I got a picture. It was a weedbed—a place I have been before—and I go around it four times, and I catch four fish, and I win the tournament. The next morning I went to that weedbed, and that's what happened. I got a seven-two, a six-five, and a four-eight."

After that, Rick had a motto sewn into his fishing vest—"There are no limits"—and began referring to fishing as his "vehicle" toward some higher goal, for which he believes he is preparing himself through a regimen of martial arts and mystic literature. "What is it the Orientals say?" he asked after our day together. "When the pupil is ready, the teacher will come."

Well, maybe. In any event, I don't think my vehicle is ready for the next leap. But I take my stand on this. There are certain people with the gift of knowing. Rick Clunn is one. So is Bobby Bryan.

Fishing with Bobby is my connection to the bridge at South Sauty. I have awarded him the title of Master of the Redneck Way because he embodies both the passion and the sadness of that old bloodthirstiness. It is a style of fishing based on killing, but at its highest evolvement, the practitioners recognize the holiness and fatality of the sport. That is what Faulkner was trying to express through the character of Boon Hogganbeck in "The Bear." Hogganbeck loved—indeed, could not outlive—the primal forest whose creatures he was bent on destroying with his unreliable old shotgun.

"The Bear" deals with the taming of the last wilderness in the Mississippi Delta and incidentally the passing of the old part-Indian countrymen like Boon. In the last scene of the story, Faulkner provided an enduring image of the conflict inherent in the frontier experience, whereby Americans both gloried in the wilderness and greedily consumed it.

This scene opens when Isaac McCaslin, a sixteen-year-old hunter, hears a loud clanging sound, "as though someone were hammering a gun barrel against a piece of railroad iron."

> Now he went on, his gun unloaded and the barrel slanted up and back to facilitate its passage through brier and undergrowth, approaching as it grew louder and louder that steady savage somehow queerly hysterical beating of metal on metal, emerging from the woods, into the old clearing, with the solitary gum tree directly before him. At first glance the tree seemed to be alive with frantic squirrels. There appeared to be forty or fifty of them leaping and darting from branch to branch until the whole tree had become one green maelstrom of mad leaves, while from

time to time, singly or in twos or threes, squirrels would dart down the trunk then whirl without stopping and rush back up again as though sucked violently back by the vacuum of their fellows' frenzied vortex. Then he saw Boon, sitting, his back against the trunk, his head bent, hammering furiously at something on his lap. What he hammered with was the barrel of his dismembered gun, what he hammered at was the breech of it. The rest of the gun lay scattered about him in a half-dozen pieces while he bent over the piece on his lap his scarlet and streaming walnut face, hammering the disjointed barrel against the gun-breech with the frantic abandon of a madman. He didn't even look up to see who it was. Still hammering, he merely shouted back at the boy in the hoarse strangled voice:
"Get out of here! Don't touch them. Don't touch a one of them! They're mine!"

There you have it, the greed that killed the buffaloes and cleared the twenty-pound cutthroats from the Henry's Fork of the Snake River and the big crappies from South Sauty. It is also the greed that led me to kill the fish that I regret killing more than any other fish except for the smallmouth bass that Jeff and I ate in Canada when we saw the Maymaygwayshi. This second-most-regretted fish was one that Bobby found and that I mistakenly thought was mine.

It happened one time when Bobby was fishing with several seriously devout Baptists from Texas, and he was not having any fun. I feel I can say this, since I am from the South and grew up among Baptists and am related by blood to many of them. Southern Baptists as a group are not much fun, and when you get into that strain of Southern Baptists from Texas, principally the ones associated with Baylor University or the church of the Reverend W. A. Criswell in Dallas, you may be in for a notably sour time. That is what Bobby had on his hands, a group of Baylor Baptists, and he did not like them at all. So when Jeffrey and I showed up at Uncas Favret's fish camp at the BBY Marina on the bayou near Leeville, Louisiana, one October weekend, Bobby blew off the Baptists and took us fishing.

We were way back in the marsh on a tidal creek that none of us had ever fished, and Bobby kept jamming his skiff over the skinny water and making us cast into the potholes in the bends of an increasingly narrow ditch. Jeff and I had long since given up on this ditch, but we kept casting because Bobby gets very irritable if you don't keep fishing in what he regards as promising water. Never mind that at certain times he would regard a wet spot in the highway as promising water.

In any event, the ditch finally straightened out for a stretch of a couple of hundred feet and way down at the end there was a spot about twice as wide as our boat, and there was a little bush growing on one side of it, this bush being the tallest piece of vegetation in several thousand acres of marsh grass. It did not require Bobby's sixth sense to see that the ripples moving across this little pool were made by a large fish swimming in a restricted area.

"There's a big one," Bobby said. "Be real quiet now."

We were real quiet and also very happy that Bobby had brought us into what we had regarded as an absolutely barren ditch. Now that he had pushed us across a mile of trackless mud and marsh grass, it seemed inevitable that a fish would be there. I put a cast into the middle of the ditch and never had a chance to set the hook, so quickly did the fish take. It dashed heroically around its little patch of home water before coming into the net. In the splendid October light, Jeff took a picture of me holding the fish, which weighed about eight pounds.

The picture turned out nicely, and it makes me sad every time I look at it. Bobby got into a hassle with the Texans over the expenses for their trip, and they left in a bad mood, taking my redfish along with everything else they could stuff into their ice chests. I had planned to use that fish as the star of a Cajun recipe that Don Marion had sent me for barbecuing a large redfish. You leave the fish whole for this recipe, but those folks reduced my fish to fillets and hauled it out of there.

I was raised by Christians, and I know that the fish is a powerful symbol of sharing. After all, Jesus used fish to feed the five thousand near Bethsaida. Still, I never would have killed that fish if I had known it was going to be used to feed the Baptists in Texas.

27
Yet Another Culinary Digression: Bobby Bryan's Cajun Firecracker Kinda Pink Fried Fish and the Grand Isle Classics of Donald H. Marion

One of the reasons I took an instant liking to Bobby Bryan was that he struck me as a throwback to the mythic characters one encountered in the hunting and fishing lodges of the South when I was a boy. He had a grizzled beard and was built along Falstaffian lines. Nothing on his body or in his tackle box came from Orvis. He communicated through jokes, stories and, when confronted with sloppy casting or a lack of zeal, a blizzard of insults. Even though he had caught thousands of fish in his fifty-eight years and now released more than he kept, he regarded losing a fish as an astonishing tragedy. His vocation and his avocation had merged. As sole owner and chief designer for

Lightnin' Lures, Bobby made fishing lures for a living, and in his spare time, he used them.

And in keeping with the tradition of the old sporting camps of the South, what Bobby could do in a boat was nothing to what he did in front of a stove. Here is his recipe for fried fish and French-fried potatoes.

Mix yellow cornmeal and cayenne pepper. As for the amounts, Bobby says, "I pour in the cayenne pepper until my cornmeal turns kinda pink."

Roll the fish in this and fry it, preferably outdoors in a large vat of oil over a butane-fired fish cooker.

Sprinkle a little of the kinda-pink mixture over the sliced potatoes. Do not coat the potatoes, but rather use enough of the mixture so that the potatoes feel sandy to the touch. Fry them, too.

Juanita Bryan, Bobby's wife, makes a more scientific version of kinda-pink breading by combining five pounds of cornmeal, one cup of salt, three ounces of cayenne pepper, one ounce of black pepper, one tablespoon of garlic powder, and one tablespoon of onion salt.

"That's not enough pepper," says Bobby, who recommends doubling the cayenne or, if he is feeling feisty, quadrupling it. "Red pepper doesn't really burn your mouth," says Bobby, whose taste buds are fireproof, "but it sure does help the flavor."

My original host for south Louisiana fishing was Donald H. Marion of Houston, formerly of New Orleans. It was while fishing out of Grand Isle aboard Don's boat, the *Donna Gail*, that I saw him dance around with the snapper hook in his hand. That incident notwithstanding, he is a skilled fisherman and, more than that, the luckiest man with whom I have ever shared a boat. Luckiest when it comes to catching big fish, I should add, not necessarily when it comes to boats. In fact, Don's boats are often afflicted with mechanical or flotation problems. You could not really count as lucky the day Donald and another fellow got caught in a freak storm whose ninety-mile-per-hour winds carried off the windshield of the *Donna Gail* and washed their tackle, rods and fish box overboard. They saved themselves by clinging to an oil rig.

But it is Don's cooking that concerns us here. He has many recipes for grilling large creatures of the land and sea. His recipe for barbecued red-fish is the best I know for a fish over ten pounds. His recipe for barbecued shrimp is just handy to have around and not as complicated as Paul Prudhomme's.

Here is the recipe for Don Marion's Barbecued Redfish.

First, melt eight tablespoons of butter in a saucepan. Add one-half cup chopped onion, two cups chopped celery, one-quarter cup chopped bell pepper, and sauté until the celery is tender.

Then combine the following in a blender:

> Three cups canned tomatoes
> One tablespoon ketchup
> One teaspoon chili powder
> One tablespoon Worcestershire sauce
> One-half lemon, thinly sliced
> Two bay leaves
> One clove garlic, minced
> One teaspoon salt
> A dash of red pepper

Blend this and add to sautéed ingredients.

Take one whole redfish. Salt and pepper the fish and dredge inside and out with flour. Make a shell out of aluminum foil on a cookie sheet or some other large tray. Place the fish inside the shell and pour the sauce over it. Put lemon slices on top of the fish. Put the tray inside a barbecue smoker over medium-hot coals. Baste often, making sure the fish does not dry out. A large fish may require more of the liquid, in which case double the above recipe.

Here is the recipe for Don Marion's Simple Barbecued Shrimp with the Mosca's Variation. Mosca's is a venerable Italian restaurant on the highway between New Orleans and the bayou country.

Get shrimp in the shells with or without the heads on them, as you wish. Dust these shrimp heavily with fresh paprika and then cover them with black pepper until you can hardly see them.

Melt a mixture that is half margarine and half butter and let it cool. Then pour it over the shrimp and let stand for two hours.

Cook at 450 degrees for ten minutes. Turn the shrimp and cook for ten minutes more.

Pour off the butter and cook five minutes more. Then pour the butter back on and dust again with paprika.

Mosca's marinates its shrimp in a mixture of one cup olive oil, five cloves of garlic, three bay leaves, three tablespoons of dried rosemary, one tablespoon of oregano. For the last five minutes of cooking, it simmers the shrimp in wine.

This is a more subtle dish, but I like the firehouse simplicity of Don's basic recipe.

28
Living Legends II: A Prince of the Sport

As befits a prince of the sport, he started fly fishing on a stream called Enchanted, and nothing much happened until he came to a place called the Bullfrog Pond.

"There was a hermit there," Charles K. Fox remembered. "We got to talking to this hermit and I got to fooling with this fly rod. Those were the days of a six-foot leader with two dropper loops. We put three flies out. Well, the hermit helped a little bit with the casting, and you'd flop the rig out and there would be three rings. It was just a question of whether you hooked three trout, two trout, one trout. But action on every cast. They were in there thick. There was one landlocked salmon among them that I happened to catch. So that's really the start of it. Those were the first fish I ever caught on a fly."

He was an old man when I met him. That happened on the first day Dick and I fished together, which was also the day I caught my first trout on a fly rod. We had stopped by the meadow near Fox's house on the Letort and watched brown trout spawning over the redds that Fox himself had created by hauling in eighteen tons of river gravel, one load at a time, in a battered Volkswagen. As Dick predicted, the old man appeared after a while and joined us on one of the fish-watching benches he had built alongside the stream. Later, Dick said that Charlie had also come to make sure we were obeying his hand-lettered signs warning against fishing over the spawning trout. The signs were not backed by any law, but rather by Charles Fox's moral authority as Keeper of the Letort. Dick said that of all the living masters of fly fishing, Charlie was the most amiable and self-effacing.

But I knew little of the history and literature of fly fishing at the time and did not appreciate Charlie Fox's place in the process by which Americans gradually displaced Britons as leaders in the sport, nor did I understand that Fox's meadow was a place of legends. Briefly, the Catskill anglers of the Thirties and Forties had introduced a new, more sophisticated style of dry fly and nymph tying after studying the works of British masters like Skues, Halford and Marryat. After the "Catskill school" had its day, the Pennsylvania anglers associated with the Fly Fishers Club of Harrisburg came to dominate the sport, principally through the advances that Alvin R. Grove, Jr., Vincent Marinaro and Charles K. Fox made in the use of tiny flies for difficult fish in clear water. Most of those advances were perfected by Marinaro and Fox, who used the clear waters that flowed past Fox's meadow as a laboratory for studying how wild brown trout react to "minutiae"—that is, the tiniest of insects and the flies that imitate these insects.

The place of the Pennsylvanians is summed up in *McClane's New Standard Fishing Encyclopedia* as follows: "He who would implement, by today's standards, the most refined application of Cotton's immortal exhortation to fish fine and far off must now sit at the feet of the three Pennsylvania masters of the minutiae, Fox, Grove and Marinaro, who will certainly some day seem as legendary to us all as Hewitt and LeBranche are already beginning to seem within the decade of their death."

By the time Dick and I went back to have lunch with Charlie and his wife, Glad, a few years later, I was better read on fly-fishing history. I knew enough to be dazzled when Charlie began talking matter-of-factly about his outings with Edward Hewitt and George LaBranche. Charles Fox knew LaBranche. LaBranche, in turn, had corresponded—and argued—with Theodore Gordon (1854–1915), the consumptive bachelor and failed accountant who had established himself as the father of dry fly fishing in America by the time he died alongside the Neversink in upstate New York. As for Hewitt, he was famous as both the most popular writer and most inflated ego in the first half century of American fly fishing. He seriously believed that the nymphs he tied were so deadly that he could clean out a stream with them, if he chose. But as Charlie related, the man's enthusiasms were not limited to the stream.

"I was interested in the history of fly fishing, and I was very, very fortunate to have met some of the real greats and become pretty close to them," Charlie said.

"It wasn't all my doing," he added. "Mother was a very attractive widow, and Hewitt liked Mother, see. So he would visit. He'd come over here trout fishing, but there might not be too much trout fishing involved.

"Oh, he was something. I'll never meet another man like that. He was a genius. He had tremendous information about everything. You could bring up a subject, and he was an authority on it. It was just unbelievable.

"He got to know this section pretty well and he liked it, along with his interest in Mother."

These stories were like gold to Dick, particularly the part about Hewitt and Charlie's mother. The movement of the Catskill fly fishers down the spine of the Appalachians to inspire the next generation of angling innovators was an important event in the history of fly fishing in America. To think that Hewitt, who was famous for what one writer called his "opinionated crankiness," had started it all in hopes of currying favor with a comely widow was a vivacious footnote in the studiously ascetic annals of the sport. So much for the incompatibility of *amore e pesce*, at least in southern Pennsylvania.

It was a clear September Sunday when we visited Charlie and Glad Fox. They still lived in the little house overlooking the meadow that Charlie built in 1956. Dick had baked a pork roast and a pumpkin pie, and he took over Glad's kitchen to serve lunch. Charlie had taken a bad fall a few months before, and Glad had been so badly crippled by arthritis that she was hardly recognizable as the lithe brunette in hip boots pictured in Charlie's books. But she was a person of almost ethereal sweetness, and the lively couple loved being fussed over by Dick. They both took wine with the meal, and the four of us listened as Charlie told the story of his life as a fisherman.

In the late Twenties, he said, there were by some estimates only a hundred or so skilled dry fly fishermen in the United States. It was a tight fraternity that always traded gossip about promising streams. So as Ed Hewitt pursued his interest in Mrs. Fox and the trout in her vicinity, he began bringing down other prominent New York anglers. They had already been fishing Brodhead Creek in the Poconos, but the richer waters of southern Pennsylvania astonished them with brown trout up to fifteen pounds. The group included a number who had used Ed Hewitt's place on the Neversink, a revered Catskill stream, as a fishing headquarters. Young Charlie Fox met Colonel Ambrose Monell, who caught a salmon in 1912 that was among the first to fall to a dry fly in North America, and John Alden Knight, the inventor of the famous and probably fraudulent "solunar tables" for predicting when fish would bite.

But his favorites were Hewitt and LaBranche, the latter a New York stockbroker and champion yachtsman who wore a tie, vest and deerstalker cap for his fishing. The name of LaBranche's favorite fly, the Pink Lady, may suggest another of his interests. His fly-fishing aesthetic was summed up in the comment "Fly fishing is closely allied in my mind with music."

"They were very, very interesting," Charlie continued, drawing a picture from a Thirties movie of two dapper gents aprowl in the countryside. "LaBranche looked like a model, sort of a Hollywood model, very dapper, and he was smart, and he loved to kid Hewitt. He knew just how to get Hewitt going. That was the damnedest pair you ever wanted to be around."

Fox got directly from LaBranche the story of how he became a millionaire. Hearing that the United States Navy was going to make a heavy investment in submarines around the time of World War I, LaBranche loaded up on the stock of the then little-known Electric Boat Company of Groton, Connecticut. He departed almost immediately for an extended salmon-fishing trip to an isolated camp on the Restigouche, leaving instructions for his secretary to sell the stock if it made a modest gain. But she was unsure about the exact figures and sent a series of increasingly frantic telegrams: "Electric Boat at four. Should I sell?" "Electric Boat at eight. Should I sell?" Flooding rains had ruined LaBranche's salmon fishing, but also stopped delivery of the telegrams. By the time he emerged from the woods, he was set for life.

Hewitt and Fox first met when Charlie invited Alfred W. Miller, a famous fishing writer whose pen name was Sparse Grey Hackle, to address the Fly Fishers Club of Harrisburg. Hewitt accompanied him and soon became enamored of the rich fishing around the nearby town of Carlisle. That town and the surrounding Cumberland County lie atop a bedrock of limestone. This porous rock is laced with the largest overflowing springs east of the Mississippi and north of Florida, feeding streams of fabulous biological richness such as the Yellow Breeches, Big Springs, Cedar Run and the Letort Spring Run.

To a large degree, the story of dry fly fishing in the past forty years is the story of what Charlie Fox and Vince Marinaro did on the Letort. Indeed, an important part of the story of the spread of fly-fishing-only streams begins with Charlie's purchase in 1945 of a meadow that included a 2,200-foot stretch of the north bank of the Letort.

Charlie knew that Gifford Pinchot, a pioneering conservationist who was twice governor of Pennsylvania, had started the first special-regulation trout stream in 1934 at Fisherman's Paradise, a state park in central Pennsylvania. But no one had ever tried to regulate fishing on waters that flowed through private land by imposing stricter catch limits and dictating the fishing methods and baits that would be allowed.

Charlie dreamed of the day when some streams could be set aside for fly fishing over wild fish. But even half a century ago, the politics of trout fishing was clear. Mainstream conservation organizations and state wildlife bureaucracies viewed fly fishers as selfish elitists who wanted to make it hard for the average guy to take his kid out on the weekend and catch a few fish paid for by his tax dollars.

"Here in Pennsylvania, we had a well-organized, big sportsman's club, and they were bitterly opposed to it," Fox recalled of his initial effort to get the state to set aside some waters for wild trout. "They liked to chase the fish trucks. That was their game. They couldn't catch anything but newly stocked trout. That's what we were up against." For their part, the state fisheries people had a simple philosophy: "Give us the money and we'll give you the fish."

Finally, Charlie Fox came up with the idea of end running the state regulations by getting the landowners on the Letort to agree to restrict the catch on their properties to two fish per day. The

Pennsylvania Fish Commission agreed, somewhat reluctantly, that the scheme was legal on the grounds that private landowners could define the "terms of trespass" by which they allowed fishermen to cross their section of the stream bank. In order to get three local fishing clubs to endorse the idea, Fox agreed that bait fishing would be allowed. His immediate goal was to cut back on the killing and to get the state to quit dumping its hatchery rainbows among the wild brown trout of the Letort. The principle of special regulations on streams that pass through private property had been established.

"That was the first one in the country. I had signs printed. We couldn't have flies only. Bait would be permitted. Barbless hooks was part of it. A limit of two killed. This thing had wonderful notoriety in *Outdoor Life*.

"We based this on the property owners. The property owners could control things. They said, 'You can trespass here, you can fish here, provided you abide by the following rules.' After the *Outdoor Life* article, it started at other places. In due time it really caught on."

Indeed. Today there are special-regulation trout waters throughout the country, although no one seems to know how many miles of streams are now for fly fishing only. But the number is growing, and the issues of political fairness are not quite as clear-cut as in years past. For example, by one estimate, there were a hundred dry fly purists in the United States in 1929. Clearly setting aside a stream for them was hard to justify from the standpoint of social equity. By 1986, there were an estimated one million fly fishers, and in 1992, the number had risen to three million.

Even so, state game officials must walk a tight-rope. There is no question that restricting a stream to fly fishing only and imposing catch-and-release regulations increases the fish population, provided the water quality is good enough to support reproduction. But the number of taxpayers who have the equipment and skill to fish such waters is still relatively small. Moreover, only about 500,000 of the three million fly fishers are hard-core purists.

So in Pennsylvania and most states, the fish and game officials zealously produce hatchery trout and defend the rights of bait fishermen, as they probably should. The balance usually works out the way it does in Charlie Fox's neighborhood. The best mile and a half of the Letort is fly-fishing-only, and the management practices favor wild brown trout over stocked trout. Four miles away, on the Yellow Breeches, one mile is set aside for fishing with flies and other artificial lures, while the remaining twenty-nine miles of the stream are open to bait fishing and receive thousands of stocked trout every year.

The Yellow Breeches and the Letort were central to the friendship of Fox and Marinaro, a friendship that began shortly after Marinaro moved to Harrisburg to take the job he would hold the rest of his life as an attorney in the state legal department. They were drawn together by a mayfly hatch that occurred each year on the Yellow Breeches around June 15.

"Vince was brilliant," Charlie said. "I was editor of the *Pennsylvania Angler*, and one day a dapper little fellow comes in there, and he wanted to see me. He said, 'I want to talk to you about an article you wrote about the Yellow Drake [mayfly].'

We called them sulfurs after that. He wanted to know more about it. Where were the wonderful hatches? And so I was impressed with this fellow and his interests and everything. And then learned he had no car. He said he didn't know where to go anyway. So I said, 'Well, let's get together. I'll take you out on this stream.' He said, 'Well, in return you come to my place, and my wife will have dinner ready for the two of us.'

"So I took him up on the Breeches somewhere, I guess, the first trip, and we had a good time. He was interesting. The meals were good, too."

"You were both fly fishers at this time?" I asked, for I knew that Charlie had gotten his start as a bait caster fishing with his father for bass and muskie.

"Oh, yes," he said. "We were pretty well advanced, too. I didn't know it at the time, but Vince was a fine bamboo rod builder, and he was a fine fly tier. We enjoyed each other's company, and I got to know him real well. I recognized that here was a brain and I didn't argue with him. Hell, if we had a difference of opinion on something, I just folded up. He was too much for me."

Many men, including me, have dreamed of living their lives for fishing rather than work. Charlie Fox came close to doing that. He worked as a deputy sheriff, a hotel manager, an outdoor writer, anything that would keep him close to his streams. He sold a farm he had on the Yellow Breeches because the water there was too dingy for good dry fly fishing, and in 1943 he bought beside the Letort a grassy plot dotted with thorn apple trees.

He built a small shack beside the stream, consciously copying Walton and Cotton with their fishing house on the Dove. Sometimes Marinaro spent as long as a week at a stretch in the shack, obsessively studying the brown trout of the Letort. Up to that point, most dry fly fishing was based on the insects of the air, the mayflies and caddises. Marinaro and Fox discovered that there were some trout that fed almost exclusively on insects of the land—grasshoppers, ants, beetles, crickets and so on. Fox was the first to give the flies that imitated these insects the name "terrestrials," a term that is universal in fly-fishing terminology today.

The two men showed that trout could be taken on smaller hooks and with lighter tippets than had ever been used before, drawing on connections with fishing buddies at Du Pont to get the finest nylon filaments then available. As synthetic fibers gradually replaced the old "gut" leaders made from silk-worm filaments, they rode the first of several waves of technological revolutions to sweep fly fishing during their careers.

But there was one tribe of persnickety trout that eluded them, feeding on some mystery insect that neither Fox nor Marinaro could identify. After lunch, we adjourned to one of Charlie's streamside benches, and he related how this played out.

"Vince was camping up here, and I said, 'Vince, catch some of these damn things, so we'll know what they look like.' So he put up two stakes with a net strung between them."

With Fox's urging, Marinaro set out to try to figure out which of the ants, hoppers and other, much tinier insects in their net was attracting the Letort trout.

"I had a fly-tying kit in the cabin and I told Vince to get busy. The next day I came in, and Vince was beside himself. He said, 'I know how to take these fish. I know what they're taking, and I've got the fly tied up for it.'

"I said, 'What is it?' and he said, 'It's a jassid.'

"I said, 'I've never heard of a jassid,' and he said, 'It's a kind of insect.'

"He said, 'I'll show you.' He cast out and said, 'He'll take it,' and he took it.

"Then I went upstream to a place where I had spotted five trout the day before. I put the Jassid on, and I got all five."

Joe Brooks, a well-known writer for *Outdoor Life*, got wind of this tiny fly imitating an insect only one-eighth inch long and so obscure as to have escaped the notice of generations of expert fly tiers. The Jassid fly, imitating a family of insects once called Jassidae and later renamed Cicadellidae, was not of much use on waters other than the Letort. But the artistry of its conception, reported by Brooks in *Outdoor Life* in 1958, established the fame of Fox and Marinaro and the dominance of the new Pennsylvania school of fly tiers.

Like all friendships, that of Fox and Marinaro had a script. Charlie was quiet and patient and generous, Vince testy and grudging and, like many geniuses, self-centered. Marinaro had been a concert violinist at age ten. He had given up the instrument but not the temperament of the child star. Glad Fox never forgot the angry letter he wrote Charlie when he heard she and Charlie were getting married. Apparently, he feared it would inhibit Charlie's ability to drive him to nearby streams.

Like many friendships, this one also had a balance point and a secret. Marinaro's book *A Modern Dry Fly Code* won more acclaim than Charlie's *The Wonderful World of Trout*. Marinaro was a better tier and rod builder than Fox. But Charlie caught more fish and bigger fish. That brings us to a secret that has seldom been disclosed outside the tight little circle of Cumberland anglers who gathered around a bonfire in Fox's meadow every year for "the last supper" at the end of trout season. The secret jumped out of Charlie's mouth so quickly it seemed to surprise him.

"Vince couldn't catch trout," he said, laughing nervously. "I shouldn't have said that, I guess. He had trouble . . . that business of leaving the fly sticking in 'em.

"He wasn't as good at catching as he was at tying flies and making rods and talking and so on. He had a couple of little weaknesses, and one of these weaknesses was when a trout took his dry fly he reacted too hard and too fast. Instead of just hooking him easy, Vince would leave a fly sticking in him."

Suddenly I remembered a passage in *A Modern Dry Fly Code*. Marinaro had written of the "nervous pressure" he felt on seeing a rise and the "violent reaction" that often produced "a sudden parting of the ways between me and the trout." I had thought on reading the passage that Marinaro was simply observing the shopworn tradition whereby fishing writers depict themselves as bumblers. Not so. He was doing that rarest thing among fishermen. He was telling the truth about his own shortcoming. The father of modern dry fly fishing, the author of what has been called "the first original American contribution to fly fishing," was making a confession that has led me to revere his memory. He was a practitioner of the South Sauty heave.

In their personalities, Fox and Marinaro demonstrated the amiable and obsessive styles of fly fishing. Followers of the amiable style have the fun, but it is the obsessives who make the discoveries that enable the rest of us to catch fish and who most often wind up wounded in the ego wars that so fascinated Dick.

Dick had heard that Marinaro died embittered because his book was ignored when it was first published and not even the veneration that marked his later years made up for that.

"Vince would have liked publicity," Fox said. "He was built that way. He felt he didn't get his due in the early days."

Yet like many fishing innovators, he was torn between the desire for adulation and the desire to keep the magical secrets that allowed him to look down on lesser fishermen. In the beginning, he was almost maniacally secretive about the Jassid fly on which his fame rested, withholding it even from the small fraternity who met at Fox's shack on the Letort.

"Vince wasn't too free with material things," Charlie said. "He was a little more free with what he had to say than with gifts. There were only two ways that several local friends that we fished with could get a Jassid. There were some thorn apple trees in the meadow, and every now and then Vince would try to reach a little too far and get his backcast in the thorn apple tree. They'd always make note of that and after he got out of there, why they'd try to find his fly. And the other way was they'd see him leave a fly on the strike sticking in a fish. They'd look for a fish coming up right around there. That's how they got their Jassids."

Dick pressed on about Marinaro's crankiness.

"He wasn't the kind of person you wanted to get into an argument with," Charlie said. "He rubbed some fellows the wrong way."

"He never carried a grudge—just to his grave. Some people say that," Dick remarked. "I don't know."

Charlie paused for a moment. "Well, we loved each other, and he recognized my weaknesses, and I recognized his problems. It ended up that we fished together an awful lot."

He said this in a tone of nostalgia and finality, as if the vanished friend were before him in all his genius and crankiness, the complete man. It was toward the middle of a mild afternoon. Charlie said he would like to go down along the river.

We sat on a bench near which Trout Unlimited had erected a plaque, but its inscription—a mundane tribute to Charlie—did not catch the importance of the place where Marinaro and Fox coached Ernie Schwiebert in how to catch trout on flies. On the other hand, it is a tall order to ask any inscriber of plaques to describe just why we should honor a spot where there occurred significant breakthroughs in a thoroughly inconsequential activity.

The old man sat on the bench and tried to explain what happened there. It was a place where technological advances in tackle enabled fishermen with an unusually keen understanding of insect life to test their discoveries in an unusually rich stream over a strain of brown trout that were unusually receptive to dry flies. We had Herbert

Hoover to thank for those brown trout being there, Charlie said.

"I beg your pardon," I said. I was beginning to be exasperated with the fact that my hobby kept intersecting with my least favorite President. It seems that Hoover was on his way to Carlisle to fish, and the Pennsylvania fishing authorities, as slavishly eager to please as those in Virginia, dumped 150 brown trout into Cedar Run. From there they were introduced into the Letort and other nearby Cumberland County streams. As it happened, these were Loch Leven browns from Scotland, which were supposed to be "free risers" in comparison with the more stolid German browns. For all I know, this may be anti-German propaganda, but in Cumberland County people take the superiority of Loch Levens as gospel and will fight you over it. That is all right with me, since the story turned out to have the kind of churlish ending I prefer in a tale about our thirty-first President. Hoover, after putting everyone to a lot of trouble, failed to show.

"I came into this thing at just the right time to see these wonderful advances and to be able to capitalize on them and I appreciate that so much. Those days are gone. They'll never come back," Charlie said.

Out in the stream, not fifteen feet from us, a trout started rising. The bubble it left was the size of half a golf ball, meaning that it was a fourteen-incher. It takes a fish of seventeen inches or better to leave a bubble the size of half a tennis ball. That is what Charlie Fox said.

He talked about how the insecticides and fertilizer and silt from the farms are breaking links in the chain of life that connects trout to the bugs of the world. He spoke of the suburbs that are pressing in toward his meadow. He talked dyspeptically of the fly-fishing club called the Letort Regulars that tries to honor his devotion and Vince's genius by holding the kind of meetings Vince hated.

Then he said this: "It's sort of a rare treat to see a trout rise in here now. In the old days, you'd see fish popping all up through there. One ring wouldn't finish spreading before another would interrupt it.

"I don't get any pleasure out of fishing this stream. I'll come down here and I'll think of a fish I got here or a fish I got there. It's so different now. All that's left are memories.

29
Living Legends III:
The Lord of the
South Branch

Dick loved to argue, and it really irked him to lose the argument that I got him into with his main fishing hero, Ben Schley. We had gone up to Shepherdstown, West Virginia, to visit Ben, a spry and gallant man in his mid-seventies who had spent his career with the Fish and Wildlife Service of the Department of the Interior. Ben said there was a regrettable error in a magazine article in which I quoted Dick's favorite saying about the Rapidan—that it had never been stocked and that its brook trout had been there since the Ice Age.

"I know that the Rapidan was regularly stocked with brook trout back in the Thirties and probably through the Forties," he said. "I personally have stocked brook trout in there from the Leetown hatchery out here."

Since Ben's family had been in the Blue Ridge since God dug the rivers and since he had once been in charge of all the fish hatcheries in the

United States, I figured he might know what he was talking about. So I asked him to tell me more. But I could see that Dick was squirming.

"You've got to remember, too," Ben said, "that most of these mountains have been burned over time and time again. There was a drought through the Alleghenies probably about 1937 or '38 when many of the streams went dry, and those that didn't became very, very warm. The local people would often burn the mountains so that they would get a job putting out the fire. Really. I was a fire warden in Morgan County, West Virginia, at one time, and we paid them twenty-five cents an hour, and they would literally start fires so they would have a job. Then they also burned them so that grass would grow and the cattle they were grazing could eat. So I would doubt that the brook trout in the Rapidan or in many of those streams are genetically the same fish that they were initially."

"Oh, listen, may I say in self-defense that that is almost an *ad hominem* attack," Dick said with a halfhearted chuckle. He muttered something about his own "bent toward hyperbole and poetic license." The real point was that these trout were not like "trout that were brought in."

He continued: "These fish have been here since the Ice Age. Now, I'm not saying genetically intact or pure or anything else. I'm saying that we've always had brook trout, we've *always* had brook trout. That's my point . . . these fish go back to the Ice Age."

"Well, that species does," Ben said helpfully.

Dick saw his chance. "Okay," he said, "that's essentially what I'm saying." Then he made the mistake of turning to me. "I don't even think you said that they are genetically the same fish. I don't think that's what you said."

"No, I said that," I said.

Dick's face fell. "You quote me as saying the fish go back to the Ice Age?"

"I think I referred to them as hardy little genetic warriors, in fact," I said.

Ben was laughing out loud now.

"Since the Ice Age they've been *evolving*," he said in a patient, teacherly tone. "There've been changes, Dick. They've broken down racially. There are probably a thousand different races of brook trout."

He had us, and he knew it. Then seeing how the air was going out of Dick, he let him off the hook by adding a final observation about the Rapidan. "There may be some original blood there in that particular stream. I don't know."

Dick brightened immediately, and on the drive back to Washington he spoke warmly of Ben. Without mentioning our Ice Age debate, he also added that Ben had almost single-handedly wrecked a blockheaded plan by the Virginia Department of Game and Inland Fisheries to convert our beloved Rapidan into a pay-for-play stream. Under this scheme hatched in the late Sixties, bait fishermen would have been turned loose on the stream, checking out through a concession stand where they would pay a fee for every fish taken. Their money would be used to pay for hatchery-raised rainbows to replace the fish that had been taken out. The fish were to have been restocked on a daily basis, thus reducing one of the great wild streams in America to a holding tank.

Later, Ben had shortened his career at the Department of the Interior by speaking out against the government's plan to build the Tellico Dam on the Little Tennessee River. He had also opposed his superiors at Interior on stocking policies for the White River in Arkansas. He had fished in Newfoundland, Yugoslavia and New Zealand and instructed both Dwight Eisenhower and Jimmy Carter in casting and tying. He was the inventor of the Schley Crayfish, a fine fly for smallmouth bass.

In his social views, Ben was an ardent liberal, but like many mountaineers, he had a soft spot for the Republicans. Even though Hoover was gone from the Rapidan by the time Ben got there, he thought I was too hard on the old man in my writings about the river. "He always killed two fish for breakfast, and that was it," Ben said. "I just feel a kind spot in my heart for him even if he did cause the Depression."

"Ben is certainly one of the most gentlemanly fishermen I have ever known," Dick said. "He has never been preoccupied with numbers or size, and although he's fished all over the world, he's told me any number of times that there's no experience any more satisfying to him than to go out during the White Miller hatch on the Potomac and catch the eight- or ten-inch smallmouth. He doesn't care about numbers. He told me the other day that he had caught the largest bass he had caught in two years out of the Potomac and it was twelve and a half inches. That doesn't bother him a bit. If he catches a bigger fish that's just an added delight, an added fillip.

"He's concerned with the creation and preservation of the resource and not with going out and catching a fish. I don't think he ever kills a fish. He's a very good caster. He uses relatively inexpensive tackle. Every time I ever fished with him he fishes with the same outfit. He fishes with an Orvis Spring Creek rod which is nine-three for five, and he's got an old Pflueger reel. I don't think he ever bought a fly in his life. He ties his own flies. He doesn't tie up a whole lot of flies and put them in boxes like I do. If he's going out fishing this afternoon he'll stop and tie three Crayfish and three Fuller Brushes. He just doesn't carry a large inventory of flies. He's utilitarian in his fly tying. He ties flies to catch fish. I tie flies to tie flies.

"Ben's a real stickler for getting fish on the reel. He told me there were three things he liked about me: that I put every fish on the reel, that I was not competitive and that I reel with my left hand. He can't stand anybody reeling with their right hand unless they're a left-handed caster."

I had never heard Dick speak in such adulatory terms of anyone, particularly someone who had disagreed with him and carried the point. But I, too, found Ben a man of great charm. His angular build, his sharp features punctuated with a neat mustache and his well-formed sentences reminded me very much of my friend Tennant's late father, Richebourg Gaillard McWilliams. Mr. McWilliams, an elegant South Alabamian who died in 1985, had started me on the road to being a writer. Like Ben, he was a great storyteller, and I thought how much the two men would have enjoyed knowing one another.

So I was naturally pleased when Dick called a few weeks later in a state of some excitement. Ben had invited us on an overnight canoe trip on the South Branch of the Potomac River. On the Potomac, this was as close as you could get to an invitation from the owner; Ben Schley caught his first fish from the river in 1919. For our canoe trip, he had in mind a remote, indeed almost inaccessible stretch where the stream squeezes through the rocky passes of the West Virginia mountains. Ben had taken the largest bass of his career there, a six-pounder.

We set a date, and this immediately prompted a crisis in the Blalock household. After his hospitalization in Florida, Dick had lost fifty pounds or so, but now his weight was back up. I would not ask the exact figure, but I guessed he would go 260, at least. Dick's grown sons, both in their twenties, began lobbying Sigrid, their stepmother, to order Dick not to go. Sigrid was nervous, and to tell the truth, I had a few grim fantasies about floating Dick's body out of the wilderness.

But the relish with which Dick began planning our menu and assembling the gear overcame my misgivings and Sigrid's. Last-minute calls from the children failed to stop him, and before long we found ourselves overnighting at a bed-and-breakfast in a West Virginia town so remote that teenagers stood under the streetlights to watch cars pass. We met Ben and his companion, an amiable young contractor named Bill Howard, at the boat landing on Saturday morning, and there Dick unveiled his prize purchase for the trip.

It was a pair of large plastic barrels that Dick said were used to ship mushrooms from China. He had purchased them from a surplus store for $2.50 each, making them the most inexpensive "dry bags" that any canoeist ever had. Dry bags are an essential part of canoe camping. They keep the clothing, tents and sleeping bags from becoming soaked. They must be absolutely waterproof, and a good dry bag or dry box costs $100 or more.

As Dick chortled over the inventiveness of this purchase, we committed our possessions to the mushroom barrels, screwed down their circular lids and lashed them into the canoe, and off we went.

Things did not go particularly well that first day. We stopped to fish a long, rocky beach. Dick got a heavy strike and played the fish nicely, preening under Ben Schley's gaze.

"You notice I've got it on the reel, Ben," Dick said. "You always said you like the fact that I put every fish on the reel and cranked with my left hand."

"I always crank with the right," said Ben. "On bonefish and salmon, you can't take up line fast enough cranking with the left hand, unless, of course, you are left-handed."

"Oh, I thought you cranked from the left."

"No, you must have me confused with someone else," Ben said amiably as Dick's fish came into view. "My goodness, that's an exceptionally large chub, Dick. I thought you had a nice bass."

The trash fish and all that talk about cranking had, in turn, made Dick cranky. Then our canoe filled up with water, and that made him wet.

Early on, I noticed that a canoe with a Blalock-sized weight in the bow does not steer well. As the day went along, our craft got more logy and increasingly reluctant to answer my efforts to guide us through the rapids. I had just discovered that in addition to Dick we had about twenty gallons of water in the boat when we struck a rock in a stairstep rapids and broached.

"Hold on, hold on," I shouted, knowing that there would be hell to pay if Dick fell out of the canoe and started tumbling downstream. He was simply too big and weak to keep himself from getting bashed on the rocks. An awareness of the folly of the trip settled on me.

Then, at last, we got a little bit lucky. We were aground on the rock that had broached us. It supported the downstream side of the canoe, tipping us just enough so that the canoe began taking water over its upcurrent rail. In no time, we had filled up and settled solidly against the bottom. As disasters go, this one wasn't bad. The water was only about a foot deep. The mushroom barrels that contained our clothes and bedding were awash, but only one of them came out of the boat and went bumping downstream along with assorted fly boxes and cushions. The important thing was that we were upright, and Dick was still sitting in his seat, even if there was water up to his knees.

We got the canoe bailed out, retrieved most of our gear and caught up with Ben and Bill, who had found a campsite. With considerable chagrin, Ben reported that he had tripped getting into the canoe and broken his rod. Fly rods are such fragile things that even the best fishermen break a few, but it is a dispiriting business. We overturned Dick's canoe on the beach and found the hole that had caused us to take on water. We had a little scotch and bourbon, and I went off to fish the evening rise, thinking that would cheer me up.

But I returned to find Dick in an extraordinarily crestfallen state. The lids on his $2.50 mushroom barrels were not watertight. Our clothes and bedding were soaked. Bill had loaned Dick a sweater against the evening chill, but Dick's various maladies had left him susceptible to cold, and he felt he might have to stay up all night tending the fire.

As it happened, I had packed my sleeping bag separately in a small dry bag from L. L. Bean. Like many products sold by the heirs of Leon Leonwood Bean of Freeport, Maine, it had the quality of performing as advertised. To make a short tale of it, I spread a parka on the floor of our tent and opened my sleeping bag to form a large quilt, and Dick and I slept side by side in the closest communion of our friendship. The joke I had made in the cabin on the Rapidan about sharing a sleeping bag with Dick had come horribly true. I discovered that for a large, lethargic man, Dick did an extraordinary amount of thrashing. He had a symphonic array of snores, wheezes and gasps, some of them soaring to crescendoes of rock-concert volume. I have since likened it to sleeping with a water buffalo. But considering the travails of the day, it was not as bad a night as expected, and as I was awake for most of it, I was able to be on the stream not long after first light.

I will always remember that morning's fishing on the South Branch. It was one of those rare moments in fishing—or in life, for that matter—when you can feel the weight of acquired knowledge and take pleasure in the fact that it is adequate for the problem that confronts you. The problem in this case was a lack of surface-feeding activity. No fish moved to any of the standard streamer patterns, either.

But by and by, I saw some subtle bumps in the surface over a slot of deep water that ran parallel to the steep, forested shoreline. These bumps were the tiny, almost invisible wakes made by fish swimming just under the surface, but never breaking it. In the morning, moving fish are generally feeding fish. But these fish were not eating bugs. I also ruled out minnows, since I saw none hopping on the surface in an attempt to escape the bass.

I knew that in trout streams this subsurface feeding is a dead giveaway that the fish are taking "emergers"—that is, nymphs that are struggling toward the top in preparation for shedding their husks and taking flight. I also knew that smallmouth bass liked to eat the nymphs of dragonflies and large mayflies and that Clouser's Swimming Nymph was a fly tied for mid-Atlantic smallmouth streams. I happened to have several Clouser Nymphs in my box. I tied one on and cast it carefully toward the surface disturbances along the shady bank. I started catching bass or sunfish or rock bass on every cast.

These were fish that I would not have caught a year or so earlier because I would not have noticed the surface disturbance, and if I had, I would not have known what it meant. Even if I had known what it meant, I would not have known what fly to try. Even if I had known which fly, I would not have had it in my box. So I felt good about the fish I was catching, and I felt even better when Bill appeared from upstream and commented on the luck I was having.

"Have you tried a Nymph?" I said with the sweet, ballooning hubris that blossoms in the heart of every successful angler, especially in the presence of someone who is not having as good a day. I waded over and offered one of Clouser's magical concoctions. Bill caught a few fish, too, but their feeding slowed once the sun got high enough to wash the entire river in light. The little slot of dark water where I had prospected with my nymph now lay exposed to our sight, and it had lost its magic.

Back at camp, Dick was drying his clothes in the sun and setting up Ben with the extra fly rod he had brought along. I repaired the bottom of Dick's canoe with duct tape, and we had a pleasant, leisurely breakfast during which Ben and Dick entertained one another with lies about their individual and collective importance to sport fishing in America.

When we stopped for lunch, Dick had an extraordinary stroke of good luck. He got to participate in the verbal mugging of a Republican. This happened when Bill Howard revealed himself as an ardent supporter of George Bush and an opponent of abortion. Ben and Dick tore into him, and just when things might have gotten a little too testy, Ben put everyone in a good humor by revealing that his pique with Bush on the abortion issue had led him to join both Planned Parenthood and the National Organization for Women. Dick allowed that he was almost certainly the only male member of NOW in Shepherdstown and maybe in all of West Virginia.

To my surprise, Dick began telling Ben and Bill about how his children had feared that our outing might kill him. But he said that if he could survive a leaking canoe and a soaked sleeping bag, he probably had more time left than they gave him credit for. I took out my notebook and jotted down a few phrases to help me remember that moment. This was something I seldom did on fishing trips, but I did it that day. This is what I wrote: "Dick reveals that his children tried to get him not to come on this trip. Sense of him grasping for the sweetness of life." And on another page: "Dick—sense of sweetness and shortness of time."

After lunch, the fishing was very slow. Dick and I loafed along, letting Ben and Bill go ahead of us so we could watch Ben fish. The sight of Ben Schley casting from a canoe in the canyon of the South Branch is an elegant thing to have in your memory.

When we came to a particularly enticing piece of water, Dick tied two small streamers in tandem and cast into the green shade along the shore. He caught a double that turned out to be two of the brilliantly colored sunfish called pumpkinseeds. Those were the only fish he caught that day, and he was immensely pleased with them. I took a picture as he lifted these small, beautiful fish into the boat. I have it still.

30
Living Legends IV:
The Genius of
Three Mile Island

Dick had more opinions than could be contained in mere conversation. Besides, there were long periods when I and his other cronies were tied up with work. During those times, his telephone and his typewriter were busy. He loved talk shows and letters-to-the-editor columns. He made no grandiose claims about the place of such enterprises in the festival of democracy. They were his playgrounds.

As I mentioned earlier, Dick specialized in using call-in shows to torment the governor of Maryland, William Donald Schaefer, about a proposed highway that threatened to dump silt into Paint Branch, a trout stream near Dick's home in Silver Spring.

Then, in 1990, Dick set his sights on a new villain, one Donald E. Calaway of St. George, Utah. Mr. Calaway had penned the following letter to *Fly Fisherman,* one of Dick's favorite magazines.

"After reading Lefty Kreh's 'Clouser's Deep Minnow' in the July issue, I couldn't resist writing. Once again, not only has someone reinvented the jig, but you compounded the plagiarism by running the Umpqua 'Sub-surface Dynamite' advertisement on the page facing the tying instructions. Shame on you."

On the journalistic side, Calaway had a point. Both Lefty and Bob Clouser, the inventor of the Deep Minnow, had a business relationship with Umpqua Feather Merchants, Inc. Lefty was a paid consultant to the company and Bob received modest royalties for allowing Umpqua to sell the fly under his name. There was no mention of this relationship in the magazine. Indeed, Lefty's article about this "truly great fly" was on the same page with an Umpqua ad quoting Lefty saying that "Bob Clouser's 'Deep Minnow' is the most effective sub-surface fly I've ever seen." It was, in short, a case study in the relaxed conflict-of-interest standards that prevail in outdoor journalism.

Dick was amused by this back scratching, but he was not amused by Mr. Calaway's assault on the Deep Minnow. Before long, I got another call at work. "Have you seen my letter in the new issue of *Fly Fisherman?*" Dick said. "I really gave it to that guy who was attacking Bob Clouser."

Here is what Dick wrote:

"How perceptive of Donald E. Calaway to see through Bob Clouser's Deep Minnow as nothing more than 'reinventing the jig.' Where was Calaway when Lee Wulff developed his hair-wing patterns? If only Calaway had unmasked Wulff for 'reinventing the dry fly,' he might have saved me buying all those calf tails.

"Fortunately, the smallmouth bass in Pennsylvania's Susquehanna River don't recognize the Deep Minnow as just another jig. Fishing with Clouser on that river in late September, a good friend and I netted and released more than fifty bronzebacks; all were caught on Bob's Deep Minnow, and only a half-dozen were under twelve inches long.

"Like my Cherokee Indian grandmother used to say: 'Even when it ain't broke, sometimes it pays to fix it.' Sharp hooks!"

As letters go, it was a pretty good example of Blalockian exaggeration. One virtue of Dick's system of not counting fish was that we could inflate our thirty or forty fish to fifty. I *had* landed a very fine seventeen-inch smallmouth, but we had plenty under twelve inches, too. But on one point, Lefty and Dick were right. In the two or three years after we met Bob Clouser, his Deep Minnow had established itself as perhaps the most effective wet fly ever invented. Dick and I regarded Bob as the one true genius we had known personally in fly fishing. Moreover, he was *our* genius.

He was also a man of exceptional modesty.

The first time I spoke to Bob Clouser, he said the only boastful thing I have heard him say. I had called his fly shop in Middletown, Pennsylvania, to place an order for a batch of Deep Minnows.

"Have you ever used this fly?" he said.

"No," I replied. "I just read about it in *Fly Fisherman*."

"I'm not one to brag," he said, "but you'd better hold on to your fly rod when you throw one of these things in."

He was right, and before long, Dick and I were headed up the highway to fish with Bob on the Susquehanna. I came to think of this as industrial-strength fly fishing, because Bob favored a stretch of the river that passed beside the abandoned mills of Bethlehem Steel. This vast rusting hulk occupied the eastern bank of the river, while the western side was a goose-harboring array of small islands and forested sloops. To the south, always within view, were those enduring symbols of industry run amok, the mushroom-shaped smokestacks of Three Mile Island.

This landscape of industrial decline also symbolized the liberation of Robert Jay Clouser. He was forty-four years old in 1982, when Acme Supermarkets decided to close the store that employed him as a butcher. Karl Jung once congratulated a middle-aged man on getting fired, because in the view of the analyst it meant the man could get on with his life. So it was with Bob Clouser when they closed his meat counter.

Lefty Kreh, then the outdoor editor of the *Baltimore Sun,* had already learned of Bob's innovative flies and of his skill as a guide. He encouraged Clouser to open a fly-fishing shop and publish a mail-order catalog advertising the flies he had invented. These already included the Clouser Swimming Nymph, the Clouser Crayfish and the Clouser Hellgrammite.

Bob was a self-taught naturalist. He invented flies by studying the river closely to see what the fish ate and then tied flies that not only looked like the local fauna, but also moved the way those creatures were moving *at the moment* they were being eaten. All genius is simple. It involves close observation and a momentous act of self-trust. The average fisherman, myself included, approaches a stream with the idea that all the appropriate flies have long since been invented. A genius approaches it like a brand-new world.

I had known Bob for some time before I learned his place in the each-one-teach-one chain of knowledge that binds the Pennsylvania school of fly fishing. His father gave him a fly tying kit when he was fourteen. At sixteen, he got a driver's license that enabled him to make his way from his home near Harrisburg to the waters of the Letort and the Yellow Breeches. In those days, Vince Marinaro and Charlie Fox were in their prime, and Ed Shenk was another kid who had signed on as their gofer. Bob Clouser did not know he was going among legends of the sport. He was a boy on the lookout for men who knew how to catch fish.

"I used to follow Vince Marinaro around and try to learn how in hell to catch fish, because Vince was good on the Letort, and I knowed Vince pretty good and he used to call me the kid that deviled him," he said. "I fished a year and half before I caught my first trout. I had the right kind of flies. Didn't know how to use 'em. I just kept deviling those guys.

"But you got to learn somehow, and you learn by watching and copying is what you do. So you follow a guy around who knows how to catch fish and then after a while you pick it up."

From Marinaro he learned the skill of minute observation of aquatic life. Like Marinaro he had the ability to disregard the accumulated misinformation traded back and forth by other anglers on the waters they fished.

As for casting, I have my own theories about where Bob acquired the smoothest, most powerful basic fly-fishing motion I have ever seen.

"You are trying too hard," he would always tell me when as I put out a fifty- or sixty-foot cast. Then he would pick up his rod and boom out a seventy-foot cast with no double hauling or other fancy motions.

"It is all timing. You don't have to put a lot of muscle power in it. Just give it a little punch."

This from a man whose forearms look like Popeye's.

"Bob," I said, "your 'little punch' is a little different from mine. I did not spend twenty-five years throwing beef carcasses around a meat locker."

Dick's stamina waned after our trip on the South Fork, and he looked forward more and more to our outings with Bob. Dick and Bob had in common that they were both crusading letter writers. Dick was tormenting the National Park Service about the stocking of hatchery trout in Big Hunting Creek near the Presidential retreat at Camp David. He believed the hatchery rainbows were crowding out the wild brown trout. Bob was trying to limit the catch of Susquehanna smallmouth to two fish a day over fifteen inches. He believed the traditional limit of six fish and ten inches was decimating the river he had fished since boyhood.

Bob had acquired a word processor, and he wrote passionate, ungrammatical diatribes accusing the bureaucrats and biologists of the Pennsylvania Fish Commission of gross ignorance and of bending to the whims of Pennsylvania's army of meat fishermen. Then he would sign these screeds very sweetly, saying either "My personal gratitude" or "With great respect." Such combinations of insult and flattery always appealed to Dick.

Bob, by the way, was delighted with Dick's letter to the guy who accused him of reinventing the jig. That led us to discuss how Bob had came up with the concept of the Deep Minnow.

"A lot of that I think was through watching spin fishermen fish Rapalas and watching the action of a Rapala or any kind of a darting lure that will dive. You could pull it real hard, and as soon as it would stop, a fish would take it. But it would never stop on the same plane."

This was an example of Bob's ability to separate out, by observation, the decisive elements or unique qualities of a common fishing situation. In this case, Bob Clouser had invented his wonderful fly by analyzing the success of another genius, an alcoholic trout fisherman from Lake Paijanne, Finland, named Lauri Rapala.

Rapala was a commercial fisherman who could not obtain an adequate supply of live minnows. So he carved a piece of wood into the shape of a minnow and covered it with foil and attached a lip to the front of the lure so that it moved through the water with what the outdoor writers call a "seductive wobble." The lure looked like this:

Most fishermen, including me, thought the wobble was the secret. What Rapala knew and Bob figured out was that the lure's real secret was that it moved through the water in different "planes"—that is, at different depths. When the Rapala is jerked hard, it will dive for the bottom because of the increased pressure against the protruding lip. Then, when the pressure is decreased, the natural buoyancy of the body, which is made of balsa wood, causes the lure to rise toward the surface. Many lures wobble, but only the Rapala planes between the bottom and the surface like a submarine.

And Bob observed that this lure's quality of changing depths depending on how hard it is pulled is a quality possessed by no existing fly. "Like a regular streamer fly, you throw a regular streamer fly out, it always stays where it's at," he said. "If you pull it real fast, it stays right there even when you stop it. Even a jig, when you stop a jig, it darts. It heads for the bottom. It tries to hide. It goes faster than it did before."

Bob tried different ways of adding lead to the standard streamer fly to make it dive for the bottom or rise toward the surface, depending on how fast it was being pulled through the water. Nothing worked very well. For one thing, if lead was wrapped around the shank of the hook, the fly simply settled toward the bottom on an even keel, rather than making a nose-first dive like the Rapala or a lead-head jig. Then one day in 1987, a fishing tackle company sent him some tiny lead barbells. Bob came up with the idea of attaching one of these barbells crossways just behind the eye of the hook. This is what happened.

"I brought it out on the river, dropped it in, and that thing went nose first to the bottom, and you strip it, it would go nose first the other way. I said, God, this might be what we're looking for.

"The first patterns were imitations of minnows. They were blues and grays and white with either silver flashing or some kind of flash like what the minnows looked like. The fish out here had never seen them, and gosh, you could get twenty bass to one over your old patterns like Zonkers and stuff like that.

"Then I just started experimenting with different colors, according to the sky, the lightness and darkness of the water, muddy water and clear water. But it's the darting motion that makes them fish attack it. Well, you've seen yourself—a big long pull, then a pause, and as soon as that thing turns itself to go hide, the fish grabs it right away. It has a motion that no other streamer fly has. Some guys call that thing a jig. But you cannot jig a fly or a jig on a fly rod. It just doesn't work that way. You can't let that thing bounce on the bottom and lift it. You can't do that with a fly rod. But it's just the motion that the eyes give it. I think the eyes are really the secret of the fly, that plus the sparseness of the pattern to let light shine through."

This happened in 1987. Bob Clouser kept his invention to himself for a year or so. When Lefty Kreh came up from Baltimore to fish his stretch of the river, he dropped a couple of his creations into the hands of the master and told him to try them that day.

"When he came in that evening Lefty said, 'This is one hell of a fly.' He said, 'It's so damn good, we've got to tell everybody about this.' I said, 'What the hell are you going to call it?' He said, 'Think of a name.' I said, 'I don't know.' He said, 'Well, it goes deep. Let's call it Deep Minnow.' "

Fly Fisherman magazine unveiled the fly as Clouser's Deep Minnow. So far over eighty species of fresh and saltwater fish have been taken on it. But in fly tying, there is no such thing as a patent that anyone is bound to respect. So while Umpqua pays Bob a fee for use of his name, there are plenty of people selling Deep Minnows without doing that.

On the other hand, Bob Clouser's name will last a long time in the world of fly fishing. And he got Dick Blalock as a public defender, a fact that Dick made clear when we were back at our motel that evening, and he was explaining why a retired butcher had won a place in his fly-fishing pantheon.

"Bobby Clouser, first of all, is one of the sweetest guys I've ever met, and he's a hell of a good fisherman. He's a wonderful guy. He's not well educated. He's not terribly articulate. But he certainly has created. It's devastating. It's devastating everywhere from a little old modest brook trout stream down to the Florida Keys. He reinvented the jig is what he did."

I told Dick to hold on. Was it not he who had written a national magazine defending Bob against a man who accused him of reinventing the jig?

"Well, yes," Dick said, "but I'll be goddamned if I was going to let somebody I never laid eyes on criticize the only legitimate genius I've ever known."

Dick liked Bob, and as his stamina was fading, he also liked his boat. Bob had taken a seventeen-foot johnboat and built a large carpeted casting platform in the bow. It was big enough for one person to stand up and cast and another to recline and watch.

Dick chose to do that quite a lot. He would lounge around and talk while I hammered out casts and Clouser poled the boat slowly down the river. Then when Dick got up the energy I would step aside and let him cast for a while.

One day the fishing was particularly hot in the morning, but my reflexes were off. I was blowing strike after strike, an embarrassing performance, since Bob had begun to brag on me as one of his more expert clients in fishing the Deep Minnow. By midday when I started to get my touch back, a windy front was marching up the river. It was part of the general disturbance, we later learned, caused by the arrival of Hurricane Hugo off the Carolinas.

The fish got very sulky, but because Bob knew the river so well, he kept putting me on to prime spots where we could generally pull one or two strikes. It was that kind of fishing, punch and move, punch and move. Finally we came to one of our preferred areas, a place where a long gravel bar ran out from a grassy point.

Dick had not been fishing, but he got up and annouced that he wanted a try a popping bug. We had not seen a surface strike for hours, but on the other hand, fishing the Deep Minnow takes an amount of concentration that Dick was not likely to muster at the end of a tiring day. The wind was pushing the boat faster than Bob liked, so we came quickly into the best water.

Dick flipped one cast up against the grass, and he got an extremely hard strike. It is funny how you will remember a particular strike here and there or an individual catch. In a lifetime of fishing, these are the moments of punctuation.

Dick often referred to that fish, which struck with unusual ferocity and fought extremely hard, as one that gave him memorable satisfaction. I remember it, too, because right after striking, the bass shot toward the sky in an abrupt vertical leap. I can see the fish hanging in the air, like an exclamation mark.

31
Spies, Flies and the Mystery of the Blalocks

Dick was proud and a little amused that he was listed in *Who's Who in the CIA*. This cheaply printed booklet was published in Berlin in 1968 by a firm believed by Western authorities to have ties to East German and Soviet intelligence. The book caused a stir at the time because it blew the cover on some genuine American spies who were working abroad under the cover of other U.S. government agencies. It also raised embarrassing questions for American diplomatic and military officials whose names appeared, but who were not really CIA agents or working in intelligence in any way. The book was highly inaccurate. Its author had simply combed through government directories and listed every State Department employee and military officer who might conceivably have an intelligence connection.

Dick insisted that was the case with him. He had once attended a CIA training center in Front

Royal, Virginia, where Foreign Service officers received instruction in security procedures. He had also been stationed in such hotbeds of conflict and intrigue as Lebanon, Algeria and Yemen. The booklet listed Dick as having served in Army counterintelligence, and I thought I had heard him mention something about military intelligence training, too.

"I was commissioned in the Corps of Engineers, not intelligence," he told me firmly when I asked him about it. But he also said that after he left the Foreign Service, he had turned down an attractive offer to work in the Middle East for an American oil company. Two CIA agents had called on him at his apartment in Foggy Bottom and made it clear that the Agency felt that he knew too much sensitive information to be bouncing around in that explosive part of the world. The implication was that a former American diplomat might be vulnerable to blackmail or kidnapping by terrorists who wanted to wring information from him. In the end, Dick said, their veiled threats had intimidated him into turning down the job.

Frankly, it sounded strange to me that the government would be so interested in a retired diplomat. Maybe he was not just a retired Foreign Service officer. I began to think about the way Dick had telephoned me and introduced himself as a brother fisherman right after I had taken over the Washington bureau. In times past, it was common for intelligence agencies and the FBI to keep dossiers on journalists in prominent jobs. Domestic spying and other hanky-panky had supposedly ended when Senator Frank Church and the Senate Intelligence Committee investigated CIA abuses in 1975. On the other hand, anyone who understands the history of the CIA or, as in my case, ever met William Casey knows that you can never be confident that those guys are running a clean shop.

I showed Dick's entry in *Who's Who in the CIA* to a reporter on the intelligence beat. "It's a classic spook's profile," he said. "He had a long series of postings in lively places. That's one tip-off for people with Foreign Service cover. They never come home. That's because the State Department doesn't want Agency people making policy. I can't be sure, but if I had to guess, I'd say yes, he's Agency."

Of course, you run into a lot of American spies, active and retired, around Washington, and they have social lives like anyone else. They seem to favor Georgetown and the Virginia suburbs. The European intelligence services, most notably the British, have always been interested in keeping tabs on journalists who cover foreign affairs. So was the KGB in its day. The Israeli agency, Mossad, is particularly active in leaking intelligence reports and trying to plant stories when it serves its country's interest. It is not something that a journalist wants to be paranoid about, but neither do you want to be naive if someone with a whiff of spookiness turns up suddenly in your life. Real-life spies are not particularly clever, so you can usually tell when you are being milked or spun. Dick showed none of the signs. But if the CIA was putting people into the buddy business with journalists, it would be worth knowing. In any event, I told my colleague, it was I who had kept the friendship going. "That's what they always want you to think," he said with a laugh.

Of course, there's a strong connection between spies and flies. Ernest Hemingway's son, Jack, parachuted into France with a fly rod during World War II. He wanted to sample the streams his father had told him about while he carried out his behind-the-lines spying. He wound up in prison.

The late A. J. McClane apparently had an active relationship with the CIA while serving as angling editor of *Field & Stream.* The environmental writer George Reiger, a friend of McClane's who also worked for *Field & Stream,* gave the details in an obituary essay published after McClane's death in 1991. It seems that McClane was a favorite sergeant of General Walter Bedell Smith in World War II. After the war, Smith became ambassador to the Soviet Union, and McClane, who had studied fisheries biology at Cornell, went to work at *Field & Stream.* "And when Smith became the nation's first director of the Central Intelligence Agency in 1950," Reiger wrote, "it was natural for him to think of Al's job as perfect cover for foreign missions."

McClane made no effort to hide his friendship with Smith, who is mentioned in several articles as a fishing companion. But it was not made precisely clear that the CIA chief and the man from *Field & Stream* both believed that—as George Reiger put it—a "career as an international angling editor provided ideal camouflage for foreign intelligence. Upon returning to the states, the editor would tell his readers about fishing opportunities in country X or Y—and his debriefing officer, sometimes 'Beedle' Smith himself, about the latest military or political goings-on there."

Then there was James Jesus Angleton, the

infamous chief of counterintelligence operations at the CIA during the 1960s. He was, by reputation, a fanatically meticulous dry fly fisherman. He also spent his last years fishing the troubled waters of the CIA headquarters at Langley, hoping to snare a Soviet mole he believed to be betraying his best secrets. That bit of business had destroyed his career and perhaps his sanity by the time he died in 1987. Angleton's biographer, Tom Mangold, described him as a "world-class" expert with the dry fly. I would have to see that for myself. Every account I have ever seen described Angleton as a joyless and methodical fisherman. Perhaps it is no accident that his favorite poet was that grim genius T. S. Eliot. In any event, as Mangold says, the analogy between Angleton's hobby and spycraft was obvious.

"To study [Angleton] the fisherman is to study the hunter of Soviet intelligence agents; the sport and the craft require equal parts of patient dedication, intellect, pure obsessiveness, and the cunning that comes with experience."

Friends spoke of seeing Angleton move along the stream like a bony old heron. They recalled the care with which he covered every seam of water. "Fishing was not a superficial effort to be in the sunlight and the water," said Cord Meyer, another old hand at the Agency. "It was a total effort to understand the ecology and win," Angleton's daughter said, adding that he favored cutting open the stomach of small trout, emptying the contents into a cup and then tying a fly to match what he found. He spoke to her of the "science of fly fishing."

He often fished at night for the big, predatory brown trout he favored. Caroline Marshall, a poet who knew Angleton on the Brule River in Wisconsin, wrote about an encounter with him:

" 'Browns are vicious, atavistic creatures,' he says. . . . 'They eat mice and frogs, baby chipmunks, their own kind.' He stretches forefingers away from thumbs to demonstrate, matching them in a flame-shaped arc. It must be five or six inches wide. 'This is the mouth of one,' he says. His eyes gleam. 'Look what it could snap on to.' He describes the life-sized mouse lure he uses when the moon is down and mist a lid on the river."

She concluded: "I saw him one night when I was a child—coming suddenly wet, slippery, and silent as a huge brown in from the dark, trailing rain, his fedora pinched and dripping, pulled low over his eyes, a fisherman wholly unlike others."

And wholly unlike Dick Blalock, to be sure. For one thing, Dick regarded brown trout as saintly creatures. Whenever Angleton's name came up, Dick ridiculed both his obsessive style of fishing and the grandiose paranoia of his worldview. But Dick had his own more modest obsession, and it seemed to confound him every bit as much as Angleton, the old spy, was confounded and haunted by his obsession with finding the Russian mole in the CIA.

Angleton embraced a belief in the existence of that mole as fervently as some people embrace a belief in God or the healing power of rock crystals. He did this on the basis of evidence that was just about as ambiguous as that which confronts us in the realm of theology or mysticism. Angleton decided that the mole existed on the testimony of a KGB defector who may himself have been a double agent sent by Moscow to warp Angleton's mind by feeding him lies. For his part, Dick had embraced a belief in his father as an embodiment of pure evil. Like Angleton, he seemed able to look at the question from only one angle.

"My father was a mean son of a bitch," Dick told me one day, "and that's being as nice as I can be. It was frightening because he was so volatile, so goddam explosive. He didn't know how to disagree in socially acceptable ways. He had to be abusive. He was not a skilled person, but he was a verbal bully. He was a verbal terrorist, for God's sake."

When Dick was getting ready to take on his adversaries in Trout Unlimited or when he got through to one of his favorite call-in shows, it was easy to see in him the ghost of his disputatious father. Dick would argue with a post, as we used to say in Alabama. He enjoyed argument as a form of social discourse, as a means of getting attention and as a way to exert his dominance. He had a temper, too. But at bottom, he was not a mean or disagreeable person like the father he described.

Dick was also sophisticated about psychology and relationships. He was one of those people who had learned from his own therapy, and he had learned from his life in the trick-mirror worlds of government and diplomacy. I had noticed, however, that his analytical powers failed him when it came to his father. He spoke of the old man's anger and their sour relationship as if they were natural phenonema, with a force and genesis that lay beyond explanation. Dick returned often to the subject of his father. Early in our friendship, he had spoken of his old man's hunting and fishing skills with pride; but the conversation I remember best took place much later, on a cold, rainy day in the early spring. The new season had stirred our hunger for fried fish, and we were at a friend's pond in Virginia catching bluegills for the pan. Despite the weather, the fish were moving toward the spawning areas in the weedy shallows and biting right along.

Dick said that nothing he had done—from winning a football scholarship to Oklahoma, to leading a combat platoon in Korea, to serving in the Foreign Service—had pleased the old man. He recalled a visit that he and his first wife and their small children made to his father's retirement home in Mississippi around 1967 or '68, when Dick was in his late thirties and back in the States on home leave. Dick and his wife got into a minor argument in the kitchen. His father was working in the yard.

"It was kind of like in the spring, and the window was open, and my wife and I were exchanging some fairly sharp words. He came over, and he said, 'What's going on in there?'

"I said, 'I'm talking to my wife, and it's none of your concern.' What would you think he would do in a situation like that?"

I said I thought his father would turn around and walk off.

"Well, he went and got his pistol. He was going to blow my head off. That I talked back is what it was. I didn't toe the fucking line somehow. I mean he went and got his goddam gun. He was going to kill me. That was his first impulse, at least, to shoot me. And I told that story to my shrink and he said, 'Well, it's not all that unusual.' "

"It's fairly unusual," I said.

"Yeah, I think it's a little bit un-goddam-usual," Dick said.

As much as he hated the man, Dick seemed drawn to know more about him. He made a trip to Bledsoe County, Tennessee, an area near the Smokies where many Cherokees had remained when the main body of the tribe moved to Oklahoma on the Trail of Tears in 1838. Like the other "civilized tribes," the Cherokees included many families with English surnames, including that of Smith. Dick's great-grandfather Thomas F. Blalock married a woman named Nancy Smith, who according to family lore was one of the Cherokee Smiths of Bledsoe County. In 1897, this couple's son, Thomas F. Blalock, fathered a son named Jesse Alonzo Blalock. He was Dick's father.

"My father was absolutely the most mysterious human being I ever met in my life," Dick said. "The other thing about my father was that not only was he kind of mysterious and sinister, my father was a frightened man. There was something very ominous about the outside. He was very alert to strangers. When I was a child, I can remember my father going to the window and peeking out from behind the blinds when he would hear someone on the street outside.

"Several things happened that suggested that there was something in his background, sort of like a feud or something like that that I was going to have to contend with.

"Everyone called him Blalock," Dick continued. "My mother called him Blalock. My grandmother and grandfather called him Blalock, and all we knew was that there was this Indian ancestry, and over the years I guess he revealed the fact that he was from Tennessee, and just in bits and pieces he told me that he was from Bledsoe County, Tennessee, and that his mother had died when he was quite young, had died of what he called brain fever."

Then as if it were of a piece with the mundane genealogy that he had just recounted, Dick dropped a startling revelation into his narrative.

"I really don't know too much about my grandfather except he was a peace officer. My father took great delight in accompanying him on some of his peace officer activities, and I believe my father was thirteen years old when my father went along with his father to arrest somebody. He walked up on the front porch and somebody stuck a shotgun out the door and blew my grandfather's head off. Right there in front of my father. When I start thinking about the influences on my character formation I think what a hell of an experience that would have had to have been."

I had known Dick quite a long time and heard him talk a great deal about his father before this story ever came to the surface. When it did, Dick told it with extraordinary matter-of-factness. Yet it seemed to explain so much. Consider the rage that surfaced in the father when Dick told the newspaperman about shooting his father's "rifle." Was this not a spontaneous eruption of the rage that thirteen-year-old Jess Blalock must have felt when he saw a similar weapon kill his father?

Jess Blalock's impulse to pull a pistol on his own son years later might have had its roots in that experience, too. People can reenact traumatic experiences, often in disjointed and irrational but highly symbolic ways. In such people, the unconscious mind seems to believe that it can purge a painful emotion by reliving it. For example, if a gun had done you great harm by removing a loved one, there may be an impulse as an adult to use a gun to destroy a loved one in a perverted effort to preempt the pain that life has taught you to expect.

"Psychologically, there has to be a reenactment link here between him seeing his father shot and pulling the gun on you," I told Dick.

"Yeah," Dick said. "I never thought about that."

But of course he had thought about it, for all those years that the mole of childish pain had burrowed through his memory. There would come a day when I, too, would think harder about this matter of unfinished business between fathers and sons.

32
Amare o Pescare: An Essay

There or four weeks after Susan and I got married, I got up before daylight and drove a hundred miles to fish all day in nasty weather at a place called Okomo on the Coosa River. Years later, just before we divorced, Susan told me that she remembered waking up alone around ten with the rain beating romantically against the window and our orange cat curled up at the foot of the bed and thinking, "What kind of marriage is this going to be?"

Quite recently, I was on vacation on a tropical island with a voluptuous and passionate woman. Our room overlooked a fabulously landscaped pond bordered by boulders imported from the neighborhood of Mount Fuji and stocked with the large Japanese carp called koi. I spent many hours on our ninth-floor balcony. My companion said she wished I would look at her with the longing gaze I directed at the koi. She observed that I watched these fish with such devotion that I must be in the throes of interspecies male bonding. Had I failed to notice, she asked, that when viewed from above, a swimming fish looks exactly like those magnified sperm you see in sex education films? She had a point, especially when scores of koi were swimming madly toward the bread balls fashioned from the toast I saved each morning from the room-service tray.

On the last morning of our trip, I got up early so I could keep an appointment to meet the keeper of the fish ponds. I had managed to introduce myself to him, and he promised to let me go on his feeding rounds, so I could get a close look at his koi. He was very proud of these fish and eager to share their history.

Koi are carp that have been bred in Japan for hundreds of years for decorative purposes. Some are gold. Some are the soft gray of good flannel. Some are orange and black, as garishly spotted as leopards. Depending on the pattern and brilliance of its pigmentation, a garden-variety koi can fetch $500 or more. As I stood on a rock beside a palm-shaded pool and photographed these extravagantly colored fish while my lover slumbered in our bed, I thought this: "My God! I am doing it again."

In this case, I was not even fishing. I was looking at fish. Here is a fact I have had to face about myself. I am a person who needs to be near fish pretty often in order to be happy. Usually this involves fishing. Sometimes it may involve simply being in the same vicinity with them or handling objects that are associated with their capture. When I am home alone I like to scatter my tackle across the floor and play with it. I may pretend I am working on it, performing preventive maintenance, but it is really playing.

Through study and personal experience, I have learned that in our culture there is a traditional tension between men and women over the issue of fishing and over sports in general. I do not claim that one side or the other is right. I simply report that this exists.

These conflicts extend across class lines. The "golf widows" at the country club feel just as aggrieved as women left behind on bowling night. Bowling leagues and tennis ladders do not exist solely because of an innate human need to compete. They are designed to enable men to say they *have to* be somewhere other than at home or the shopping mall. There is a reason, by the way, why men behave badly and start fights when they are shopping with their wives. One recent survey found that shopping is the least favorite activity of American men.

Even so, fishing seems to be a particularly contentious issue. I can cite many examples. Twenty years ago, just after the first generation of bass boats was introduced in the South, my friend Charles Salter, a fishing writer in Atlanta, told me that these boats had spawned a rash of divorces throughout the region. By 1992, one manufacturer, Skeeter, was running an ad in which an attractive woman in tight blue jeans faced the camera and offered some comments about her husband's affection for bass fishing. "Six months ago, we bought a new Skeeter fishing boat, and if he'd ever drag his buns out of it," she added, as the camera slowly pulled back to show a smiling fellow beside her, "I might introduce him to my new boyfriend, Bob, here."

The message intended by the boat manufacturer is clear. Fishing is so much fun and our boat is such a fine one that some men—maybe *you*—would be smart to give up this handsome, sexy woman for the pleasures they represent.

Hunting, spectator sports, even playground bastketball all carry an aura of male exclusivity. In the movie *White Men Can't Jump,* the wife and girlfriend of Wesley Snipes and Woody Harrelson rarely get to accompany them to the games that represent the primary incomes of two families. There is also a men-only flavor to the watching of professional football, although in this case the physical body of the absent husband may still be present in front of the television set. But fishing is different, according to Maureen Dowd, the brilliant *New York Times* writer who has long threatened to write a feminist tract under a title suggested by her friends, "Man: Beast or Burden?"

"Fishing is not like tennis, where you can play doubles or he's gone for an hour or two," she says. "It's more than a sport. It's an escape mechanism akin to the leathery male preserve of the English men's club."

On the White House beat, Maureen Dowd spent what she describes as "torturous" days following George Bush and his buddies as they fished, hunted, golfed, played horseshoes and tennis. Along the way, she established herself as an expert observer of that gender labeled by our *Times* colleague Anna Quindlen as "bears with furniture." "The playing fields are one of the fault lines in the battle of the sexes," Dowd wrote after observing a round of Bush's hyperactive "golf polo." In that article, she went on to record the

First Lady's attempt to penetrate the Presidential buddy system.

"Earlier this summer, Barbara Bush confided in a group of reporters lunching at the White House that she was taking golf lessons. Her husband had suggested she do so, she said proudly, so that they could play together in Kennebunkport. The First Lady is always eager to find ways to spend more time with her husband.

"But the Bush vacation has provided a sad tableau of the rejection that every woman of average sporting abilities has faced in her life: Men, by and large, prefer to play competitive games with other men.

"Mrs. Bush has been seen tagging behind the President's foursomes, playing her own fledgling game with her friend from Kennebunkport, Betsy Heminway.

"The President took devilish delight, on Mrs. Bush's first outing at the Cape Arundel Golf Club, in stopping his own game and urging reporters to watch Mrs. Bush and Mrs. Heminway take their wobbly shots on the 18th green.

" 'We'll make her nervous,' the President said mischievously. Asked why he did not play with his wife, Mr. Bush replied: 'We're going down life's path hand-in-hand for many years, but golf—we go our separate ways.'

"Mrs. Bush was clearly annoyed at her husband for putting her in the glare of network cameras. 'That's so mean,' she muttered, adding that the reporters were 'lucky' not to be married to Mr. Bush.

"When the President, pressed by journalists, finally agreed to play with his wife, the disillusioned First Lady shot back: 'When? Just like he's going to garden with me one day.' "

As Mrs. Bush's sarcasm suggests, Bush often seemed to be frantic to get out with the fellows. It did not matter whether he was going to play horseshoes on the South Lawn or shoot quail at a rich friend's ranch in Beeville, Texas.

Do men behave this way simply because they want to avoid the company of women? There may be a more subtle and charitable explanation. Whatever their romantic attachments, men and women need some degree of intimacy with people of their own gender. Women seem to achieve this naturally in the course of daily events, and when they ask one another how they are doing, it seems to be a real question rather than a ritual prelude to some bit of business. Men seem to need an excuse for intimacy, such as drunkenness, or a formal structure in which to achieve it—an athletic competition of some sort, a lodge meeting or, better still, a hunting or fishing expedition. Setting intimacy aside, some men may need this structure to communicate at all, and the often tongue-tied Bush may be a case in point.

According to George Bush, he and his 1988 campaign manager, James A. Baker III, shared their most intimate moments in duck blinds over the years. They had been friends for two decades when, in the spring of 1992, it became apparent to everyone in Washington, D.C., that Mr. Bush would lose the 1992 election unless Baker left his post as Secretary of State and returned to take charge of Bush's stumbling campaign. But it was several months before Bush and Baker could get away on one of the outings where they traditionally have their heart-to-hearts and decide what they are going to do. The scene of their 1992 retreat was a trout stream near Pinedale, Wyoming, and it was there that President Bush finally told his closest friend that he needed him at the White House. This happened in July, by which time Bush was far behind in the polls. He might still be President if he had been able to pick up the phone and pop the question to Jim Baker in April.

Leslie Fiedler, the literary critic, caused a storm of scholarly debate and no small amount of private anxiety by suggesting that there is a homoerotic element in male expeditions. Our literature is full of what he saw as latently homosexual bondings—Huck and Jim on the raft, Ishmael and Queequeg aboard the *Pequod*, Isaac McCaslin and Boon Hogganbeck and Major de Spain at their camp in the big woods where it was possible to hear what Faulkner called "the best of all talking." Fiedler's famous essay "Come Back to the Raft Ag'in, Huck Honey" and the subsequent publication of his book *Love and Death in the American Novel* in 1960 terrified a lot of men, including me. Around that time, I was writing my first long fiction, a hunting story highly derivative of "The Bear." After reading Fiedler, I spent days poring anxiously over my novella, trying to figure out if what I thought was a story about a boy and a dog was really a story about a boy and a boy.

Over the years, I decided I ran into fewer hints of repressed homosexuality around hunting and fishing camps than I did in hanging around high school football coaches, priests, Army sergeants and those Brits who get overly nostalgic about boarding school. Still, heterosexual males are confused about why they want to go off by themselves and play. In this light, it is possible to see the men's movement, with its thunderdrums and wildman retreats, for what it really is: a support group for guys who want to get out of the house but are afraid their wives and girlfriends will either deny them permission or taunt them, as the feminist comedian Carol Montgomery did on a television talk show devoted to male-bashing. "How many guys over here male bond?"she asked the audience. A few fellows timidly signaled her. "Three of these guys raised their hands," she hooted. "The rest are going, 'Is that a homosexual question?' "

According to some recent books by women, the roots of male bonding and male exclusivity have more to do with male selfishness than sexual preference. Cris Evatt explored these issues in her book *He and She: 60 Significant Differences Between Men and Women.* "I wanted women to know and believe that men are self-centered, and I also wanted men to know how self-forgetful women can be," she said in a newspaper interview about the book.

It causes men stress that women do not want them to go off by themselves, she added. That is why they seem to ignore women's complaints. "Actually, men are not ignoring us. They are just trying not to have a panic attack. Some men can handle women better than others, and the confirmed bachelor is someone who can't handle women at all. I know a man like this who can't live with a man or a woman. He lives with a very placid male golden retriever. This dog is not dead, but he is very quiet."

I do not endorse male self-absorption. Again,

I simply report it. Actually, I am not so sure that women really mind men going off so much as they object to what we might call the Cult of Macho Bullshit. I suspect this is why so many women detest the writing—or more precisely the thought and cultural fallout—of Ernest Hemingway. His work depicts the most desirable part of life as what men do with other men. The celebration of a man or men alone reaches its most extreme form in *The Old Man and the Sea,* where even the fantasies have to do with Joe DiMaggio's body parts and the only prominent female figure is the Virgin Mary.

Even in the less segregated Hemingway works, the main activities—fishing, hunting, fighting wars or bulls—are undertaken by men. The female characters are secondary, but usually described in a way that caused casting directors to think of the appearance and libido of the young Ava Gardner. Hemingway's world was not unlike that which reached its most extreme expression in the gymnasia of ancient Athens. There the games, the conversations, even the most psychologically complex sexual relationships all took place among men. Like the Greeks, Hemingway tried to invent what his biographer James R. Mellow called a "masculine Eden" free of women, specifically Hemingway's tiresome mother, Grace, who liked to put Ernest in dainty dresses when he was a toddler.

For what it is worth, Mellow concludes that Hemingway was not gay, although his book includes an intriguing photograph of the author and a group of naked matadors at an all-boy picnic in Spain in 1931. Papa was worried that he might be homosexual or that other people might interpret his erotically charged celebrations of maleness and book titles such as *Men Without Women* as evidence that he was. In his review of Mellow's book, *Hemingway: A Life Without Consequences,* Philip Caputo concluded that Hemingway's "masculinism" did not represent "forbidden desire but a motif or theme squarely in an old American literary tradition. The male hero must escape society—usually associated with women, marriage, domesticity—for the wilderness, the sea, the road, the battlefield."

Clearly, Philip Caputo and Leslie Fiedler differ on whether this lighting out for the territory represents boys being boys or the pursuit of a homoerotic paradise. But either interpretation rests on the existence of masculine worlds that women simply do not understand. This interests me because when it comes to fishing, the assumption that women just don't get it is manifestly untrue. All writing about fishing stems from Dame Juliana Berners and *The Treatise of Fishing with an Angle,* published in 1496. Scholars, mostly male, have recently called her authorship into doubt. Perhaps we can attribute that to jealousy, as few writers have better expressed the primal joy of the sport: "It will be a true pleasure to see the fair, bright, shining-scaled fishes outwitted by your crafty means and drawn out on the land."

For good measure, Dame Juliana also issued the first written instructions in Britain on fly tying. The first American to explore the importance of imitating aquatic insects to fly tying and to make flies based on the study of nymphs in a home aquarium was Sara J. McBride, who lived near Rochester, New York. She wrote about her experiments in 1876, thirteen years before Theodore Gordon, the "father" of American fly fishing, caught his first brown trout, and three-quarters of a century before Ernest Schwiebert pioneered "matching the hatch." C. F. Orvis invented the prototype of the modern fly reel and gave his name to the most famous firm in fly fishing. But his daughter, Mary Orvis Marbury, handled the firm's fly-tying business and published a landmark book, *Favorite Flies and Their Histories,* in 1892. It is credited with standardizing the names and patterns of American flies, and when she died in 1914, Britain's *Fishing Gazette* said she ranked second only to Dame Juliana among women in the sport.

So much for the masculine provenance of fly fishing. But if women were present at the creation of the sport, male writers gradually masculinized it. No one bothered to declare Mary Orvis Marbury the "mother" of American fly fishing. In *Trout Magic,* Robert Travers said that you did not run into many women on the trout streams because men did not want them there. Even so, there are eighteen million women who fish. Scientific Anglers, a tackle company, estimated in 1992 that there are over 200,000 American women who fly fish regularly. Thirty percent of the people enrolling in Orvis's weekend fly-fishing schools were women. That alone comes to twelve hundred women a year who are learning the basics of fly fishing. What amounts to a refeminization of the sport has brought a few troglodytes out of the bushes.

Fly Fisherman published an essay entitled "The Yuppie Invasion" that decried the growing popularity of fly fishing among the affluent young of both genders, but its author's ire seemed focused on the presence of women in the temples of the sport—in this case the spring creeks near Livingston, Montana.

"One of the pleasures of that [spring creek] fishing is the chance to compare notes with the serious anglers who have traveled from all over America and the world to fish there.

"Four of us were discussing the relative merits of the Henry's Fork and the Bighorn over lunch on Armstrong's Spring Creek when a procession including a Porsche, an Audi, a BMW, a Volvo and a Saab pulled into the parking lot. Five women and one man emerged and suited up. They headed off upstream, presumably to fish. For the remainder of the day I kept coming across the women in the party, none of whom were fishing. They were sitting on the bank holding expensive rods, discussing life, sipping white wine and nibbling from a wheel of Brie.

"I engaged in conversation with one of the encounter groups and learned that it was the man's birthday and the five women had traveled to Montana for the event. Armstrong's Spring Creek, the Valhalla of fly fishermen, being used to stage a scene from *The Big Chill.* Does fly fishing really need people who think *Pteronarcys californica* is a new type of varietal wine?"

For my money, the women's use of the setting was admirable. To start with, it left more water for the dyspeptic author, and it is hard to think of a famous male fisherman who has not spent a fair share of his time sitting on the bank and drinking. But it put the writer, one Gerald P. Lenzen, in a bad mood.

"A year later, I was back on Armstrong's," he continued. "A woman fishing the riffle below me was playing a good fish. I walked down and offered to net it for her, hoping to get a photo of what was obviously a large trout. She declined my offer and told me that she would call her husband to net the fish. Reaching into her vest, she removed a whistle and deafened me with an ear-splitting blast. Her hapless husband, who had no doubt flunked obedience school, failed to appear. After ten more minutes, a twenty-one-inch brown trout surfaced, firmly hooked through the base of the dorsal fin.

" 'Oh my, I *foul-played* him,' she announced.

"Foul play, indeed. It is time to get these people back into the lofts, sushi bars, and aerobics classes where they belong. If we don't, what will be next?"

I found this a hugely, even nakedly informative piece of writing. What could be worse to a man like Gerald P. Lenzen than women sitting around on the bank of a sacred stream talking about life? The answer turned out to be a woman in the stream, hooked into a big fish and declining to be helped. Like racism, this kind of bigotry involves making a fault out of behavior common to all people. For example, foul-hooking a fish is a routine occurrence. You often see it on the television fishing shows. As for whistles, I used one when my boys were small to stay in touch when we were spread out along a stream. I have even seen whistles in the fly-fishing catalogs. They are usually in the section that has flasks for people who like to sit on the bank and take a nip while visiting with their friends.

I suppose there are gender differences between the approaches of male and female fly fishers, but a clever essay by Mary S. Kuss entitled

"Jesus, Pete, It's a Woman Fly Fishing" made me wonder how firmly rooted in fact they are. Kuss has turned all the standard clichés on their heads in telling of her experience as an addicted fisherperson since childhood. It started when, as a six-year-old, she pestered an uncle into taking her fishing and saw a sunfish take her bait, provoking shouts of "Pull, pull, pull!" from her instructor. "When I finally did, it was too late, the sunnie had spit out the baited hook. I think I've spent the rest of my life searching for that fish, catching many others but never the one that got away on that fine spring day."

In adolescence, she turned to a friend's father for fly-fishing instruction. Later, she sharpened her skills on a trout stream near her Pennsylvania college. "Then I fell in love with, of all people, a nonfisherman." During courtship, he learned to fly cast and went fishing with her. Then after the marriage, he went less and less. "One day I asked him why," Mary Kuss reports, "and he looked me right in the eye and said, 'Why should I go fishing? I caught the fish I was after.' "

Mary Kuss's husband meant to flatter her by saying she was the only "fish" he needed to catch. But he touched on an important point. Most of us, like Kuss, are struggling to reconnect with something we glimpsed long ago. "One of the most remarkable characteristics of fly fishing," she concludes, "is its capacity to become an obsession."

Here, I think, we may encounter a true gender difference among people who fish. Although Kuss seems an exception, men are generally more susceptible than women to obsessions with inconsequential pursuits, I believe. So are a lot of writers, according to any number of stories from

Moby-Dick right on through *The Bridge on the River Kwai.* The reason may lie in the masculine capacity for self-indulgence defined by Cris Evatt. The "masculine Eden" that Hemingway imagined was, after all, a place where men could do whatever they wanted to for as long as they wanted without regard for the preferences or claims of women.

It took me a long time to confess to my self-centeredness and even longer to relax about it. A couple of years after Susan and I divorced, I had a dream in which she said to me, more in resignation than anger, "You're just looking for an excuse to go fishing." And I answered. "I don't need one." When I awakened, I realized, happily, that this was true.

For the record, I want to say that most of the women I have known, including my former wife, were as reasonable and tolerant about my fishing as anyone could be expected to be. The problem is that I often felt an unreasonable need to go fishing.

I would not argue if you called this a childish need. Indeed, it is a yearning that I first felt on the morning after the trip to South Sauty and wished that instead of going to school I was going back to the bridge where I caught the crappies. I doubt I felt anything so powerful until the day I saw Pattie Wright on the beach at Panama City when I was sixteen. Since then my life has been blessed with a thematic question: *Amare o pescare?* To love or to fish?

It was on the shores of Lake Como in northern Italy, a place where both loving and fishing are woven deeply into the traditional culture, that I discovered an arresting linguistic fact. In Italian, *pescare* has two meanings. The second is "to try to find the meaning of." In Italian, the word for "fishhook" is *amo,* which links it to the noun for love, *amore.* Clearly, I am not the first to fish in these mysterious waters where we try to hook out the meanings of sport and love.

And I guess I have discovered the truth of what Mary S. Kuss discovered. When couples in which only one partner fishes have a conflict, the real issue is usually the amount of time that is spent and the degree of obsession exhibited. The Skeeter commercial was saying the same thing, in its rough-hewn way. Something has to give.

John N. Cole, in his autobiography, *Fishing Came First,* put his cards on the table concerning this conflict over priorities by recounting the following conversation with his father:

" 'I don't know what's going to become of you, John.' My father shook his head, his eyes angry, his fists in knots. 'The only two things you care about are fishing and women. Nothing else means a damn thing to you.'

" 'Well, you got them in the right order,' I said."

It is possible to argue that in the matter of fishing and women, John Cole and I come out at the same place and that he simply expresses it more honestly. Susan would have liked me better if I had spent more time in art galleries and the garden. After the divorce, a woman I had been seeing happily for some months said the time had come for us to compare our calendars to determine when I would be around and when I would be fishing. Things trailed off after that.

But let this testament show that I do not want to line up with Mr. Cole in believing a fishing life has to have separate compartments. My mother and my aunt Grace and the granny woman who taught me about limit on crappie were beside me the first day I fished. Between my father and mother, she is by far the more avid and more skilled fisher. She has caught bigger bass than anyone else in the family, and over the past twenty years, I have spent more time fishing with her than with my father. As a girl growing up in Alabama, Susan fished with her grandfather, and part of the magic of our courtship was that it took place on waters she had known since childhood and that I could not have fished those private lakes without her. My girlfriend in college was at home on the waters from the Tennessee River to the Gulf of Mexico. The biggest fight we ever had was when I told her that a snapper trip out of Destin, Florida, was going to be for men only. Fortunately, my brother and his wife overruled me.

So I have learned not to regard fishing as a male preserve. The fact that thousands of women are taking up fly fishing is historically apt, flowing from a tradition that dates back to Berners, McBride and Marbury. It is also inevitable, I think, since fly fishing is the most feminine branch of fishing, relying as it does on touch, intuition and a more relaxed, nurturing and uncompetitive feeling for the quarry and its home. Perhaps that is why men discover fly fishing when they age past the point where, as Tom McGuane puts it, they are simply "running on testosterone."

Mary S. Kuss says that many of the women coming into fly fishing "do it as a way to spend time with a boyfriend or spouse." But I am not sure that is the norm. For every woman I know who fly fishes with her husband, I have met a single woman who fly fishes on her own or with a mixed group of male and female friends. This, like the enrollment figures at the Orvis school, suggests there may be a deeper trend in play here, and it is beginning to show up in the demographic studies.

Divorce is increasing in every age group, but most rapidly among people aged forty to fifty-four. Divorcées in this age group increased from 1.5 million in 1970 to 6.1 million in 1991. The numbers are increasing because people who get divorced are staying single. Digging into these figures, Jane Gross, a *New York Times* reporter, found that women are staying single in greater numbers and more happily than men.

She interviewed a forty-six-year-old woman in Kalamazoo who "comes and goes as she pleases and spends the money she earns without reproach," much of it on her horse. Jane Gross also found a fifty-five-year-old man near Detroit who complained: "Some of these women, it's an ego trip for them. It's hooray for me and the heck with the other guy. They don't know how to share. Fine and dandy. Let them do their own thing."

How long will it take this wave of role reversal to overtake the traditional stereotype of the clinging woman? A very long time, I would guess, because it is deeply embedded in our culture, as evidenced in a pivotal scene in the movie *Out of Africa*. In that scene, the character based on Denys Finch-Hatton is the mouthpiece for the traditional male view. He and his lover, Karen Blixen, the Danish woman who wrote under the name Isak Dinesen, are sitting by a campfire. Her desire to be married and his desire to follow the freebooting life of the African hunter are in collision.

She: "When you go away you don't always go on safari, do you?"

He: "No."

She: "You just want to be away."

He: "It's not meant to hurt you."

She: "It does."

He: "Karen, I'm with you because I choose to be with you. I don't want to live someone else's idea of how to live. Don't ask me to do that. I don't want to find out one day that I'm at the end of someone else's life. I'm willing to pay for mine, to be lonely sometimes, to die alone if I have to. I think that's fair."

She: "Not quite. You want me to pay for it as well."

The real Denys Finch-Hatton was a charismatic, emotionally distant man who was apparently able to sustain the life of radical freedom that he described. We will never know how he would have emerged from the midlife passage, because he died at forty-four, alone, in a plane crash at Voi, Kenya, in 1931. But in today's America, women know what Jane Gross found in her reporting among the 14 percent of the middle-aged population that is divorced. Most men talk a good game of a-man's-got-to-do-what-a-man's-got-to-do, but when they get a little bit lonely they get clingy and pitiful. The Finch-Hatton model is valuable for men of my age group because it suggests that it is important to be honest about your selfishness and not to talk the talk unless you can walk the walk.

So here is where I came out as I entered my fiftieth year.

We are not on this earth for long. Part of what a midlife crisis is about is figuring out what gives you pleasure and doing more of that in the time you have left without asking for permission or a financial or emotional subsidy from anyone else. I believe in a balanced life. I do not want to fish all the time. I am extremely fond of people in general and women in particular. In fact, as I get older I more and more prefer their friendship and company to that of men. But I have learned that I am also a person who has to be able to go fishing whenever I can and for as long as I want to go. It is a silly thing, but there it is.

The day may come when I do not care to fish anymore. That day is not here yet, but it could happen. Just as I outgrew the Redneck Way, I find that I do not much like to go to the streams in Pennsylvania and Maryland where Dick introduced me to trout fishing. I prefer the rivers out West or the saltwater flats in the Keys or on the Gulf Coast. And sometimes when I am in the West or on the coast, I feel like I have had enough after a day or two. Anything is possible in the life of a man if he lives long enough. Even maturity.

33
George, Jimmy and Herbert

George Bush invited me to go fishing.

It happened because I saw a report on CNN that showed him fly fishing from a boat on a stream near Kennebunkport. It seems there are a few sea-run browns in the headwaters of one of the coastal streams there. I thought Bush threw a pretty good line, so I wrote him and requested an interview about fly fishing. The recession was just taking hold. I was curious, among other things, to see if Bush was going to develop a Hoover problem, casting happily while the economy and his political support went to hell.

I got back a very nice letter, dated August 8, 1991.

"Dear Howell:

"I am flattered that you would like to have my experiences on fly fishing—flattered because I am not a good fly fisherman at all. I like the sport, but I have only done it a couple of times:

once with Jim Baker in Wyoming, and once with Alan Simpson, also in Wyoming. I've got some outstanding reels and fly rods, but what I lack is fly-fishing experience."

He went on to describe his fondness for catching bluefish off the Maine coast. "We take them on bait-casting reels and light rods and twelve-pound line." Bush said he would be happy to be interviewed about his "enthusiasm for fishing generally," but I should not take that film clip as evidence of expertise in my favorite branch of the sport. "The point of all this is that I would not be a good subject for even half a chapter for any book if the topic is fly fishing."

The letter impressed me in one way and gave me pause in another. I admired the President's candor about his fly-fishing experience, his preference for light tackle and the general modesty of his tone. But I was taken aback by the news that Alan Simpson, the Republican senator from Wyoming, was a fly fisherman. So much for the ennobling influence of the sport. During Bush's term, Simpson established himself as the meanest man in the Senate. True, his hatefulness had a kind of Dickensian grandeur. But there was no way you could follow his rantings about women, the environment and civil rights and still believe that fly fishing in the mighty temple of the Rockies is guaranteed to purify the soul.

Speaking of souls, Herbert Hoover wrote a book entitled *Fishing for Fun—and to Wash the Soul.* He was a surprisingly spiritual man, but like Bush, he had a politically fatal attachment to the idea of the Presidency as a passive stewardship. I think history will remember both as well-meaning men who did not understand that the President must be an active guardian of the people's welfare, more attuned in hard times to the suffering of the poor than to guarding the economic pieties by which the wealth of their class is preserved. Neither seemed to grasp the lesson of Franklin Roosevelt's Presidency. The stability of American society depends less on defending the rich against imaginary threats than on providing a decent standard of living for the unfortunate. If Bush had been as worried about the fact that he could see homeless people in Lafayette Park from his bedroom window as he was about lowering the capital-gains tax, he would still be President. Similarly, if Hoover had been as concerned about hunger in Alabama as he was about the depth of trout pools on the Rapidan, he might have won a second term.

Hoover's book came out in 1963, near the end of his long, grumpy retirement. He died in 1964 at ninety. The preface captures the tone of Hoover's last three decades. He had put together this slim collection of his speeches and magazine articles on fishing, Hoover said, because an editor suggested its publication would be a relief "from the daily grind of trying to find out why the Communists get that way."

It is a curious book, revealing Hoover to be both a fly-fishing elitist and a meat fisherman so dedicated that he made killing fish a political virtue. Americans believe "they have a divine right to unlimited fish," he said. "They have inherited this notion from ten thousand generations of free fishermen."

In an essay entitled "The Class Distinction Among Fishermen," Hoover put dry fly fishermen at the top of his pecking order, followed by wet fly casters, spin casters and, on the lowest rung, users of live bait. In what sounded like a personal confession, Hoover added that "toward the end of the day when there are no strikes, each social level collapses in turn down the scale until it gets some fish for supper." In other words, fishing in the final analysis is about food.

Despite this retrograde tendency, Hoover made it clear in "Fishing Presidents and Candidates" that he was a snob about fly fishing. He reported—"with a slight egotism!"—that only he, Teddy Roosevelt and Grover Cleveland "had been lifelong fly fishermen before they went to the White House." A mixed lot of chief executives that leaned heavily to Democrats like Wilson and FDR went after the "common fishes," he sniffed. With a surprising lack of feeling, Hoover needled his predecessor and fellow Republican Calvin Coolidge for failing to progress from worms to dry flies in his trout fishing.

The best part of Hoover's book is a few paragraphs in which he elaborated on his well-known remark, "Presidents have only two moments of personal seclusion. One is prayer; the other is fishing—and they cannot pray all the time!"

In the book, he began by ruminating on the appeal of fishing for Presidents. Most are first drawn to it, he said, because of the "political potency of fish" as a signal that a candidate has the common touch. Once they are in the White House, something else sets in.

"That Presidents have taken to fishing in an astonishing fashion seems to me worthy of investigation. I think I have discovered the reason: it is the silent sport. One of the few opportunities given a President for the refreshment of his soul and the clarification of his thoughts by solitude lies through fishing. As I have said in another place, it is generally realized and accepted that prayer is the most personal of all human relationships. Everyone knows that on such occasions men and women are entitled to be alone and undisturbed.

"Next to prayer, fishing is the most personal relationship of man; and of more importance, everyone concedes that the fish will not bite in the presence of the public, including newspapermen.

"Fishing seems to be one of the few avenues left to Presidents through which they may escape to their own thoughts, may live in their own imaginings, find relief from the pneumatic hammer of constant personal contacts, and refreshment of mind in rippling waters. Moreover, it is a constant reminder of the democracy of life, of humility and of human frailty. It is desirable that the President of the United States should be periodically reminded of this fundamental fact—that the forces of nature discriminate for no man."

Hoover predicted the attractions of privacy and discipline that would attract Jimmy Carter to fly fishing. But he was not so prescient when it came to George Bush. Here was a President who hated solitude, got itchy on any Saturday when his schedule allowed a quiet day in the family quarters with Mrs. Bush and generally preferred gregarious pastimes to solitary sports.

Before considering Bush and Carter in detail, I should note that the sports and recreations of a President sometimes crystallize in the public mind as a controlling metaphor for his regime. There was Ike the genial golfer and casual fly fisherman. With Carter, the attack of the killer rabbit on his fishing skiff in Georgia and his collapse while jogging created an image of haplessness that hardened into a governing electoral reality when the helicopters that were supposed to rescue the hostages in Teheran crashed in the desert. In the 1992 campaign, Bill Clinton's decision to play golf at a segregated golf course in Little Rock fed into public suspicions that he was a Democrat who espoused one set of values and practiced another. Could a few more sporting gaffes Carterize—or Bushwhack—the Clinton Presidency?

In his successful 1988 campaign, Bush demonstrated that Hoover was right about the "political potency" of the fish as a symbol of the common touch. He cannily presented himself as a bass fisherman, a fan of country music and a muncher of pork rinds. But once in office, he reverted to his true enjoyments. My guess is that his decision to deliver comments from a golf cart as he dispatched American boys to the Persian Gulf helped produce the image of elitist detachment that crippled him in 1992. Similarly, Bush did not grasp that it was unseemly for a petroleum millionaire to be ripping along in his gas-guzzling Cigarette boat when he was waging what many Americans suspected was a war for oil.

Bush detests any kind of psychological analysis of his motives, tastes or behavior. He calls it "being put on the couch." He once complained to Marlin Fitzwater, his press secretary, that Maureen Dowd of the *Times* was studying his golf game too closely. "I saw her giving me the Gail Sheehy treatment," he wrote in a memo to Fitzwater. "Indeed, she was trying to figure out what makes this crazy guy tick." It is not surprising, then, to read what *Newsweek* found in its post-election report on the 1992 race. "When campaign honchos Bob

Teeter and Fred Malek told Bush more than a year ago that he should quit playing golf and riding in his speedboat because it furthered the image that he was out of touch with voters, Bush paid little attention."

Apparently, hubris and overconfidence are viruses that breed in the ventilation system of the Oval Office like some exclusive form of Legionnaires' disease. Even Carter, a religious man whose faith called for self-abnegation, sometimes slid over into self-congratulation. Yet in the course of his Presidency he moved from amateur to expert status in fly casting for trout and in fly tying. In 1991, the museum of the Jimmy Carter Library in Atlanta mounted an exhibit called "The Tie That Binds." The displays included the fly-tying desk that Carter used in the White House and was still using in retirement at Plains. It was clearly the workplace of a craftsman. Plenty of people would argue that fly tying is the ideal hobby for a micromanager and that if Hoover's Presidency failed while he flailed the waters of the Rapidan, Carter lost the 1980 election by spending too much time at this very desk on the second floor of the White House.

Carter, of course, was a more sensitive President than the architect of the Depression, even if he did bring us Depression-level interest and inflation rates. Anyone who puts his book *A Sporting Journal* alongside Hoover's can also see that he understands the mechanics and psychology of fly fishing on a much deeper level.

"It levels people out," Carter said when I visited the exhibit at the library. "The trout don't give a darn if you're President of the United States or a local farmer or a high school kid. It's a disciplinary thing, too," he added, noting the constant pressure to learn "a little more about how currents behaved, what kind of trout will take a certain kind of fly at a certain time of year or what the temperature of the water does or how a cloudy day affects it or how I can approach a pool without my shadow or silhouette being outlined against the sky. If you read a whole book on it and only come up with one suggestion, it adds to your repertoire and so you become increasingly effective. But then you realize that nobody can ever master the sport. Even Lee Wulff hasn't mastered the sport. He's still learning, he tells me."

Carter made this comment shortly before Wulff died. He had used the Presidency the way any smart fly fisherman would—to get expert coaching. He fished with Wulff, George Harvey, who taught a well-known fly-fishing course at Penn State, and Dave Whitlock, a consummate fly tier and fisherman who was hired by L. L. Bean to direct its effort to cut into Orvis's business. In 1980, Carter asked a number of experts, including Ben Schley and Ed Shenk, to Camp David for a fly-fishing clinic. He also invited Vince Marinaro as the featured speaker, providing at least one occasion at which the old fellow could feel he was getting the recognition he deserved.

I had first met Carter in 1973, when he was governor of Georgia and I was assigned to cover him for the *Atlanta Constitution*. Our fishing careers had many parallels. Both of us fly fished for bluegills and bass in our youth and then became devotees of the sport upon moving to Washington. Big Hunting Creek was a school for both of us, although Carter told me that as President he visited Camp Hoover and the Rapidan only once.

The arc of his career can be detected in artifacts in the Carter Library. They have there a picture of Carter splashing water with a boat paddle toward the infamous "killer rabbit" that tried to climb into his skiff when he was fishing on the Carter farm near Plains early in his Presidency. The photograph shows a spinning rod in the boat with a bobber attached to the line. The President as bait fisherman. The library has this photograph in its files, but it is not on display.

What is on display is a frame of varnished wood that is used as a drying reel for fly lines. Carter built it in his workshop on the day after he lost the 1980 election. The object bespeaks the therapeutic values Carter found in fly fishing after a crushing defeat and his desire for top-to-bottom mastery of the sport that reshaped his attitude toward fishing.

"It's hard to talk without derogating other kinds of fishing, which I also enjoy," he said. "I really enjoy fishing with a plastic worm for bass in the warm-water areas in South Georgia and Florida. I don't want to derogate that, but at the same time, fly fishing to me opened up just a new panorama of challenge. Because you had to learn the intricacies of streams, of currents, of water temperature, of different kinds of fly hatches, how to tie your own flies, which you wouldn't ordinarily do in other kinds of fishing, and then try to match whatever fly is hatching off and experiment. It's a matter of a kind of stalking, a great element of patience, because the consummate fly fishers really spend a lot of time observing a pool or a stream or current run before they ever put a fly in the water."

This brings us back to my fishing trip with George Bush. It is hard to imagine Bush going into that kind of detail with his fishing. He is an active rather than a contemplative man. But let it also be said that while fishing brings out the testy side of some people, it was just the opposite with Bush. He was such a genial and considerate host that I found it hard to square that behavior with his lackadaisical performance and mean-spirited policies. He was also, by every sign I know, a deeply snake-bit fisherman.

For one thing, by the time we got to the Washington Navy Yard and climbed into the bass boats that would take us down the Potomac toward Mount Vernon, the wind was really honking through the trees. It was early morning on a cold March Saturday, and out on the open water, the wind chill must have been in the teens or lower. Luckily, the guide in my boat, Bob Denyer, had a snowmobile suit in one of the storage compartments. Since the President was in the other boat, I did not have to worry about protecting the leader of the free world from frostbite. But there was not a word of complaint from Bush, even after our long run with the open boats banging unpleasantly across the chop and him with nothing but a light windbreaker for cover.

We fetched up in a cove that offered a bit of shelter from the wind. The boats were close enough for conversation, and the President soon dispelled any idea I had that when the chief executive gets ready to go out there is somebody from the National Oceanographic and Aeronautics Administration to tell him how many layers of insulation he is going to need. Bush said he got up around five in the morning and asked his wife if he ought to wear his long underwear. She said no and rolled over and went back to sleep.

The wind kept building. The sun was weak. Bush's windbreaker was too thin and the skin on his gloveless hands looked chapped and papery. I was now squarely up against a novel etiquette problem. If the President of the United States has been kind enough to invite you somewhere, it is difficult to say to him that this is not a very good day for it and you would really be just as happy going back to the White House and having a cup of tea. It is even more difficult to say what I really thought, which went something like this: "Sir, you are sixty-eight years old, which is just old enough to be my father if you happened to be an early breeder. I would not have my father out here in nasty weather with inadequate clothing."

Bush, for his part, seemed pretty content. He proved to be handy with both spinning and bait-casting tackle. To my surprise, the security forces did not get in our way or interfere with other fishing boats or with the joggers who passed along a trail on the shore. I caught the first fish, a small bass still pale from the long, dark winter. After an hour or so, Bush caught a fish. I think there was one other taken by the party, and after four or five hours, the President said we could go in.

It turned out that the Secret Service and their helpers from the District of Columbia police had run aground with the twin-screw police cruiser that was going to take us back upriver into the teeth of the wind. They got it unstuck, and I was happy to get out of the open boats and into the cabin. There were no seats, and Bush and I were standing side by side, chatting about the fishing. I could not help noticing a loud whomp-whomp-whomp sound when the pilot tried to open the throttles on his diesel engines.

"Sounds like you bent a shaft when you went aground," the President said. There was no reprimand in his voice. He had the matter-of-fact tone of an old Navy man who knows the sound of a bent shaft when he hears it. So we went back upriver at a fast idle.

I admit I lost my courage and did not ask Bush about the theories of Dr. Juice, a Minnesota physican who was interviewed in the *Wall Street Journal* in 1990. Dr. Juice, aka Gregory Bambenek, invented Dr. Juice Hand and Lure Cleaner. This product is intended to mask a fish-repelling amino acid called L-serine. It seems that Dr. Juice took a fingerprint from the President at a bass-tackle exposition show that Bush visited in Springfield, Missouri, during the 1988 campaign. The *Journal*'s conclusion: "George Bush is a walking L-serine factory . . . his fingerprint on the bait will stink up the water with L-serine and send fish zooming in the other direction."

Maybe it was too cold on the Potomac for Bush's bass to smell the Presidential secretions. But that lone fish did little to dent the general air of pessimism that prevailed all day among Bush's attendants. They carried themselves like parents taking an insistent kid on what they know is a hopeless mission. Even so, I was surprised with the blunt consolation one of them offered to Bob Denyer when he said he regretted not having been able to put the President onto more fish on one of his rare days off.

"Oh, don't feel bad," a White House photographer told the guide. "The President never catches anything." That day, he was lucky not to catch pneumonia. But he might have taken the weather and the bent shaft as an omen for the rest of 1992.

34
Blalock Among the Burcaucrats

Dick's resignation from presidential politics took a lot of us by surprise. Ron Ashmore announced it in the Trout Unlimited newsletter in the space where Dick's column, "Leader's Lines," usually ran. Ron used the headline "Leaderless Lines" and apologized that it read like a eulogy.

"Our fearless leader and president, Dick Blalock, has resigned. For the last three years (one over the limit), Dick has served as president, outing chef, nursemaid, cajoler, bully, spokesman, coordinator, and evangelist spreading wild trout, catch-and-release gospel among the heathens. You name it and Dick has been it. Of course strong leaders step on toes and Dick has wound the hackles of some guys the wrong way. Dick has served our chapter well and for my money rates as the best president our chapter has had."

Of course, Ron was as devoted to Dick as I was. Another way of reporting Dick's resignation might have been to say that the President-for-Life stepped down just before the colonels came out of the barracks to shoot him. Many of the people who want to be officers or directors in something called Trout Unlimited tend to be bossy and vain. Naturally this put them in collision with Dick. Also, some were jealous of the publicity Dick was getting. The *Washington Post,* the suburban newspapers and local television had discovered Dick as their dial-a-quote source on conservation and the fly-fishing fad. The local Charles Kuralt imitator went along on one of our Rapidan outings to tape a piece for his Sunday-morning show. Dick wound up as the star, sitting Yoda-like on a rock and dispensing crystal droplets of wisdom.

I was worried that Dick might go into a post-resignation depression, sort of a Trout Unlimited version of Nixon at San Clemente. In fact, stepping down as president of the chapter freed him to do the one thing he liked better than arguing with members of TU. That was tormenting government officials. In my time as a newspaperman, I have run across a number of citizens who were good at this, but Dick was in a class by himself. When it came to bureaucratic boxing, he was Muhammad Ali.

At the time he resigned as president of the National Capital Chapter of Trout Unlimited, Dick was already well engaged with the Maryland Department of Transportation. It seems that one Lowell K. Birdwell, the state's secretary of transportation, had decreed that $221 million would be spent to build a road called the Inter-County Connector to speed passage between the seats of Montgomery and Prince Georges counties, which abut the District of Columbia on the north and east, respectively. Opponents pointed out that this road was parallel to and only four miles distant from the existing Beltway and therefore had more to do with pork than transportation.

Its other flaw was that it would pass within a few hundred yards of Dick's town house and cross over his beloved Paint Branch Creek in three places. Under Maryland's classification system, this was a Class III stream, meaning that it had naturally producing wild brown trout.

"These are urban trout!" Dick said. "Think about it! These trout live closer to the White House than any other trout in America, and they have survived both Ronald Reagan and George Bush, the worst environmental presidents in history."

Dick was truly infatuated with the proximity of these fish to the White House. When Teddy Roosevelt and Grover Cleveland were in office he said, it was possible to catch trout only a few blocks from the executive mansion by fishing up Rock Creek from the M Street Bridge in Georgetown. Congress wisely set aside the Rock Creek Valley as a national park in 1890, creating one of the most beautiful urban parks in the United States, trout or no trout.

The wooded valley that contained Dick's stream had the same kind of potential. It was the most desirable undeveloped parkland left in the suburbs around Silver Spring, Maryland, and Paint Branch still had a chance of keeping its trout. As a recreational resource for the future, the area was special enough to merit protection on environmental grounds more substantial than its proximity to the Blalock manse. But even I had to admit that it was not exactly the prelapsarian paradise that Dick described in the *Washington Post*.

"It's more than just a trout stream," he said. "It's deer, turkeys, pheasant—a garden of Eden. And to ruin it just so somebody can get from Rockville to Laurel at the speed of light, well, to tell you the truth, I don't know why anyone wants to go to either place."

Dick led troops of state legislators, county officials, newspaper reporters and televison crews on well-publicized hikes through his creek bottom. Lowell K. Birdwell and his sponsor, Governor Harry Hughes, left office without ever starting the first bulldozer. That brought Dick's talk-show nemesis, the famously autocratic William Donald Schaefer, on to the scene as the new governor. He tried to placate Dick by writing him a personal letter promising to "do everything within reason to maintain the water quality required for trout spawning" when the road was built. Dick recognized a bureaucratic brush-off when he got one. He responded by tormenting the man incessantly. Every time the hot-tempered governor went on the radio, which was often, Dick was there. Sometimes he called in as "Dick" and sometimes he used his middle name, Culmer, as a nom de radio. This enabled Dick to double his air time, even though the hosts and producers of the shows knew what he was up to. One producer had even given Dick a special number so he could pop through the telephone traffic and stir things up when the show got dull. Schaefer was a notorious bully, known for asking and giving no quarter in his exchanges with voters. Of course, the governor knew very well that Dick was out to provoke him. So Dick regarded it as a crowning triumph when he finally pummeled Schaefer into his on-the-air complaint about being able to hear the "hate" in Dick's voice.

Dick thought making the governor whine in public was the equivalent of one professional gunslinger staring down another. His happiness was complete when he reported proudly that an article with his picture had been posted like a most-wanted bulletin in the state offices in Annapolis.

Gradually local politicians and the smaller newspapers began swinging to Dick's side. I knew victory was in his grasp when the *Montgomery Journal,* the most important suburban paper, ran a color picture of Dick, with waders and fly rod, on the banks of Paint Branch. It covered a third of the front page of their feature section under a headline that said: "The Last Fishing Hole: Dick Blalock's Urban Trout Stream." By 1991, public opinion and Bush's recession had put the Inter-County Connector into an indefinite stall. As of 1993, neither state nor federal highway authorities have had the political will or the money to start construction.

Now that he had tasted blood, Dick got seriously rambunctious. He dragged me up to Big Hunting Creek one day to show me the latest outrage that had come to his attention. In the name of erosion control, someone had started shoring up the banks of the stream with crossties and big hunks of gray quarry stone. It was a breathtaking defacement, considering the history of the stream and the fact that it passed through national park land. Franklin D. Roosevelt had built his retreat, Shangri-La, on the mountain slope above Big Hunting. Later, the place was renamed Camp David, and the creek became home water for two fly-fishing presidents, Dwight D. Eisenhower and Jimmy Carter.

Dick started the usual blizzard of letters and soon found out that the superintendent of Catoctin Mountain Park had allowed a local conservation group called CAMPER to put in the erosion-control structures. It turned out that CAMPER, an acronym for Catoctin Area Mountain Park Environmental Resources, had a lot of politically influential citizens from the nearby town of Frederick among its members. Over the years, they had used their clout to shape the fish management policies of both Catoctin Mountain Park, which was supervised by the National Park Service, and an adjoining state park. They had also encouraged the Maryland Department of National Resources to dump one thousand rainbow and brook trout into the stream each year. In Dick's view, the hatchery fish competed with the native brown trout for food and spawning sites.

Once again, Dick's blizzard of letters was taking hold. The chief of Maryland fisheries, Robert A. Bachman, one of the most respected trout biologists in the country, earned his doctorate with original research showing how hatchery trout muscle aside wild trout. Bachman knew Dick well. They had first met years earlier when Bachman was doing a fish count on Paint Branch. Dick, not understanding they were on the same side, came storming out of the woods and chewed him out for tampering with his fish. As a scientist with a bias toward wild trout, Bachman had responded honestly when Dick complained about the stocking in Big Hunting. He wrote that "the management of Big Hunting Creek is not consistent with the cold water fisheries policy of the state of Maryland." But the policy had been altered, he said, because of "political" factors. That, of course, meant pressure from CAMPER and its friends in the state legislature.

Along about this time, I was in Jackson Hole for a fishing trip and noticed that a local rancher was in trouble for digging a garbage pit on federal land that adjoined the Teton National Park. When I got home, I told Dick I did not see how it could be legal to put crossties and rocks in Big Hunting since the same laws apply to federal land in Maryland and Wyoming. On January 23, 1991, Dick wrote the inspector general of the Department of the Interior. He included his usual rant about the stream structures, but his main argument focused on two details. CAMPER, a private organization, was sending out fund-raising letters as franked mail from the Catoctin Mountain Park. Moreover, the visitors' center at the park was "selling curios, maps, and other articles for the benefit of CAMPER." Dick was especially proud of his last sentence, a bureaucratic zinger. Would the inspector general like to examine these "questionable management practices" or should Dick go ahead and write the General Accounting Office?

In a few weeks, Dick called in full strut. The Department of the Interior had just informed him that the superintendent of Catoctin Mountain Park had decided to take early retirement. Moreover, the regional council of Trout Unlimited was holding a meeting in Thurmont to discuss how to press Bob Bachman to end the stocking in Big Hunting. It was going to be on Saturday, and we made a date to drive up together.

It was an interesting drive. The tape recorder was rolling, and we were doing one of our usual interviews about the world according to Blalock. We were talking about his Foreign Service work in Lebanon in the hot old days, and Dick said that I should turn the recorder off so he could satisfy my curiosity about the CIA. After the agents told him that as a former diplomat he could not go into the oil business in the areas where he had served in sensitive diplomatic posts, he told them fine, but he had to make a living. The Agency obligingly signed him up as one of its vast network of domestic observers at $10,000 a year. The position was a payoff for complying with the Agency's threat and involved no work. This was back in the days when the Agency had plenty of money and did what it liked. Then the Church Committee came along and discovered that there were hundreds of Americans getting such retainers, in clear violation of the Agency's charter. Dick lost his sinecure and started selling insurance part-time to supplement his Foreign Service pension. I thought this was a fascinating story, if true.

The Saturday meeting was at the Cozy Inn. Dick and Rick Duffield reported on their routing of CAMPER. The other star of the meeting was one of Dick's longtime rivals in TU, a guy from Baltimore who had once served as a national officer of Trout Unlimited. Dick and this fellow were backing different candidates for membership on some kind of council. They went back and forth in a tedious way while the other two dozen folks emitted groans and occasional pleas for mercy. I wrote "Battle of the Blowhards" in my notebook. Then the chairman of the meeting came up with what I thought was a brilliant, even Blalockian idea. He appointed Dick and his opponent to serve together on a committee to discuss stocking practices with the fisheries department.

On the way home, Dick seemed as contented

as Br'er Rabbit after he had been thrown in the briar patch. "He's abrasive, overbearing and an authority on any subject that comes up," Dick said of his partner on the committee. "He and I fight like cats and dogs. I can't stand but one person like me in an organization."

35
Dick's Good Day

The fourth Saturday in February was a big day on Dick's calendar. Each year on that day, the Washington Suburban Sanitary Commission gave out boating permits for its two reservoirs in suburban Maryland. The commission dispensed these permits on a first-come, first-served basis. Permit holders were allowed to leave a canoe, rowboat or small sailboat at lakeside from the first of March until the end of October. Each boat had to be locked to a numbered mooring stake. It was important to Dick to get a low number, because those stakes were nearer the parking lot.

Since his hospitalization in Florida, Dick had gotten heavier and increasingly short-winded. He had developed a mysterious catch in his hip that made it impossible for him to walk more than a hundred yards without great pain. The failure of his hip ruled out most stream fishing for Dick, but he could still canoe around a water-authority reservoir near his home and catch sunfish and the occasional bass. One day, he took some visiting crony out, and the guy caught a seven-pound smallmouth. He called me at work to tell me that this monster proved Tridelphia Reservoir to be an underappreciated gem.

It was a pretty lake, although savagely over-fished because of its closeness to Washington and Baltimore. Also, it spooked me a little that Dick was devoted to it despite his mishaps. We were up there one cold Saturday in March and Dick fell in the water as he was climbing out of the canoe. With his circulatory problems he was always worried about hypothermia, and we both agreed it would be foolish to get back in the canoe and make the half-mile trip across the lake to the parking area. We flagged down a car on a nearby road and made it back to our car before he got too cold.

Not long after that he called me at work on an even colder day. He liked to go to the lake during the week because there were fewer fishermen. On this day, because of the weather, Dick had the place to himself. There was not another car in the parking area. This seemed fine until he capsized immediately after shoving off. Luckily, he was near the boat ramp and was able to scuttle out of the water. But he discovered that he could not rise to his feet. He crawled a hundred yards on his hands and knees to his battered Chevrolet. He managed to hoist himself against the side of the car and get his key in the lock. Once inside the car, with the heater on, he had to wait forty-five minutes before his shivering had subsided enough for him to drive.

"A few more minutes and I would have been too hypothermic to get into the car. I guess I would have died right there in the parking lot unless someone found me in time," he said. Leaving his swamped canoe and tackle behind, he drove home and changed clothes, returning in the afternoon to drag the canoe up on the bank and salvage as much tackle as he could. He said he was not sure how many reels and other expensive items remained in the lake. Sigrid, a high school art teacher, was at work while this happened, and Dick said he had not decided whether to tell her about his misadventure.

Dick did tell anyone who would listen that in 1992 he intended to get the number one stake, so that he could drive his car up beside his canoe. This would save him from carrying his gear, including an electric trolling motor and its heavy battery, across the parking lot. As the fourth Saturday of February approached, Dick began writing an essay about his plans for *Riffles*, the TU newsletter to which he still contributed.

The secret, he said, was to get an extremely early start so as to avoid the rush on Saturday.

"In fact, the rush begins *before* Saturday; this year [1991] the first stake seeker parked alongside Brighton Dam Road at 2:15 on Friday afternoon. Several other vehicles were spotted in line well before midnight.

"Watershed authorities have worked out a super-efficient system for dealing with the large numbers who show up on the designated Saturday. Vehicles line up on the aforementioned Brighton Dam Road, then at 6:00 A.M. Watershed Manager Mike Grear passes down the line and hands out plastic numbers, not unlike what occurs at the neighborhood ice cream parlor on a summer evening. At 7:00 A.M. motors begin to rev and the first cars pull into the fifty-nine spaces at the parking lot at watershed headquarters. The most humane touch is the long picnic table where coffee, doughnuts and juice are served. Promptly at 7:00 A.M. Chief Patrolman Larry Iager begins calling numbers, and minutes later, those whose numbers were called can be on their way. This year, I pulled out of the parking lot at 8:05.

"Since 1987, I have shown up on the appointed Saturday to insure that I got a preferred mooring stake. That year, I rolled out of bed at 5:00 A.M. and was assigned number 51. This year, I again planned to get up at 3:00, but at 2:15 A.M. an alarm went off in my head, so I sped to Brighton Dam Road and quietly pulled into line. This year, for the first time, I dozed off and slept until Mike Grear rapped on my window and handed me number 49.

"Looking ahead, I've started shopping for an RV—one with a wide, soft bed, a built-in kitchen and a TV system. After all, if I hope to get a number lower than 49, I'll have to be in line on the fourth Friday rather than the fourth Saturday next February."

Dick did not obtain the RV, but he did trade his ratty old Chevy for a nice Blazer. He planned to leave his house at 11:00 P.M. on Friday evening and sleep overnight in his vehicle.

On Saturday morning, I was writing at home and missed an early telephone call. Around 10:00 A.M., the phone rang again. It was Rick Duffield.

"Sigrid is trying to reach you. Have you talked to her?" he said.

"No," I said.

"I've got bad news. Dick is dead."

Early Saturday morning, the police had spotted Dick's car in a grassy area beside a roadway. He was slumped at the wheel. The car had apparently coasted to a stop after he was stricken. He had never made it to the line of cars parked on the Brighton Dam Road, but he had received his number, alas.

36
Rivers of
Remembrance

Dick left handwritten instructions for his memorial service. Sigrid found the document—a sheet of lined notebook paper—among his files. Apparently he had written these instructions after they returned from the trip to Florida on which he had almost died. He asked to be cremated. He wanted an Episcopal priest to preside at a service to be held within a week of his passing. He requested that the program include a space for "remarks by friends."

The service was set for Friday evening at a funeral home near Silver Spring, Maryland. Sigrid chose three speakers, one from each sphere of Dick's life. The first was a sweet fellow who sold insurance with Dick and said that Dick was a man who would not tell a lie or lose a friend in order to make a sale. The second was a member of Dick's bridge group, which was composed of retired Foreign Service officers. He said that from first to last, Dick was distinguished in that company by the extraordinary sharpness of his mind. I was the third speaker. I spoke for the fly fishers.

I had taken the day off from work and spent it at my word processor. The eulogy had to sum up Dick's life as an artist of our sport, and I had to try to get it right. Late in the afternoon, I printed out my remarks and read them aloud to make sure that I could get through them without choking up. Then I drove through the rain to the funeral home. There was a very large turnout of Dick's friends from Trout Unlimited and a respectful delegation of his adversaries, too, including the fellow from Baltimore with whom he liked to argue. Ben Schley was there, too, as were Ron Ashmore, Carl and Pat Geyer, and Rick Duffield. As I sat through the first two eulogies, I rested my gaze on a small urn on the altar. At first I thought it was decorative. At some point, I realized that it contained all that was left on this earth of Dick Blalock.

Most of the fly fishers present knew that I was working on a book in which Dick figured prominently. He had made sure that all of them read the magazine article in which I first portrayed him as the wizard of the Rapidan. I began by recalling the bond that started forming between Dick and me on our first trips to the Rapidan and Big Hunting.

"Who can explain what goes into the making of a friendship?" I said. "Perhaps, being distant from my father and brother, I wanted the support of an older man. Dick Blalock had a cherub face and wispy white hair. He suffered chronic pain from the heart surgery that he had several years before. But he had a great zest for life."

I recalled the familiar stories about Dick's battles with his doctors over his weight, about his love of good food and good talk, especially his own talk. I told how I had been working on the chapter about Dick's boyhood fishing experiences in Oklahoma when Rick Duffield called with the news of his death. I read from the chapter the long passage in which Dick spoke of the "wonderful, wonderful, wonderful relationship" formed with his Choctaw friend on their trips to Sheep Creek.

Then I spoke the rest of the eulogy as follows:

> As I read his words today, I think how typical it was of Dick that this reminiscence about fishing should end with his memory of something that was more important to him than the fish. That was the quality of friendship.
>
> Our friend Richard Culmer Blalock was in the course of his rich life an intercollegiate athlete, a soldier, a diplomat, a businessman. He was a husband and father, and no one stood closer to his heart than Sigrid, the children that each of them brought to a marriage that meant so much to him, and the grandchildren upon whom he doted.
>
> It is my role this evening to speak of another realm of Dick's life—the rich years of his maturity when he became a passionate advocate for the environment and an expert on the sport of fly fishing. But his skill in those areas rested on something larger and more important.
>
> Dick Blalock was an expert in the art of friendship. He demonstrated that in addition to the precious bonds of family, a man in the course of his life can be father and brother to those with whom he has no familial kinship.

He was a wonderful mentor for younger men, but he did not limit the circle of his friendship to men. There was nothing he liked better than to sit on a rock with Pat Geyer and discuss her career in investment banking while Carl was off flailing the water.

As a friend, Dick was an individualist who respected individuality. He liked renegades and artists who march to their own drum, and yet he also admired those who achieved success in traditional careers.

He was, as I say, an expert at friendship, but he also prided himself on the quality of his adversaries. He relished the fact that Governor Schaefer—his favorite target—knew him by the sound of his voice on the call-in shows.

He delighted in battling bureaucracies. Big Hunting Creek and Paint Branch are better streams for that. And he is the only person I know ever to defeat the circulation department of *The New York Times*.

He enjoyed the political jockeying in Trout Unlimited. Only a few weeks ago, he told me he always got in an argument with one particular fellow because in any meeting there was room for only one ego like his.

He had a big ego, but he was not vain or jealous. When it came to fly fishing, he was very modest, especially in the presence of that select few who were his fishing heroes—people like Ben Schley and Bob Clouser and Lefty Kreh.

I admired Dick's courage. I think he was more ready for this day than any of us here. I come from a death-fearing family and I was impressed with the resoluteness with which Dick confronted his illness. I do not mean that he was immune to fear and pain. But he did not let his illness curb his life. He did not live under the shadow of death. He lived in the sunshine of expectation.

Only last summer, he defied all good advice and made an arduous canoe trip with me and Ben Schley on the South Branch of the Potomac. I have never seen a happier man or had a jollier time.

The last conversation Dick and I had was to plan trips to the Rapidan in March and to Jackson Hole in July. He said that if I didn't mind he would take care of the menu for the Rapidan, and as it was spring we should have shad roe and roast pork and brandied sweet potatoes.

On the streams that Dick and I fly fished together, he taught me a lot. With his passion for life, he helped me come to terms with my own mortality. As I approached fifty and began to worry about the loss of youth, Dick's example showed me that the last chapters of a life can be as full as the first. I thank him above all for that gift. For Dick understood that life itself is a gift. We cannot control its length, only its quality.

That attitude was central to his concept of fishing. It is an attitude that in my book I call—in capital letters—Blalock's Way. Those of us in this room who were lucky enough to be on a stream with Dick all know the central teaching of Blalock's Way. Fly fishing is not about catching fish.

Let me quote Dick's words on this subject. "I've arrived at the point where fishing has become a social experience. I enjoy going out with people I like to be with. I'm to the point that the only thing that's important any longer is to be fishing water where there are fish, and if I don't catch any of them, more power to them. I don't count the quality of the experience by the number of fish I catch. I can go out and have a wonderful day and not catch any fish. I don't want to go out here and fish dead water. It's important that there be fish there."

In the last few years, Dick said this with increasing frequency—that all he asked was to be fishing over good water. In the land of memory, there are many rivers, and they all hold good water. It is always the right season there—one of the times that Dick loved—like spring on the Rapidan or White Miller time on the Potomac or high summer on the Madison or golden October on the Yellow Breeches. The fish are always rising for us on these good waters, and there is always time for that thing which was sweeter to Dick than the fishing itself. There is time to sit on the bank and be at ease with our friends.

In memory it will be as it was in life. Dick Blalock will be talking, and we will be listening. We can be with him there on the rivers of remembrance, because he has been with us here on the waters he loved.

37
Last Ride Together

Bill Dunlap told me that I had to persuade Sigrid Blalock to let us put Dick's ashes in the Rapidan, and when she asked me to help her select a place, I offered to drive her up to see the big pool where Dick caught the legendary twelve-inch or thirteen-inch brook trout. I knew he would be happy there. But Dick's children wanted a spot that was closer to home and easier to get to. They settled on Hunting Creek, and that seemed a good choice to me, too. It was, after all, the site of Dick's last conservation victory and his final joust with the bureaucracy.

Sigrid rode with me, along with George Hall, her son by her first marriage, and his wife, Kyoko, a scholarly Japanese woman of whom Dick had been very fond. As we loaded up, Sigrid and I joked about the amount of gear Dick and I would cram into that same vehicle for a one-day trip. She put the urn containing Dick's ashes on the backseat, and I managed to knock it off. There was no harm done, and it seemed fitting that our last ride together began unceremoniously. Dick was not a formal man, and I felt he might like the idea of his burial urn rolling around on the floor of a four-wheeler in which we had often set out for Hunting Creek.

Mike, one of Dick's two sons, was there ahead of us, and he had picked a shaded riffle a hundred yards below the Elbow Pool. Dick and I had fished there often. Above the riffle, there were three rainbow and two nice brook trout holding in the deep water under an overhanging tree. As Dick's daughter Laura read "Crossing the Bar," I saw a fish rise, but I could not tell if it was a brook trout or one of the rainbows.

George spoke then, recalling the gentle way in which Dick had introduced his two daughters, two sons and two stepsons to fishing. He told of the places they had been together with him—the Shenandoah and Lake Brittle in Virginia, the Yellow Breeches in Pennsylvania and Deep Creek Lake in Maryland. George said Dick knew how to take a kid fishing without insisting that the kid think it was the greatest thing that ever happened. "Dick never assumed that your experience fishing was the same as his," George said, "and I'm grateful for that."

Upstream from where we stood was one of the crosstie revetments that Dick had hated, but at this spot, there were two flat boulders that jutted into the stream and bent the current into a natural channel of fast, bumpy water. Mike walked out on the boulders and unscrewed the cap from the urn and dropped a plume of gray ash upon the water. It bloomed briefly across the surface, and when I went down to the water, I saw that a few grains of heavier silver ash had settled to the bottom and glistened in the crevices of the submerged portion of the boulder on which I stood. I reached down and touched these last molecules of my friend and only later did it occur to me that I might have taken a pinch of this material and transferred it to the Rapidan, the stream where our friendship began.

But I am glad, on balance, that I did not. Dick entered many rivers in his life, and it was the right of his family alone to choose the last one. As for me, I believe he is in all the waters we knew together, and on some good day, I will enter them, too.

I am not ready yet. For one thing, I'd like to know if the house of the future contains sons and daughters of my sons and if these little people would like to go down to the river someday and follow an old man along Blalock's Way and hear the story of the twenty crappies and learn the magic by which we may shoot a line across the water like the weightless tongue of time itself.

38
Aging the Heart

It is the nature of reporters to see things through to the end. So it was that I loaded my waders and the little two-weight rod I bought from Dick for $100 and set out on the familiar drive to Thurmont. I had to attend the last meeting ever called by Dick Blalock.

Along the way, I had an appointment with a man who worked for the Department of the Interior. He promised to tell me the entire story of what had happened at Catoctin Mountain Park after Dick wrote the inspector general.

"It was Dick's letter that triggered all the changes in the park," he said. The auditors found that under an informal and highly improper agreement with the former superintendent, CAMPER had taken in over $200,000 a year in rentals from cabins in the park. This was money that was supposed to go into the federal treasury. So far as could be determined, the money had been spent on improvements within the park and for charitable purposes. Otherwise the superintendent who took early retirement might have been in far more serious trouble. As it was, the inspector general found around a dozen violations of Department of Interior procedure in a place that is regarded as one of the jewels of the National Park Service because it adjoins the Presidential retreat at Camp David. The new superintendent had severed all connections with CAMPER and put rentals of the cabins back under control of the rangers. Oddly enough, the stream structures that so offended Dick were installed legally, because CAMPER, with the support of the old regime, had secured the proper permits. But it was clear that the new superintendent, a by-the-book ranger with long experience in the big parks in the Rockies, viewed them with dismay and thought they would never have been allowed in the parks out West.

The meeting was in the American Legion Hall. It, too, was part of the fallout from Dick's letter. The subject was whether to continue the stocking of Big Hunting Creek. About a hundred people had turned out. A lot of them were already hopping mad when they came through the door. I recognized a number of wild trout advocates from Trout Unlimited chapters in Washington and Baltimore. They were aligned against members of CAMPER who were still confused over how they had lost control of a national park that had been run like a small-town fishing club. Both the CAMPER folks and the local fishermen from Thurmont were upset about outsiders meddling with their stream and about the prospect that Big Hunting Creek might not get its annual infusion of easy-to-catch hatchery trout. Then they would be left to face those wily stream-bred browns and the native brookies.

The Maryland Department of National Resources had sent in a facilitator, a guy in a flannel shirt who introduced himself in a flurry of therapy-speak. There was a lot of oily talk about his "contract" with the audience. Everyone would get to speak and he would not take sides and he would get all of us out on time. Dick would have hated this guy, I thought, then immediately realized how wrong I was. He would have chewed him up with relish. We had here the perfect living monument to Dick: an all-day argument over how many and what kind of trout ought to live in the stream containing his ashes.

I spotted Bob Bachman, the Maryland fisheries director, standing in the back of the room and sidled over to tell him how Dick would have regarded his presence as a tribute to his epistolary skills. "Dick's letters had a way of making you focus on what you really think," Bachman said with a chuckle. Then he went up to address the group. He began with a question: "Why is it that so many of you feel so strongly about Big Hunting Creek?" Since I knew the answer, I thought I would spend the rest of the afternoon fishing.

There was a trout rising under the hemlock that leaned over the stream just above the place where we had scattered Dick's ashes. I had spotted a big brook trout in there that day. It was a difficult cast, but I managed to get a drag-free float right up against the base of the tree. The fish struck, and I missed it.

Upstream at the Elbow Pool, I found another fish rising steadily. I got down on my knees and cast so that my fly line landed on a long rocky beach and my leader curved out to the right, draping over a boulder so that only the fly and about two feet of tippet touched the water. It was a perfect cast, if I do say so myself. The fish took immediately, and I played in the largest brook trout I had ever seen in Big Hunting. It was twelve inches easily.

I made another cast to the same spot. It landed as nicely as the first. Again I got an immediate strike. This brook trout was even bigger. Maybe I measured this fish before letting it go, and maybe I didn't. I can tell you this. It was a big brook trout, probably thirteen inches. I am pretty sure of that. But who's counting? The last thing I am when I am fishing is competitive. I do know this for sure. Dick Blalock caught a thirteen-incher one time, when we were up on the Rapidan. He measured it carefully and I was there when it happened. You can take that to the bank, no pun intended.

I can tell you this, too. Dick was a good friend, and he never disappointed me, except maybe in one thing. I know an investigative reporter who has access to internal CIA directories and also knows how to tap into the old boys' grapevine over there. I had him run Blalock for me, and it came up negative. "He's not on any of the highly classified internal phone books," my friend said. "He was not an overt. If he was under deep cover, he was not on any known track. He's not known to anyone as an NOC—what they call a nonofficial cover." My friend also said the Agency could have paid him for his cooperation in the deal he described. They did a lot of that back in the Sixties and early Seventies. But he was not someone they would have used for light or heavy lifting, either before he was in the Foreign Service or after. "There's just nothing there," he said. "I'm sorry."

In a way, so was I. Secretly, I guess I had harbored the hope that I was important enough to spy on and that our friendship had an aura of intrigue. Journalists are prone to vanity, and we do like to think of ourselves as threats to power and foolishness. So it was fun to imagine that in writing about Reagan I had provoked some old renegade dinosaur at Langley and he had called on Dick to check me out for old times' sake. It was amusing, too, to see Dick as a fly-fishing spy, a potbellied version of James Bond's old CIA side-kick, Felix Leiter. Also, I am a taxpayer like any-body else, and for once I would like to feel I got my money's worth. If I could just believe that my government sent me a companion so useful and brave, then I would pay every tax they could dream up for as long as I live and know that I came out ahead.

But in the end, he was simply my friend and I was his and that was enough. You see, Dick Bla-lock helped me finish up some things that started a long time ago. He put a fly rod in my hand, and he showed me what could be caught if I learned to use it. He also taught me that when you get to a certain age you better balance your books with the people you love. I thought about that during the reunion fishing trip that my brother Jerry and I took after he and my dad and I had settled our feud for good. We were down along some dark bayou in Louisiana with Ben and Jeff and Jerry's son, Mike. Jerry and I told about adventures and misadventures that had occurred years ago, when we were very young, and these boys, our sons, who are men now, were not yet in the world. We spoke of fish caught and lost, of boats bought and sold, of storms endured, of lines broken and tackle destroyed, of friendship embraced, of lore imparted, of great lies told on waters long since impounded in the still, unrippling lakes of memory.

Then, from out of nowhere, my brother said, "Tell about the time you broke the tip on my new bamboo fly rod." And that is what I have tried to do.

INDEX

Page numbers in italics indicate illustrations.

The author with his father, W.S. Raines, and brother, Jerry, at Guntersville Dam Alabama, 1948

The author with the twenty crappies from South Sauty Creek, Alabama, 1950

Dick Blalock on the Rapidan River, Virginia